How to Get
Happily Published

How to Get Happily Published

FOURTH EDITION

* * *

Judith Appelbaum

HarperPerennial

A Division of HarperCollins*Publishers*

HarperCollins books may be purchased for educational,
business, or sales promotional use. For information, please
call or write: Special Markets Department, HarperCollins
Publishers, Inc., 10 East 53rd Street, New York, NY 10022.
Telephone: (212) 207-7528; Fax: (212) 207-7222.

FIRST EDITION

Library of Congress Cataloging-in-Publication Data

Appelbaum, Judith.
    How to get happily published / Judith Appelbaum.—4th ed.
      p. cm.
    Includes bibliographical references and index.
    ISBN 0-06-271544-5 — ISBN 0-06-273133-5 (pbk.)
    1. Authorship—Marketing.   2. Authors and publishers.
  3. Publishers and publishing. I. Title.
PN155.A67   1992
070.5′2—dc20   91-58282

92 93 94 95 96 PS/MB 10 9 8 7 6 5 4 3 2 1

*For writers everywhere who could use encouragement,
and for Alan, who specializes in that.*

Contents

A Foot in the Door

The Sale and Its Sequels

The Self-Publishing Option

Money

Endnote

Resources

Acknowledgments

HUNDREDS OF PEOPLE in and around publishing provided valuable information and advice for this book. My warmest thanks go both to those who are mentioned in the pages that follow and to those whose contributions the book reflects indirectly, including:

Bob Adelman, Alfred H. Allen, Carolyn Anthony, Robert E. Baensch, Nicholas Bakalar, Ann Banks, Virginia Barber, Marvin G. Barrett, John Baskin, Walter L. Bateman, Sheila Berger, Susan Bergholz, Louise Bernikow, Meredith Bernstein, John Berry, Janice Blaufox, Georges Borchardt, Ruth Brengel, Richard P. Brickner, Selma Brody and Diana Brown.

And Robert Cassidy, Carol Cohen, Janet Coleman, Gay Courter, Page Cuddy, Ginger Curwen, Joann Davis, Kenneth C. Davis, Julia della Croce, John P. Dessauer, Paula Diamond, Paul D. Doebler, Arnold Dolin, Jane Dystel, Robert J. Egan, Lisel Eisenheimer, Martha Fairchild, Paul Fargis, Jenny Feder, Cheri Fein, John Fischer, Zelda Fischer, Joan Foster and Len Fulton.

And Jonathan Galassi, Elizabeth Geiser, John Gilbertson, David Glotzer, Elizabeth Gordon, Annette Grant, Judith Grossman, Hannelore Hahn, Elise Hancock, Stuart Harris, James B. Heacock, Bill Henderson, Susan Hirschman, Berenice Hoffman, Elaine Hughes, Hayes Jacobs, Alison Jahncke, Tony Jones, Joan Kahn, Irwin Karp, Laura Katz, Mimi Kayden, Ralph Keyes, Rhoda

Koenig, Diane Kruchkow, Mary and Robert Lane, Georgie Lee, Bill Leigh, Tom Lewis and Lydia Link.

And Tom Loven, Miriam Madfis, Rich Marchione, Richard Marek, Elaine Markson, Peter McCabe, Ken McCormick, Karin McQuillan, Walter Meade, Kate Medina, Lisa Merrill, Robert R. Miles, Tom Montag, Joseph Montebello, Helen Moore, Richard Morris, William Morris, Jennifer Moyer, Julian Muller and Raymond Mungo.

And Jean Naggar, Victor Navasky, Kenneth P. Norwick, William Novak, Carol Ohmann, Don Passer, Christina Paterniti, Molly Peacock, Jean Peters, Ryan Petty, Christine Pisaro, Terry Pristin, Alice Quinn, Eleanor Rawson, Eric L. Reiss, Stephen F. Roth, Pat Rotter, Marc Sacerdote, Richard Sandomir, Karl Schumacher, Eleanor Shatzkin, Leonard Shatzkin, Mike Shatzkin, Robert Shnayerson, Maggy Simony, Ruth Sonsky and Miriam Steinert.

And Helen A. Stephenson, Patsy Sweely, Cindy Taylor, Carl Thorgerson, Linda Triegel, Carll Tucker, Joseph Vergara, Sharon Villines, Scott Walker, Lois Wallace, Michael Weber, Florence Weiner, Richard Weiner, Sally Williams, Stephanie Winston, Marianne Woolfe, Susan Zakin, Suzanne Zavrian, Mel Zerman and Charlotte Zolotow.

Leslie Li, Sylvia Johnson and Evie Righter all contributed to creating this new edition. To them, to my family and to Florence Janovic, my partner in providing Sensible Solutions, I owe special gratitude which it's a pleasure to express here.

Thank you all.

What's New in This Newest Edition, or Things Can Be Better for Writers

HALF-TRUTHS KEEP TOO many writers from getting what they want—and should have and probably could have. Authors slow down or go off in the wrong direction or stand stock still because they've been told:

* "We don't accept unsolicited manuscripts."
* "We'll get behind the book only if it takes off."
* "You have to have an agent."
* "Short fiction doesn't sell."
* "If the chains don't like your book, forget it."
* "You just can't make a living by writing."
* "We buy all rights; that's the deal."

Since there's some truth in these statements, the people who utter them frequently believe them. And since they believe them, you may be tempted to believe them too. Resist the impulse. As thousands of writers who've read this book in earlier editions will testify, you have the power to change or get around policies and practices that threaten to get in your way. And when writers proceed intelligently (which you will when you've read what follows), then everybody benefits—publishers, wholesalers, retailers, readers and writers alike.

Over the years since the first edition of *How to Get Happily Published* appeared in 1978, thousands of its readers have written and called to tell me about their success stories (and sometimes, of course, their failures and frustrations). These people sell articles, short stories, poems and books to publishers large and small; they publish their own books and magazines, their own newsletters and newspapers. They write full-time to make a living or part-time because of commitments in other fields.

Whether they're beginning writers or veterans, they report getting their work out to readers who like it. And they say that even when setbacks occur along the publication route, they don't feel powerless or defeated; they just figure out some way to get around the difficulties and back on track.

To help today's writers progress toward their goals, this edition of *How to Get Happily Published* takes account of new developments in the book and periodical publishing worlds and recommends hundreds of useful new resources (plus hundreds already established). It includes a whole new chapter about agents and it offers new material about ways to reach your readers in all the other chapters.

Because reaching readers is a vital ingredient in this book's recipe for success, it covers the full spectrum of publication possibilities. Focusing on writing for magazines and newspapers as well as on writing books, on self-publishing as well as on selling to established publishers, *How to Get Happily Published* assumes that you need to know about all the opportunities you have so that you can select different forms and different routes for different purposes.

You may find, for example, that the article you wrote and sold is germinating into a book, which you'll need to place and promote. Conversely, you may find that the book you wrote and sold can be publicized best through articles you write and sell.

Furthermore, just as you're apt to want to switch between books and shorter works, you're likely to benefit by placing some projects with publishing giants, submitting others to small, specialized companies and maybe even handling some through a tiny company of your own.

All these options figure in the pages that follow and any of them may help you attract receptive readers.

If you ask me, the best part of getting published is getting comments from those readers. Fame and fortune and well-turned phrases are rewarding too, of course, but nothing beats hearing from people who've read what you've written and who tell you they're better off as a result. Nothing except hearing from people who tell you that, having read your work, they got people to read their work, and those people, in turn, wrote to them to express appreciation. When you write a book about getting published, that kind of compound pleasure can come your way.

My thanks to readers across the country and around the world who've made me happy by responding to *How to Get Happily Published* in the past. I'll look forward to hearing from those of you who have comments, criticisms, stories to share or quick questions to ask after you've read this latest edition.

Judith Appelbaum
P.O. Box 204
Katonah, NY 10536

Initiation

TO BEGIN WITH, an announcement for writers, would-be writers and people who have important things to say from time to time and want to say them in print: It is largely within your power to determine whether a publisher will buy your work and whether the public will buy it once it's released.

That having been said, two questions naturally arise: Why do so many people who try to place articles, stories, poems and books with publishing firms get rejected time and again? And why do so many people who succeed in placing articles, stories, poems and books with publishing firms then find that their work never attracts a sizable audience?

The answer is surprisingly simple. Failures abound because hardly anybody treats getting published as if it were a rational, manageable activity—like practicing law or laying bricks—in which knowledge coupled with skill and application can ensure success. Instead, almost everybody approaches the early phases of the publishing process, which have to do with finding a publisher, by trusting exclusively to luck, to merit or to formulas. And when later phases come along, bringing production and marketing problems, writers too often opt out.

Such behavior is thoroughly counterproductive, but it's entirely understandable at the same time, and on several grounds.

In the first place, just like everybody else, people who write are reluctant to risk ridicule by asking questions. Seeking information

1

is an intimidating task in this day and age. We've all been raised to believe that, since knowledge is power, ignorance must be impotence, and it's shameful, therefore, to admit it when there's something we don't know.

And in the second place, we tend to proceed on the assumption that mastery of any field is the exclusive province of specialists and experts. The lay public, so the theory goes, can't expect to understand how to fix a leaky pipe, let alone how to get a manuscript from writer to reader, so people who aren't prevented from inquiring by the fear of looking silly are hindered by the fear that the information they'll receive will be unintelligible anyway. But even those who are brave and energetic enough to go in search of knowledge about getting published have not, in most cases, found the effort worthwhile. What all aspiring authors really need is an editor who has the time and the inclination to sit down with them and show them the industry ropes. What a writer gets, however, is more likely a handful of books from the oppressively large canon of works on breaking into print (which usually tell only parts of the truth and may not tell the truth at all) or a handful of books from the smaller canon of works on subsequent aspects of the publishing process (which tend to explain the way the business works without focusing on the flesh-and-blood men and women who run it and who inevitably alter the rules to fit personal and practical demands).

This book is a substitute for the friendly editor. It offers a full and frank description of the contemporary publishing picture— complete with fallible human beings in the foreground and annotated guides to hundreds of helpful resources at the back. Anyone who reads it intelligently should come away with a good general idea of the way the publishing process normally works, some valuable specific information on the ingenious tactics writers have devised to make it work for them and easy enough access to additional information about the full range of publishing options to be able to create effective publishing strategies for particular projects.

More than thirty years of personal experience in editing books, magazines, newspapers and newsletters have gone into the advice you'll find here about getting through the publishing labyrinth. And so have myriad experiences other publishing professionals shared, all of which help explain each phase, introduce the people in charge, define the unfamiliar terms, set forth the basic unwritten rules that govern progress and tell you how to discover more about whichever aspects of getting published interest you.

But at every step the main focus of attention will be on you— what you want, what you need, what you'll have to contend with to get it, how wide your options are, and how you can reach your goals most expeditiously.

This book, in other words, is designed as a launching pad for individual writers and writing projects, and its overriding purpose is to help you improve your improvisational skills so that you'll be able to switch gears when you need to, no matter what the rulebook experts say. The idea is that once you understand the query letter in context (for example), you'll see that it's a valuable tool for you and not just a time-saver for editors, and you'll choose to use it to maximum advantage. Similarly, once you've gained the confidence to obey other people's dictates only when they fit your situation, you'll draft a covering letter to an editor at *New Woman* that's quite different in tone—and perhaps in content as well— from the one you'd send to *New Age*.

New Woman may return your material, of course, and so may *New Age* and Bantam and the Globe Pequot Press, but please don't let yourself be discouraged if getting what you want involves a few false starts. To keep your spirits up on darker days, you may find it useful to dwell on three important facts:

✱ *Publishers need you at least as much as you need them.* Despite widespread suspicions of conspiracy, there's little truth in the theory that an elite circle of editors and writers concentrated in Manhattan and doing business on the cocktail-party circuit reserves every printed page for itself.

Editors do, no doubt, know established writers, and established writers do, no doubt, know editors, and, unquestionably, a lot of assignments are given out at New York cocktail parties and New York publishing lunches as well (they still exist, those lunches, somewhat subdued by current conditions but worth angling for if you find yourself with a big-city publisher interested in you).

On the other hand, (a) even the deputed leaders of the New York Literary Establishment are wary of accepting too much material from fellow NYLE members; in spite of long and liquid lunch hours, editors are always aware of the dangers of provincialism; and (b) no matter how many authors editors know, they never have enough first-rate material. In publishing firms on both coasts and in between, the quest for new ideas and new writers is considered so vital that editors-in-chief frequently chide—and sometimes threaten—their junior colleagues about it. "Unless you have three projects to propose, don't come to the editorial meeting this week; and if you miss three meetings, don't come back to work," a particularly stern taskmaster is in the habit of telling his staff.

One editor's search for good manuscripts led to a teacher named Walter Bateman who believes in "learning by inquiry." *Minnesota Monthly* published a piece he wrote about that. A chemist who read it passed it on to her husband who had studied growth in students' intellectual understanding as part of a team headed by William G. Perry at Harvard. From there the piece went to Perry, who liked it enough to show it to Lynn Lucknow, an editor he had worked with at Jossey-Bass. Lucknow then called Bateman, discovered that the article had been derived from a book Bateman was writing, and asked to see every chapter already done.

"Some of them were pretty rough," Bateman recalls, "but I sent them along anyway. Several rewrites and arguments later *Open to Question* was published. Four months after pub date it had sold over 5,000 copies." This writer happened to get a break because he'd gotten a piece into a regional magazine, but editors doggedly scan publications of all sorts looking for promising material. And of course they spend hours each day paging through the manuscripts and outlines and proposals that arrive on their desks in the hope of discovering a new writer who will boost their status with their colleagues and improve their employer's standing in the marketplace.

✱ *Editors make mistakes.* By actual count, 121 publishers said "No thanks" to *Zen and the Art of Motorcycle Maintenance.* Roger Tory Peterson's *Field Guide to the Birds* and *Lolita* were turned down too, again and again. *The Clan of the Cave Bear, The Spy Who Came in from the Cold, The Peter Principle, Watership Down, To Kill a Mockingbird*—rejected, every one. And John Fischer, for many years head of the trade (i.e., general) book department at Harper, used to tell—with the aplomb made possible by his otherwise admirable record—of the time he confidently spurned a book that went on to make publishing history.

"I hate to remember," Fischer confessed in one of his "Easy Chair" columns in *Harper's Magazine,* "when James R. Newman first told me his scheme for a history of mathematics. . . . He wanted to gather all the basic documents of mathematical thought and arrange them into an anthology which would trace the development of the science in the words of the masters themselves. It would be a big book—perhaps five hundred pages. What did I think of it?

"I told him it was impossible. Nobody would buy it; its subject was too specialized—in fact to most people (including me) downright repellent—and it would be far too costly to manufacture."

Newman's *The World of Mathematics* was subsequently issued by Simon & Schuster, having grown to four volumes from the originally contemplated one, and Fischer noted dryly that before long the publisher had sold over 120,000 sets, in addition to those distributed by two book clubs. A few years ago, the work was re-released by Microsoft Press with considerable fanfare and a $75,000 advertising and promotion budget.

The point, clearly and comfortingly, is that a rejection (which in any case is directed to your work and not to you as a person) may well reflect more unfavorably on the editor's ability than on yours.

✻ *Perseverance pays.*

Outlets for writing are multiplying rapidly nowadays, as new technology makes small publishing ventures economically feasible. And at large houses as well as small, editorial tastes are always so varied that there should be an editor somewhere who's looking for what you have to offer, as Judith Guest discovered when she tried her now famous, but then rejected, novel *Ordinary People* on a new pair of editorial eyes.

After the book was turned down by Random House, Ms. Guest sent it on to Viking, where an editorial assistant named Mimi Jones saw its merits and passed it along to her colleagues with enthusiastic comments. Viking accepted the book, whereupon it was published to good reviews, selected by the Book-of-the-Month Club and sold to a paperback house for over half a million dollars, after which it went on to make the bestseller lists and win four Oscars in its film version.

The author was delighted, for obvious reasons, that she hadn't quit while she was behind, but Mimi Jones won a full measure of joy from the novel's fate too. "It was exhilarating," she explained, "to have one of my cherished ideals finally borne out just at the point when I was about ready to abandon it: that real talent will always eventually be recognized, that a good first novel does have a chance."

Precisely because so many people inside publishing companies share Mimi Jones's desire to get valuable pieces of writing the attention they deserve, it makes sense for an author to persevere even after the acceptance stage. In fact, a wise writer will shepherd written work all the way through production and distribution until finally it reaches its readers, realizing that when the pros are prepared to do their part, it would be a shame to have a project founder because the person who created it didn't pitch in.

Please understand: there's no need for a writer to actually perform every publishing chore, but authors who make it their business to know what should be done to give their work its best shot—and when it should be done and why and by whom and how they themselves can participate—stand by far the strongest chance of winning attention from the critics and purchase money from the public. Moreover, they figure to escape the frustrations that so often arise to plague people who rely on the specialists in a big and busy organization to handle important matters for them.

In publishing, as in practically every other field of modern endeavor, "success" is a term that does, and should, mean different things to different people.

But if you set your goals wisely, with full comprehension of the framework that surrounds their realization, you can find a good measure of fulfillment in getting published, and you will encounter serendipitous pleasures at several points, for using your own wits and your own energies provides an especially satisfying way to ensure that the profoundly personal act which writing constitutes comes finally to fruition.

Getting the
Words Right

* * *

Basics

A GREAT MANY successful authors have never taken a writing course or read a writing manual, and they wouldn't want to. Instead, they rely on common-sense measures to improve their writing skills. Realizing, for example, that reading offers one good way to learn about using words, they are apt to go through several books and magazines a month and to pick up pointers on style, organization, point of view and the like from each one.

Sometimes the learning process that takes place when you read is virtually unconscious. For instance, you may barely sense that steeping yourself in Henry James novels causes you to be more careful about nuances in your own prose; but the effect will have occurred nonetheless and, at a minimum, it will have taught you something about your options in selecting language.

To make learning from reading a more deliberate act, writers often stop to examine each powerful passage they encounter in order to figure out how it achieved its impact (through a succession of startling images, a change of tense, a panoply of facts?). And to further advance their educations, many authors turn to behind-the-scenes books like Virginia Woolf's *A Writer's Diary* and the diaries left by Chekhov, Hawthorne and Thoreau, which deal directly with how a writer creates and organizes material, how private reading feeds constantly into present and future projects and how to deal with writer's block, self-doubt and the other psychological hazards of the trade. Similar subject matter characterizes anthologies like the *Paris Review Interviews*, in which writers not only talk about their craft but also reveal whether they write reclining nude on a sofa or standing up in an A & P parking lot.

Because analyzing and explaining how they do what they do appeals strongly to many writers, the common-sense approach to writing has given rise to a body of teachings based on personal experience and handed down over the years in print and through word of mouth. It's from this legacy that the following suggestions derive. For additional guidance, see "Getting the Words Right Resources."

Story Ideas—Files . . .

Writing well for publication demands, first, that you pick a subject that excites you and will attract others, and, second, that you flesh it out with examples, images, anecdotes, facts and characters. Many writers meet these requirements with the help of the pack-rat process, which involves hoarding printed materials that interest them along with scribbled notes about ideas, snatches of conversation and nuggets of information they find provocative.

In the beginning, these bits and pieces may not mean much but as they accumulate they'll start to form patterns, and eventually a number of items may cluster around a subject like (for example) building your own house. At that point, the next step is easy: label a folder with that heading and stock it with all the makings for an article or book: notes on background reading, research materials, people to interview, associations to contact, relevant data from the *Congressional Record*, preliminary reflections and angles of approach.

Any subject, it's important to understand, can be treated in numerous ways, so that even before you begin to write you have vital choices to make. Whom shall I write for, and how should I address them? What style will I use? What tone? What do I want to say, and how will I arrange my material for optimum effect?

To get a concrete idea of the range of choice that confronts you, take a subject you're curious about and look it up in the *Readers' Guide to Periodical Literature* and the *Subject Guide to Books in Print* at your local library. Then look up related headings and read around in the materials you discover. You'll find that although the topic is unchanging, each treatment of it highlights a different aspect for a different audience, and you'll come away more alert to the decisions you must make at the start of any writing project. (Furthermore, by way of bonus, you'll get a leg up on your research.)

In making these preliminary choices, some writers consult style folders in which they've filed samples of the short, pithy, anecdotal piece; the first-person report; the informal essay in social criticism; the investigative story; and other forms available to authors today. If you start such a folder for yourself you can use its contents as a checklist each time you begin work on a new topic. Perhaps that will prevent you from propping a sprightly personal reminiscence on a scaffolding better suited to *War and Peace*.

. . . and the Free Space

Some of the nicest people turn pompous when they write, probably because they've been saying to themselves, "Who wants to read what I, a nobody, have to say? I'd better do whatever I can to sound important." Unfortunately, and for obvious reasons, the attempt to impress is usually counterproductive; just as people at a party groan when someone comes in putting on airs—that old standby defense against social insecurity—readers will be put off by a manuscript that's written with pretension rather than warmth and sincerity.

To build confidence in your writing ability to the point where you can drop your poses, you might try keeping a journal. Ideally, a journal is a free space, inaccessible both to the self-critic and to the critics lurking in the great out-there. In your journal you can experiment by writing whatever comes into your mind without censorship and by following your thoughts wherever they lead, because it's not polished work you're after now, but loosening up to feel comfortable with the written expression of your thoughts and observations.

If you also use your journal to jot down quotes and facts that appeal to you, to try out different writing styles, to test and develop story ideas and to phrase your reactions to current events, you should find that it serves as a healthy complement to research, reporting and the more structured writing you produce when you begin to draft your manuscript.

Drafting

No matter how extensive your preparation, you may be struck by panic and confusion when you finally sit down to write. The best way to handle the performance jitters—however devastating they seem—is first to recognize fear as normal ("I walk around, straightening pictures on the wall, rugs on the floor—as though not until everything in the world was lined up and perfectly true could anybody reasonably expect me to set a word down on paper": E.B. White). Then take one simple step. Get something written. It doesn't have to be perfect; it just has to exist so that you will have the beginning of a rough draft to work with, and not merely a pile of notes.

The impetus to get that initial group of words out of your head and onto paper will be strong if selling what you write is the only way you're going to pay the rent. Otherwise, though, writing all too often strikes people as an activity that can fit under the heading "Important But Not Urgent" devised by Edwin C. Bliss in his *Getting Things Done*. To make sure you really do get started, Bliss and other writers suggest that you reserve substantial blocks of time for writing each day, or three times a week, or at whatever intervals are practical in the light of your other commitments and priorities.

You may finish a full morning's stint having completed one sentence; on the other hand, you may become inspired once you're involved in the work of figuring out what you want to say and saying it. But keep trying. "Many times, I just sit for three hours with no ideas coming to me," Flannery O'Connor once said. "But I know one thing: if an idea does come between nine and twelve, I am there ready for it."

Particularly for people working on book-length manuscripts, making the best use of writing time takes practice. When she was drafting her book about crime victims, writer Dawn Sangrey recalled, "Making lunch dates was good for me at first. They served to get me out of the apartment and gave me some contact with the outside world. As I got more involved in the book, though, lunch dates became an interruption. I decided to see people either for breakfast or in the evenings and to keep my days completely free for writing."

Other people work best by interspersing sessions at the keyboard with periods of physical activity (one accomplished writer gets up and dances madly around his apartment whenever he's stuck for a word or a phrase). And still others function most effectively when they think in terms of deadlines. Two professors in this last group, both of whom were carrying full teaching loads and under pressure to publish, found that a deadline buddy system ensured productivity. On target dates, each teacher was required to deliver a chapter to the other; both had finished manuscripts ready for a publisher within a year.

Just as optimum time schedules vary from writer to writer, so the physical situation an author works well within may range from a book-lined cabin on the top of a mountain to a corner of a cramped, urban kitchen. "I prefer small, messy rooms that don't look out on anything interesting," William Maxwell told an interviewer; "I wrote the last two sections of *They Came Like Swallows* beside a window looking out on a tin roof. It was perfect. The roof was so boring it instantly drove me back to my typewriter." And Susan Brownmiller, author of *Against Our Will: Men, Women and Rape,* found ideal working conditions inside the New York Public

Library in "a very special place called the Frederick Lewis Allen Room, where I was given a desk for my typewriter and a shelf for my books. I was also given the companionship of a score of writers who became my own private seminar in how to get the job done. The interrelationship of my Allen Room friends and me is too complex to detail; suffice it to say that each of us struggled together, respectful of one another's progress, in a supportive environment dedicated to hard work and accomplishment, a writer's Utopia or close to it." A set-up like that can be created by any group of writers who arrange to share some working space.

Every so often, people who want to write discover that they simply can't manage the task under any available circumstances, and in such cases finding collaborators or ghosts may be a good idea. (A ghost, by the way, should always be given corporeal existence through a shared by-line or, at the least, through an explicit acknowledgment at the front of the book.)

"Getting the Words Right Resources" offers leads to writers and editors who'll work with nonwriters on book and magazine projects (see also "Buying Advice and Assistance"). And editors have even been known to function as unpaid ghosts by reworking manuscipts they've acquired to get important ideas to an audience. But for most people ghosting isn't necessary. If you give up trying to compete with the great stylists and if you know fully what you want to say, you'll be well on the way to crafting serviceable, salable prose.

Just be careful to write as you speak, or rather, in the words of Northrop Frye, use language that "is not ordinary speech, but ordinary speech on its best behavior, in its Sunday clothes, aware of an audience with its relation to that audience prepared beforehand."

Revising

The printed materials you buy at the bookstore or newsstand have generally gone through numerous revisions. "I rewrote the ending of *Farewell to Arms* thirty-nine times before I was satisfied," Ernest Hemingway told an interviewer.

"Was there some problem there?" the interviewer wanted to know. "What was it that had stumped you?"

"Getting the words right," Hemingway said.

Thirty-nine rewrites are several more than most writers will want—or be fully able—to attempt, but you should count on revising your work up to half a dozen times before you consider it finished. To make revision easier, be generous with spacing. If you're still writing on a yellow pad or using a typewriter, double or triple space lines so you can insert words and rearrange sentences without totally destroying legibility. If you use a word processor, make your printouts double-spaced and read your words in hard copy before you decide they're final.

Instruction in the self-editing process that revision constitutes is available in several good books (see this section's "Resources"), most of which explain, sensibly enough, that it's wise to begin with the beginning. This is the time to look with a critical eye at those first few paragraphs. Did you breeze through the start just to get some steam? Do they read just as they were written—as a preliminary throat-clearing exercise? If so, dispense with them and find the spot where you really begin to address your subject in a way that will capture a reader's interest.

Devising a good lead is worth all the craft and inspiration at your command. For it's with your first sentence or two that you must convince people to read what you have to say. If you're not sure what constitutes a good lead, look hard at writing you admire. And during all your reading, be on the alert for openings that grab your attention. Try to figure out why they attract you and compel you to read on. If you can determine the causes behind the effect—a catalog of precise details, a bold question, an alarming anecdote—you will be better equipped to fashion an exciting lead of your own.

Though the lead is the single most vital section of your manuscript, each word counts, and each should be designed not to dazzle but to communicate. Keep your critical eye sharp as you continue through passages now familiar to you. Read them silently or aloud to yourself to spot places where a reader may stumble.

Finding the precise word that says what you mean is not, of course, a luxury; it is a crucial necessity. Sometimes the best choice doesn't come to mind right away, but when that happens you can leave signals for yourself as you draft: circle a word you're not sure about; bracket a choice of two phrases; put a question mark in the margin; write in TK (a printer's abbreviation for To Kum, it's an easy target for a computer search when you're ready to fill in the blanks); then come back later and get the thing right.

As you insert your changes, you may notice that entire sections should be scrapped or reshuffled, or that you short-changed a point and need to elaborate. Maybe, for example, you left out the illustrative material that would make your message clear on page 6; maybe the paragraph at the end of chapter four clearly belongs with the discussion toward the beginning of chapter two. Don't be alarmed. This kind of reworking is the norm, not the exception, for experienced writers, so you should move material around with some abandon. And if the first move doesn't work out as well as you thought it would, you can always try another arrangement until you get a smooth, effective draft.

Deleting material is, of course, psychologically harder than moving or adding it, but abridgment is frequently necessary in revision. Although you may have grown fond of a passage, if it duplicates an earlier one, something has got to go. The freedom you allowed yourself in drafting now requires that you be ruthless in pruning the redundant, the irrelevant, the gratuitously showy. And that may mean cutting your first draft by half.

Getting Criticism

To get critical feedback before you send your manuscript to an editor—from whom, by the way, you shouldn't expect a critique—you can approach a variety of people. The most obvious source for constructive criticism is another writer, either one who is at your stage of development, or a professional whose work you've read and admired.

"If you really like someone's work, why not write them?" asks Elliot Figman of Poets & Writers, a remarkably helpful group. "The worst thing that could happen is that they won't write back." Most writers are accessible to some degree (see "Resources" for directories that include addresses and phone numbers), and James Harkness found Annie Dillard, Pulitzer Prize-winning author of *Pilgrim at Tinker Creek*, to be very accessible indeed.

I had just finished reading *Points for a Compass Rose* by Evan Connell—about four times, without coming up for air—and I was rushing around to all my friends, clutching them by their coat sleeves and crying, "My God, read this!" Of course no one was paying the slightest attention. I wanted to share my enthusiasm, and I was frustrated. Then Annie Dillard published an essay/review about the book which was rhapsodic and well-written.

I sent her a note via the publisher to tell her I enjoyed the piece and agreed. She replied. We spent several weeks whooping and hollering "Connell! Connell!" and eventually moved on to other topics.

Although Annie knew I was ghost writing for the president of the university where I worked, I kept quiet about the stuff I was grinding out privately. By then I had seen essays from what came to be *Pilgrim at Tinker Creek*, and I had no burning desire to send a bundle of my mawkish scribbling to this obviously brilliant and talented writer who was knocking them out in the aisles.

I don't recall exactly how it came about that I finally did allow Annie to see a manuscript of something or other. She wrote me back an ecstatic paean to the effect that I was "obviously the best writer alive on the planet," a composer of "muscled prose," and on and on. I replied proposing marriage. Too late.

As far as the sort of comments went, they were general and supportive. Mostly she stroked my ego and let the verbs take care of themselves—a strategy, I'll add, that seems to me now not only humane but pragmatically wise. For anyone who has a certain innate potential, the most difficult aspect of learning to write is the long, dreary, often desperate silence that greets early efforts. What is needed there isn't so much criticism, constructive or otherwise, as encouragement. Sooner or later you will begin to get close analysis from editors or critics, if your manuscripts are promising enough, but not many editors or critics will hold your hand and tell you how wonderful you are in the face of much evidence to the contrary. Annie instructed me to try not to be the subject and object of my own prose, an idea I've thought about a lot and attempted to put into practice. But she told me I was the best writer on the planet first, and I suspect the hyperbole was more sustaining, hence more valuable, than the bits and pieces of "objective" commentary.

At various points in their lives, a surprising number of writers knowingly and graciously accept the responsibility of encouraging beginners. "For ten minutes of time and postage costs (they never send return envelopes), I can restore a person's faith in humanity," one established essayist says. "Lots and lots of people write me and send manuscripts. I try to read and comment on them."

Nevertheless, asking for criticism is a hard thing to do, primarily because everyone is afraid of being told their work is rotten. And this fear often makes beginning writers just as skittish about seeking comments from peers as they are about approaching literary lights. Friends can be helpful, though, even if they're not writers or editors or professional critics. In fact, when he won the Nobel Prize for Literature, Saul Bellow declared that nonprofessionals may have an edge when it comes to critical comment. Many letters from readers, he told *The New York Times Book Review*, "are very penetrating; not all are completely approving, but then I am not completely approving of myself. In recent years, I would say that I have learned more from these letters than I have from formal criticism of my work."

So consider asking friends whose intelligence you respect to act as critics of your work in progress, not by passing final judgment on it but by pinpointing strengths and trouble spots. As Cynthia Buchanan, playwright and novelist, has explained, "It's a matter of being clear to other people. What I want to find out from friends is, first, can they follow what I'm saying. Then I want to know if it's boring and where it's boring. And third, I ask whether they feel that the language is too baroque and unrealistic in places. In the long run I choose what I want to do, but I need this consensus." Buchanan has given much of the credit for her fine track record in getting published to the informal consulting system she developed for herself.

With an even smaller but equally effective criticism network, Christi Killien and Sheila Bender co-authored a salable book. Killien, who had done six novels for young people, and Bender, a leader of writing workshops, decided to write to each other about writing. Offering ideas, observations, criticism and plenty of encouragement, their letters went back and forth at least once a week for six months and eventually spawned *Writing in a Convertible with the Top Down*, which Warner published.

To initiate a feedback system that will be productive for you, first formulate specific questions. You might begin, for example, by asking people which passages they had to read twice; which sections they remember best; and which parts they would eliminate if someone were to insist the manuscript be shortened.

If you've written a story for children, the most obvious testing ground is the children's story hour at your local library. And if you're eager to get ongoing criticism of your work, you may want to join or organize a writers' club, whose members will be a ready source of reactions.

It's not hard to do that, as Linda Triegel discovered. In her case, as it happens, the impetus to act came from the first edition of this book, which she read just about the time she decided she was serious about her writing. Realizing that the author lived nearby, Triegel got together with a couple of other beginning writers she knew and arranged for the library in town to host a Q-and-A session.

"We thought there must be more would-be authors around who would come to hear you speak and, lo and behold, dozens turned up," she remembers. "We had them all sign a guest book with their addresses and a few weeks later invited them to a meeting to organize a writers' group. We read our work to one another and critiqued it as best we could. We also, right off, decided to put out a collection of our work just for the sake of seeing it between covers, and this became an annual event."

The New Fairfield (Connecticut) Creative Writers Workshop, which Triegel headed for several years, functioned in part as a source of moral support for its members. To get "down-to-brass-tacks advice" on markets and contacts and writing techniques, she eventually joined a more advanced writers' group in her area.

Meeting with other people engaged in writing has several advantages. Frequently, you'll get useful pointers. Sometimes a collaborative project will be sparked. And always your morale will be strengthened by a feeling of support and community—by the knowledge that other people understand and care about what you're doing and what you may be undergoing—as you progress through the painful process of writing itself to the pleasures of having written.

Buying Advice and Assistance

MAYBE IT'S BECAUSE of the glamour—write and you too may hobnob with the rich and the famous; write and one day they'll all look at you with respect. Maybe it's a simple semantic confusion—writing, after all, is something you could do back in first grade, so of course it will be easy to bring your prose up to publishable level. Or maybe the explanation is that people are just naturally communicative. In any case, millions of Americans are regularly seized by an urge to write. Naturally—in a culture that believes in advancement through education—lots of would-be writers immediately look for courses and manuals that will start them writing and get what they've written into print. And just as naturally—in a culture of entrepreneurs—there's no lack of individuals and institutions prepared to provide what the public wants.

The goods and services on sale can be summed up under a short list of headings—courses, criticism, computer software and books. But within these categories variations in quality are enormous. A few of the writing aids on the market promise a great deal and deliver next to nothing, while others make modest claims for themselves and then yield surprising benefits. Many, it's a pleasure to report, will honestly reveal what they offer, but only to those who carefully interpret their ads and investigate their operations.

Before you spend your first penny on any form of printed,

computerized or personal instruction, you should be able to answer these four questions:

1. Is this necessary for the successful development of my written work?
2. What exactly am I buying?
3. What value will it have for me?
4. How much will it cost, both in money and in psychological wear and tear?

The answer to Question 1 is no, and you may therefore wish to go directly from this sentence to the beginning of "A Foot in the Door." But because "unnecessary" is not synonymous with "ineffective," and because much of what's on the market can be valuable if it's skillfully selected and used, here's a guide to instructional aids.

Classes

Good teachers of writing will tell you that writing cannot be taught; it can only be learned. The teacher's role, they will explain, is to create and capitalize on opportunities for learning so that the students can develop faster and more efficiently than they would on their own. Or, as Lawrence Durrell put it in the catalog description of his course in California's International College Independent Study Program, "While nothing can be taught, the presentation of notions and ideas with precision and enthusiasm can hatch out the talents in people and thus develop them." Word it any way you like, the point is that no writing course can be worthwhile unless you exercise initiative and work hard on follow-up.

First among your required course activities will be writing, arranging words until they form a structured whole. Having written, you will then be asked to submit your work to your teacher and your fellow students for criticism. And after they've commented, you'll have to rewrite, accepting those of their suggestions that your emotions and intelligence can approve and rejecting the rest. Moreover, you will probably be called upon to offer constructive criticism of your classmates' work—which means you will have to figure out where their strengths lie and how their weaknesses can be corrected.

None of this is easy; much of it may be agonizing. And what do you get for your pains?

Motivational energy, for one thing. Whether you call it writer's block or procrastination or just plain fear of failure, the difficulties that many writers experience in getting started can be eased by the presence of an instructor who assigns, expects and encourages the completion of a manuscript.

And despite instructor's protestations, you may actually get some traditional teaching during class discussions, for good teachers will seize on particular pieces of student writing to illustrate important aspects of literary technique. They may focus on dialogue, transitions, point of view, narrative exposition, plot structure or even basic rules of grammar, but whatever the subject, it will serve to sharpen every student's critical perceptions and thus to improve the value of any comments on classmates' work and the value of changes in their own.

Most conscientious teachers not only discuss students' writing in class and with each student individually; they also turn manuscripts into teaching tools by jotting comments as they read. As director of the Iowa Writers Workshop, John Leggett edited and copy-edited each piece of student work he read, just as he used to edit books when he worked for large publishing firms. And at Yale, William Zinsser, author of *On Writing Well*, marked up student manuscripts in memorable letters of red. Katie Leishman, one of Zinsser's many appreciative pupils, describes the consequences of his technique for learning.

> In the opening lecture Mr. Zinsser asked for a five-page account of "My First Day at College." I still have my notes: Writing is a craft. Good writing is very difficult. One word is better than two. Unnecessary words = CLUTTER. In the margin I've written, "This is all *very* obvious."

All that was obvious a week later was that I had a twenty-two-page draft when Mr. Zinsser wanted five pages. No amount of frenetic snipping and repasting of paragraphs made it any shorter. So I did the only thing I could do. I put the draft and my typewriter in the car and started driving. I suppose I thought that somewhere along the road I would have a vision of the sections I could trim from the article. Then I would stop in a coffee shop and rewrite.

Five hours later I was still driving. At midnight I checked into a motel in the Berkshires and lay in bed wondering, in the middle of winter, in the middle of nowhere, which were the 1,000 critical words of the 6,000 words I had written. I spent the weekend in the bathtub, writing on an upside-down drawer which I laid across the rim of the tub. Saturday, I rewrote ten pages and threw out the rest. By Sunday afternoon I had what I thought were five pages of flawless prose. Satisfied and very clean, I drove back to school.

When I got that paper back it was bleeding—bleeding badly. Mr. Zinsser's red arrows, red question marks and red slashes were everywhere; he had excised entire paragraphs. I slunk out of the classroom, crestfallen, resentful.

That evening, when I could bear to look at it again, I retyped the piece, simply leaving out what Mr. Zinsser had cut and clarifying expressions he'd found vague. As I typed I realized that he hadn't robbed me of my say. Though the edited version ran only one and a half pages, it retained every point of the original twenty-two-page draft.

So "clutter" and "craft" and "the difficulty of good writing" suddenly became real, personal problems to tackle. In later assignments if I used a gratuitous or vague expression, I could almost see a slash or question mark welting over it. Eventually I developed my own sense of what was essential or expendable, of what was my own style and what was imitative. By the end of the course, when Mr. Zinsser joked about students in his "red pen orbit" I knew what he meant. Because, though his principles remained a crucial point of reference, each student was spinning off on his or her own path.

The fact that writing well is a path, not a destination, a process more than a goal, is perhaps the most important truth a writing course can divulge. The ongoing give-and-take with the teacher and the other students makes it clear, as nothing else can, that the effort has no end; it is possible to make progress; it is necessary to accept defeat and go on. Because teachers of writing are themselves writers they can comfort students as fellow sufferers while providing living examples of at least limited success. They are people who have won the right to take themselves seriously as professionals, and they can help you earn that privilege, too.

Carol Lew Simons, having spent three terms in Richard P. Brickner's "Free-Style" Writing Workshop at New York City's New School, summed up the benefits of writing courses this way:

> I am not, strictly speaking, a beginning writer. All my life I have written essays that loyal friends and my mother have dutifully praised; as a literature major at Antioch College I wrote very well-received critical papers; for the past four years I have been writing for a medical magazine. I decided to take a writing course, however, because I felt a gap existed between these slender accomplishments and the claim I sometimes made, more often than not to myself, that underneath it all I was a *real* writer. So far my attitudes have undergone more revolution than my writing, but this fact may suggest the major advantages of workshop courses.
>
> One attitude that has begun to alter rather remarkably is my view of writing as an activity, which has come about largely through the nature of the workshop discussions. What makes a workshop different from the scores of good literature courses I have taken is that the author is there in the room; the work is being regarded as a thing in process rather than as something that has, as doctors say, passed "into the literature"; and the people considering the work are involved to some extent in trying to do a similar task.
>
> I think, though I would never have admitted to this had I been asked, that before the workshop I regarded writing as an either/or proposition; you wrote something, revised it a little, and it succeeded or not. The workshop has made it clear that writing is something to be practiced very diligently, like the piano. One might never write as well as one wishes, but one can learn to write as well as one *can*—although only with considerable time and concentration. The workshop has given me a much greater respect for writing as a craft and a process, even as it has made me see it as an endeavor more accessible and less mystical than I had once thought it.

To find a course that's as good for you as Brickner's was for Simons, decide first—and honestly—how big a commitment you are willing to make. Depending on your age and station in life, as well as on your financial and emotional wherewithal, you may want to choose anything from a full-scale, two-year creative writing program leading to an MFA degree and a career in writing, to a journalism course or a weekend workshop (though a very short course is likely to be more useful for making contacts than for learning to write; see "A Foot in the Door"). Then, if you're contemplating a sizable investment of time and/or money, consult "Getting the Words Right Resources," read catalog copy and works by your prospective professor, talk with fellow students, and look for these hallmarks:

* A commitment from the teacher to comment individually, in detail and in person, on each student's work.
* An indication that your classmates will be at approximately your level of writing ability, so that you will be able to respect their comments without developing feelings of inferiority or superiority.
* An instructor who has published, who intends to publish again and whose work you admire.
* An absence of dogma in the course description. Teachers should be loath to mold you in their image and eager, instead, to point you toward what Brickner calls "that language which is most yours and which is yet to be made available to a readership, to help you impose your specialness in a way that's beneficial to the outside."

Correspondence Courses

Despite the fact that almost every big university now has a writing program, that more and more colleges are opening their undergraduate courses to part-time students and that continuing education centers exist throughout the country, many people who would like to get instruction in writing find it hard to attend classes.

In some cases geography is the problem; there's simply no appropriate course within a reasonable radius. In others, the stumbling block is time; personal or job responsibilities can make it impossible to show up anywhere at the same hour each week. And in still other instances, psychological difficulties arise; taking criticism in front of a group—no matter how similarly situated and how sympathetic the members—may be a terrifying and repellent prospect. In these situations, among others, a correspondence course can be worth considering as a source of motivational energy and critical reaction.

No doubt, you will do your considering skeptically, because anyone who reads the papers knows that education by mail in America today is not only a big business, but also sometimes a bad business. State departments of education usually regulate refund policies, and any school that actually lies about its faculty's credentials or its graduates' achievements is likely to find itself in legal trouble—when and if somebody institutes an action against it. But for the most part, nobody monitors the quality of correspondence-school offerings. So skepticism is entirely in order.

Fortunately, however, you can size up a correspondence course before enrolling. As proof, consider a personal case history featuring Judith Appelbaum as the Aspiring Author and a school devoted to children's literature that sought students partly through flyers in an urban supermarket. "We're looking for people to WRITE CHILDREN'S BOOKS" the flyers said, adding: "If you ever wanted to write and be published this is your opportunity." A lengthy copy block explained how lucrative the market for children's literature was and invited all comers to send for the institute's free (no obligation) aptitude test and descriptive brochure.

The aptitude test proved sensible, if hardly grueling. Starting with True/False questions ("Young people don't have any serious problems and don't want to read about any"), it proceeded through a varied series of short assignments ("Write a step by step instruction for a child on how to fly a kite, cook an egg, or plant a seed") to a request for a two-hundred-word piece about "something that happened during your childhood."

Without trying to do either badly or well, the Aspiring Author filled out the form, sent it off and sat back to study the accompanying brochure, which offered hard sell—but hard information, too—about faculty credentials and curriculum. A flurry of activity then ensued. The institute fired off a form letter accepting Judith Appelbaum as a student (and then more form letters counseling prompt enrollment). Judith Appelbaum asked for additional information about course content and for the names and addresses of graduate references. The institute responded with a lengthy, informative and personally typed letter. J.A. called the ex-students (all three of them liked the course and said it helped them develop discipline and self-confidence).

At this point the Aspiring Author was satisfied, having learned enough about the school to discount the tone of hucksterism in its ads and in its programmed correspondence (letters offering new and improved incentives to enroll kept coming for months) and to conclude that it presented a conscientious and apparently effective program of instruction.

To find a worthwhile correspondence course, send for the *Directory of Accredited Home Study Schools* (you'll see full information in "Resources"), explore the programs that interest you by carefully reading their brochures, and take a leaf from the Aspiring Author's book by conducting your own investigation of any course you're seriously considering. You'll want answers to questions like:

* What's the refund policy?
* How much is the total cost of the course—including any and all finance charges?
* What promises do they make about selling your work?
* Who's on the faculty?
* Are academic credits earned here accepted anywhere else?

Ask to talk or correspond with students; check consumer and government agencies for complaint histories; write faculty members to inquire about how actively they participate in instruction and how much individual attention you'll receive.

Though you won't, of course, need to know who your fellow students are, you should see to it that the other three hallmarks of good writing courses (see above) characterize your correspondence course too. Careful evaluation before you sign up can prevent crippling blows to your psyche and your pocketbook.

Paid Critics

Both classroom teachers and correspondence-school faculty may offer advice and assistance on marketing, but as a rule they emphasize writing well at least as much as writing to sell. This is generally not the case with criticism services, which tend to stress marketing above all else and which, as a result, can be dangerous. As you read their ads (they appear in writers' magazines and sometimes in general-interest periodicals too), keep the risks in mind.

Chief among the dangers, perhaps, is the possibility that your whole approach to writing will suffer if you heed the comments of agency critics. For what they're selling is not continuing advice on improving a work in progress but, rather, a one-shot assessment of an allegedly finished manuscript couched primarily in terms of its salability. Confronted with this emphasis, you may be tempted to stop concentrating on saying what you have to say as well as you can say it, and to focus instead on giving the public what it supposedly wants. From there it can be a short step to hack writing if you're glib and to writing garbage if you're not.

Of course, hired critics may not know what the public really wants; the chances are, however, that they'll say they do, and that, furthermore, they'll have a particular "public" in mind—big-name commercial book and magazine publishers. Now, commercial publishers may very well be the wrong audience for your work, and even if they're right for it their reactions to a given manuscript simply cannot be accurately predicted. Editors themselves are so aware of the variety of tastes in their ranks that they often refuse to comment on a book or article (even if they think it has merit and promise) unless they themselves can buy it; each is afraid to suggest changes that might be anathema to another editor.

Your money, in other words, may be ill-spent on a criticism service (though the fact that you've actually spent it will provide a powerful and destructive impetus for thinking well of the advice that it bought). And your money may also be stolen. The field is full of charlatans, people who will take what you pay and then vanish where the Better Business Bureau cannot follow. For every writer satisfied with comments sold by agents such as Scott Meredith, say, there must be scores who are bitter about the hundreds of dollars they spent for useless or nonexistent critiques.

Consider, as a warning, this portion of a letter from Great Novels, Inc., to writer Wayne B. George: "There is not enough emotion in your book. Instead of the storm in Boston clearing up right away you could have a snowdrift blocking your home in the suburbs. You are slowly starving, and the young lady who is your guest gets sick and needs a doctor. Finally you are both saved from death."

The advice may strike you as insultingly simple-minded on the face of it, but it becomes downright infuriating when you realize that Wayne George's manuscript had no snowstorm scene.

If it's criticism you want, try the approaches mentioned in the preceding chapter; if it's marketing advice, turn to "A Foot in the Door," which comes next. But if you're determined to pay for comments on your completed work, take these precautions:

* Ask your chosen critic for a current client list, and call or write some of the people on it to discuss the quality of the critic's services.
* Ask prospective critics for lists of editors who've bought their clients' work recently, and get in touch with them.
* Consult government and consumer agencies about complaints.
* Get a written explanation, in advance, of charges and services.

✱ And don't forget that the substantial sums you can pay for advice have no necessary connection with what that advice is worth.

Computer Software

Word processing programs are the best thing that's happened to writing since movable type. "If you're really serious about your manuscript and you want to do it over and over and you want to get it exactly right, the computer will help you," said Alvin Toffler, author of *Future Shock* and *The Third Wave*, in a conversation with novelist Gay Courter, who wrote a bestseller, *The Midwife*, on an IBM machine; Courter's own experience and reports from many other writers she queried bear Toffler out.

In fact, authors by the dozens have now testified that software like Microsoft Word, WordPerfect, WordStar and XyWrite lets you be remarkably flexible, experimental, demanding and productive as you draft and revise.

You say you're technophobic, mechanically backward, strapped for funds? Even so, if you don't yet do your writing on a computer and if you'd like to produce better work, try to arrange to start using one now. Choose software that your computer store features and your friends favor, so that it will be easy to get help during the learning process. And streamline that process by seeking instruction from a person as well as a manual. Maybe a writer you know will come over one morning to help you master the basic moves. Alternatively, if your budget will allow it, you can hire someone who works for a nearby computer retailer to tutor you for a couple of hours.

Experienced hands can tell you, as manuals generally don't, what you really need to learn (only a fraction of your program's many features will be relevant to your work), and they can also keep you calm if you're the sort who's skittish about newfangled electronic gizmos.

Along with word-processing software, some people get "writing software" designed to spruce up spelling, vocabulary and style.

Unfortunately, although it can strengthen your spelling, it may weaken your prose by encouraging you to obey simple-minded rules. In essence, each of these programs has a finite storehouse of words and patterns it will approve or criticize. When those words or patterns show up in your work, prescribed responses spew out. Sometimes these are helpful, as, for example, when a program takes you to task for overusing certain words or writing interminable sentences. But sometimes they're harmful, too; given the Gettysburg Address to critique, one program faulted Lincoln for using the passive voice.

The best advice, therefore, is steer clear of software that tells you what to do and make use of software that enhances your ability to do whatever you decide makes sense.

Books

Relax now. Books as instructional aids are easy to access as well as inexpensive and plentiful.

Though they tend to be similarly titled, books about writing divide into three classes: those in which the author becomes your partner in the task of learning to choose and combine words; those in which the author imparts formulas; and those in which the author explains how to find things out.

Partnership books, like good writing courses, see learning to write as an unending process in which the teacher's role is to provide fertile ground for growth. Though the authors here are often men and women of considerable literary distinction, they tend to talk humbly of their work and to speak unblushingly of frustration and failure. As a rule, they concentrate on the development of skills in four primary areas:

Reading: "What the writer wants to note, beyond anything that concerns even the critic, is how the story, its language, and all its parts have been joined together" (R. V. Cassill, *Writing Fiction*).

Creativity: "To begin with, you must teach the unconscious to flow into the channel of writing. . . . [L]ess elegantly and more exactly, we might say that the first step toward being a writer is to hitch your unconscious mind to your writing arm" (Dorothea Brande, *Becoming a Writer*).

Diction: "You will never make your mark as a writer unless you develop a respect for words and a curiosity about their shades of meaning that is almost obsessive" (William Zinsser, *On Writing Well*).

And construction: Or learning "how to put words together . . . so that the reader not simply may but must grasp your meaning" (Jacques Barzun, *Simple and Direct*).

Obviously, this approach involves steady hard labor. You can expect to be stimulated by a partnership book; to be satisfied you must experiment with its teachings (preferably in a playful, almost childlike way), and you must also absorb them, so that they color your perceptions as you work. And rewrite. And rewrite some more.

Few formula publications dwell on the importance of painstaking revision. Instead, they offer to make writing easier. Almost always the authors are professionals setting forth the fruits of their experience as a series of instructions, and they tend to utter commands with great confidence.

Generally, these writers are most trustworthy when they discuss their own activities (by outlining, for example, how they keep records or conduct interviews), and they are least to be believed when they deal with the effects of their systems on editors (beware, for instance, of detailed directions about the physical appearance of a manuscript; if you follow them, you'll signal most publishing people that you're a fledgling writer trying to be slick).

Essentially, formula publications constitute a grab bag for authors in which some of the goodies are much better than others; some may not suit you at all and none is a major gift. For, where learning to write is concerned, tips on technique and on industry mores, and gimmicks and shortcuts and nuggets of knowledge can be no more than peripheral aids. The central job—developing your individual style, substance and purpose—demands independent, innovative work.

To the extent that gathering data is part of the writing assignment you set yourself, your burdens will be eased by a knowledge of research tools and techniques. As you'll see if you explore your local public library, the current range of informational materials is astonishing; running from the *Guide to Reference Books* and the *Encyclopedia of Associations* to the *Directory of Chinese Officials: Scientific and Educational Organizations* and the *Minerals Yearbook*, the assortment illuminates the infinite targets of human curiosity and provides starting points for anybody in search of facts.

Research manuals provide starting points too, and most of those that get published offer solid information and analysis in lively prose (since they can't depend on the glamour of their subject to attract readers, they almost have to be good).

Manuals on interviewing procedures tend to be less meaty. In fact, many of them are chatty, anecdotal discussions that illustrate nothing so well as the art of padding article-length copy into book-length size. But they do serve as useful reminders that people can be excellent sources of new knowledge. And the best of them offer serviceable pointers on how to get human beings to tell you what you want to know.

Wherever you get your information, you may need help in evaluating it because, as this single example from William L. Rivers's admirable *Finding Facts* suggests, the plainest of factual statements can bear a highly complicated relationship to the truth:

[Consider] varying news stories about a simple report on gifts to Stanford University during one fiscal year. The university-published *Campus Report* headed its story:
HIGHEST NUMBER OF DONORS IN STANFORD HISTORY
The San Francisco Chronicle headline said:
STANFORD AGAIN RAISES $29 MILLION IN GIFTS
The *Palo Alto Times* story was headed:
DONATIONS TO STANFORD LOWEST IN FOUR YEARS
The student-published *Stanford Daily* announced:
ALUMNI DONATIONS DECLINE; BIG DROP FROM FOUNDATIONS
These headlines accurately reflect the stories they surmounted—which were also accurate.

Clearly, one lesson here is that the way a writer presents a piece of data determines its meaning in the reader's mind. Which brings us around once more to the reason for learning to write. You can teach yourself by following the suggestions in "Basics" or by devising others or by muddling through. You can take courses, contact critics, plug into computers and study books. But your fundamental goal must always be the same—full absorption (to such an extent that both your conscious and your subconscious choices are informed as you work) of a crucial principle: What you communicate is a function of how you communicate. Or, as Northrop Frye has explained with exemplary clarity, "The words used are the form of which the ideas are the content, and until the words have been found, the idea does not fully exist."

A Foot in the Door

***

The Plain Truth About Agents

A MAGIC WAND is basic equipment for literary agents. At least, that's what even experienced authors seem to believe. Agents, it's assumed, can work miracles. They're all-knowing, all-powerful, all-wise. Each one is intimately acquainted with the tastes and needs of hundreds of editors in New York City (and a few elsewhere). At a word from an agent, offers pour in, advances rise, promotion plans expand, ad budgets skyrocket.

Because it's way too much to live up to, many agented authors end up disappointed, even bitter about their experiences.

If you think you want an agent, therefore—as virtually everyone who writes books does—it's important to understand how they really operate as well as how to get one, how to work with one and, if need be, how to leave one and find another or function alone. This chapter covers those topics; the next chapters explain how you can place your work without an agent (yes, magazine writers do it all the time, and authors of books do it often, no matter what you may have heard to the contrary).

Submitting

"I go to 10 or 15 houses simultaneously." "I won't take a book on unless I have 3–9 houses in mind for it." "I may submit a book to 10 or 15 houses, one at a time." "Usually, I'll submit to 6 or 8 editors." "I start out with 15. As they come back, I do more."

Restated, these reports from agents might read: In the normal course of events, I get half a dozen rejections, a dozen rejections, maybe more than that, for book projects I submit.

Sometimes, of course, agents will score on the first try, and even generate competing bids (probably via multiple submissions rather than auctions, which have played out badly often enough to lose much of their appeal). On the other hand, sometimes agents bomb out completely. "Everyone talks about the books I sell but they have no idea how many books I don't sell," an agent will tell you in private. In public, the subject of failure rarely arises, but it's a safe bet that 25%, and probably more, of all agented manuscripts simply don't get bought.

What all this proves is that selling literary property is a risky business, even for the experts. And it's doubly risky for agents because they not only put their reputations on the line every time they offer a book ("We're only as good as our latest submission," says James Heacock of the Heacock Literary Agency in Santa Monica); they also gamble with their finances. Most reputable agents, after all, work on commission. Some still charge 10%; most went to 15% during the '80s; but when a manuscript doesn't sell, any cut adds up to nothing.

To make their business economically viable, many agents set up shop in their homes and most agents try to maximize the chances of success in four admirably logical ways: by choosing their clients carefully (see "Finding Your Agent," below), by placing books rather than shorter work (periodical pieces take as much time but pay less), by making the projects they handle as appealing as possible and by offering them to editors who are, in essence, their pals.

Maximizing a book's appeal can involve working with the author on a proposal for months and months. (See "Procedures" for an analysis of proposals and their uses). Agents are not equally gifted as editorial advisers, of course, nor equally willing to put in tremendous amounts of time on spec, but many of the best will critique rewrite after rewrite until a book's strengths are unmistakably apparent.

Even before a proposal is ready, an agent will start the submissions process by talking about it to editors over the phone or over lunch. If the proposal is taking the agent into a new field (it's a gardening book, perhaps, the first one the agent has handled), these editors may be strangers, people ferreted out by research and added to a contact list that numbers between 100 and 200. More often, though, agents bring new book projects to people they already know, like and trust, and who like and trust them right back.

Among the hundreds of editors in New York City and the thousands west of the Hudson, the agent may deal regularly with 30. Or, to look at the pattern from another angle, among the scores of agents in New York City and the scores more around the country, any one editor at a large house may hear from no more than 25, while editors at small firms—well-established, professional, profitable small firms—seldom hear from more than 6.

Provided that your agent is really right for your work, this is all to the good, an efficient chain of interactions between people with similar tastes and interests. If your agent is not quite on your wave length, though, it may mean that the editors who'd like your book best never hear about it.

In any case, the submissions process that good agents follow is lengthy and painstaking. Let lazier authors' reps send material out with a terse covering note—"Perhaps something here will interest you." The good agent not only introduces a book in conversation, but also writes a thoughtful, detailed, personal letter to make sure editors have all the information they need to judge a book's marketability, and convince their colleagues of it.

As rejections come in, agents may pass them along to writers in whole or in part, or they may simply dismiss them and move on. When two or three comments make the same negative point about a nonfiction book, it's probably worth rethinking the proposal, most agents believe. Advice about fiction is less useful. In fact, as the agent for several bestselling novels points out, it's generally "worth nothing unless the recommendations resonate or the editor is buying the book."

During the placement process, agents maintain files of all correspondence and records of all submissions and their outcomes. Most agents try to keep their authors abreast of a book's status but no writer should expect a weekly progress report. With dozens of clients, agents find it impossible to pay constant attention to each. In any event, some writers prefer not to know every detail of a flat-out rejection letter and appreciate having a buffer between them and potentially devastating feedback ("I encourage editors to respond in detail," says Acton & Dystel's Jane Dystel, who tries "to pass comments along constructively"). It's fine to write and ask for news if you haven't heard anything for a while, but don't launch a barrage of phone calls. And rest assured that when something sells, you'll hear about it.

Making Deals

It's when your book is accepted at last that an agent's most valuable skills come into play, for at this point a book publisher will usually offer an advance against royalties, and an agent will usually be able (as a writer probably won't) to get that advance up. Furthermore, as your business representative, an agent can sell your talents and potential to a publisher in a way calculated to get you the best possible terms throughout your contract (see "Getting What's Coming to You" for additional information on negotiations).

For the best agents, negotiating means feeling one's way, not simply following a formula. Or, as Georges Borchardt puts it, "There's very little repetition, very little that's standard"; good negotiators are imaginative, they come up with new language, new approaches. Borchardt, who represents Tracy Kidder, Stanley Elkin and Janet Malcolm, among others, sold 145 books last year for publication as originals or reprints. Advances for these books ranged from $1,500 to $1,250,000, a spread by no means unique. Advances reported by other agents run "from two figures to six figures," "from $1,500 to millions," "from $5,000 to the high five figures."

"My secret goal," says one agent, "is to get the advance up at least by the amount of my commission." Trying hard to better other terms too, conscientious agents devote a great deal of time and effort to figuring out what they want for their clients and then, in effect, they develop their own versions of various publishers' contracts. As a result, when an agent goes to a large firm like Random House or Morrow, editors there know from experience what language and provisions will be acceptable to that agent and they can streamline the negotiating process.

One negative side effect may occur, though. Points that matter to you but not to most other writers may be ignored. It's vital, therefore, that even agented authors read their contracts and discuss wish lists with their agents early on to see what's realistic and what isn't.

If, for example, you're incensed by the fact that the "satisfactory manuscript" clause gives the publisher power to cancel your deal—and well you might be—you need to know that "publishers can usually get around whatever changes you make in things like that, though it is worth trying for better definition" of their rights.

It's also worth trying to retain as many rights to your book as possible, although publishers are tending to demand more for themselves. For with skill, determination and perhaps a little luck, the deal your agent makes with a book publisher will be only one of several deals the agent makes for the book. Sales to foreign publishers, movie and TV producers and firms that reissue out-of-print titles are among those a smart, hardworking agent can generate and shape.

Ongoing Activity

Money due an agented writer will go to the agent first. Agents record payments, deduct what they're owed, and remit the balance to their clients. As a rule, they also attempt to check royalty statements but it's an uphill battle at best and only a few stubborn souls emerge victorious.

Royalty statements are notoriously impenetrable—information is missing, figures won't jibe, streams of income simply don't show up. You can solve some of the mysteries yourself (see "Getting What's Coming to You") and industry efforts may solve others over time (both the Authors Guild and the Book Industry Study Group are tackling the problem intelligently).

Meanwhile, agents expect collection hassles and cope as well as they can. But money isn't all they will keep tabs on. "I'm a partner, not a broker," says Jean Naggar, whose client list includes Jean Auel, Mary McGarry Morris and Nancy Willard. Naggar, like many other agents, sees her mission as developing a writer's career, which means shepherding books through the long and cumbersome publishing process.

At the outset, when editing is going on, the agent's role is generally minor, unless author and editor clash, in which case the agent can step in to restore peace. When the time comes for marketing, agents are more active, although the level of activity varies from person to person and book to book, as does the level of effectiveness.

"We call and nag a lot, but I don't know that it does any good," one agent says, while another reports gratifying success at a meeting with marketing people at a well-known house—which doubled a book's first printing on the spot—and depressing failure in a series of conversations with sub rights people at another—who refused to reject a remarkably low bid from a paperback reprinter.

One relatively easy way for agents to affect marketing is through authors. As "Why and How to Be Your Own Best Sales Force" will demonstrate in detail, lively, savvy writers can boost sales substantially, which is why Berenice Hoffman and others habitually help them use their contacts and energies to advantage.

Does all this sound like a full-time job and then some? It surely is, especially when you consider that most literary agencies are small, maybe one or two people (with an assistant or two or three) serving as advocate, adviser and business manager for 50 to 100 writers. So if you have an agent, make sure to express your confidence and appreciation. And if you don't have one, use the rest of this chapter and the next to decide whether, when and how to change that situation.

Finding Your Agent

Just any old agent will not do. For one thing, an agent can be a handicap rather than a help. "Everybody knows there are certain agents who send only junk," a veteran editor says, explaining that manuscripts from inept agents arrive with a strike against them. And for another thing, an agent who doesn't quite understand what you're up to probably deals with editors who won't get it either (see "Submitting," above), so that the submissions process will waste time and muddy the waters.

What you want, therefore, is a capable, well-regarded agent who truly understands and admires your work.

You can pinpoint promising agents by using directories and contacting the Association of Authors' Representatives in New York (see "A Foot in the Door Resources"), but the best way to find out about an individual agent's interests, strengths, and idiosyncrasies is through word of mouth. Long before you're in a position to hire one, you might begin investigating agents by asking published writers you know whom they'd recommend, or by calling a local author you've just read about in the paper for suggestions. Alternatively, you might contact the local writers' club, talk to your librarian, scan prefaces for comments on agents' contributions and browse through the book trade's organ of communication, *Publishers Weekly* (see "Resources").

Predictably, good agents are highly selective. Some won't even read your work unless you send it exclusively to them (although they may be all in favor of multiple submissions to editors; see "Procedures"). And many find that maintaining the level of personal service they give existing clients means turning away dozens of writers each week. Authors they accept tend to have one of two things going for them: they were referred—by an editor or a current client—or they wrote a wonderful query letter. (Occasionally, agents will take the initiative and go after someone they want to represent, perhaps a chef on local TV who seems to have an interesting new diet or a psychologist whose advice columns might make a salable book.)

For guidance on crafting good queries, see "Procedures." For more tips on targeting agents (as well as editors), see "Openings." And to get the most from the advice in those chapters remember three things:

1. Boston and Washington, Los Angeles and San Francisco—not to mention all sorts of places in between—are home to agents who are good at their work and possibly right for yours. In the era of jet travel and instant communication by phone and fax, you'd be silly to rule anyone out solely on the basis of geography.

2. People just starting out as agents are less selective than people who've been agenting for a while. *Publishers Weekly* often announces agency openings. As you pursue possibilities, though, remember that anyone can use the label "literary agent," and be especially careful to check background and terms.

3. The author–agent relationship is intimate and, ideally, long-lived, rather like a marriage. In fact, when you listen to agents talking about writers you'll hear significant-other metaphors time and again. When a client leaves, it's a "divorce." When an agent decides to persevere after 38 rejections, it's because she's "fallen in love" with a book. Trying to decide whether to take a new client on, agents ask themselves, "Can I live with this person?" When the decision is Yes, writer and agent sign a contract, a.k.a. a "prenuptial agreement."

Agency contracts are occasionally verbal and, when written, often couched in the form of a letter. Some are one page long and entirely intelligible; some run on over several pages larded with legal jargon, and at least one is more draconian than any publisher's contract that agent would let a writer sign.

If the agent you want uses a lengthy form that seems to say

"We own you forever," think about hiring a literary property lawyer to negotiate for you (using any other sort of lawyer will be counterproductive because contracts in other industries are so different). Otherwise, you can probably deal direct.

The first thing that strikes most people unfamiliar with literary agents' contracts is that the agents expect payment in perpetuity. A basically reasonable requirement given their investments of time and credibility, it is variously expressed: commissions are to be paid "for the life of agreements we make on your behalf," "during or after our tenure as representative," on "all sales for which negotiations begin during the term of this agreement and end within six months after it expires, and all changes and extensions in those agreements, regardless of when made and by whom."

But what if the agent goes out of business? What if the individual who is "your" agent leaves the agency and goes somewhere else? What if your agent is acquired by a larger company whose best clients' books compete with yours? As New York literary property lawyer Kenneth P. Norwick points out, it's wise to consider the what-ifs, and Norwick recommends asking that an arbitration clause be inserted in your contract in case of irreconcilable differences.

Just don't get so wrapped up in possible pitfalls that you forget what's really going on here. Two people with complementary skills and congenial personalities who have taken the trouble to investigate each other are joining forces to launch a book and build a career. It may not be any closer to perfect than most marriages but the proper attitude for starters is a blend of confidence, commitment and joy.

Breaking Up

Say it just isn't working out. The agent's not enthusiastic anymore. Worse, your phone calls aren't returned, your letters aren't answered, nothing has sold. Breakups do occur, sometimes to an agent's regret but usually not. Agents like clients to make the decision ("I prefer to have them fire themselves") and to seek other representation ("I've suggested to several people that they'd be happier elsewhere because I was getting a twisted stomach every time they called, because I'd lost my enthusiasm or because we'd gotten fed up with each other.").

For writers, it's a scary scenario, especially when it involves the all too frequently uttered negative overgeneralization. "Nobody's buying fiction anymore," one agent told a well-reviewed novelist. "It's hopeless. We've gone to everybody," another one said, summing up seven submissions of a coffee table title. In the first case, the novelist got herself another agent—who assured her that the fiction market had not vanished. In the second, the writer decided to proceed on her own and get a publisher interested; Viking Penguin, which apparently fell outside the "everybody" category, bought her book.

Still, both of these writers had their confidence badly shaken, at least for a while. Agents may stay calm about losing clients and helping new agents take over, but authors anguish.

This is true even if the author is the one who walks. "I worried all the way to the mailbox," a nonfiction writer says. Several of his books had been critical successes and one had made a fair amount of money, but now his career seemed stalled and his agent unresponsive. He'd written the agent a polite, appreciative note severing the relationship and he was nervous. "Will I ever get another agent? Will I get a better agent? What am I doing to myself?"

Yes, he got another agent, and one who was better for him. Although most of his books had been critical rather than commercial successes, this writer had enough pride in his work to "take the position an agent would be lucky to get me." Having "decided to give myself that vote of confidence," he carefully targeted several agents to approach and met with half a dozen. The new agent he chose worked with him for close to a year, first on a proposal that didn't sell and then on one that did—for nearly three times any previous advance he'd ever gotten.

Why the big jump? "Partly because this agent is more on my

wave length than the other one was, which means his contacts are more suited to my work."

The point deserves to be underlined. It's the right agent you want, the one who knows what you're about and likes it. If you can't find that sort of representation, you'll be better off proceeding on your own, at least until you get an offer. With that in hand, getting an agent is easier. Just remember not to agree to any specifics an editor proposes until the agent is on the case.

See the rest of this section for pointers on how to generate offers, and take heart from a statement by Putnam's executive editor, Refna Wilkin: Putnam publishes many authors who come without agents, she said. "Like all publishers, we are anxious to invest in new talent and we hope we will continue to see it."

Who Do You Know?

THE CHARGE THAT the publishing game is fixed, that you've got to know an insider if you're ever going to break into print, is part myth, part truth. The myth arises because the easiest response in the face of repeated rejection is to say that everyone but you is pulling strings left and right. It's not a large step from this interpretation of bad fortune to a full-blown conspiracy theory of an entrenched literary establishment. Those who've written superb (and fairly conventional) prose, however, are all but sure to get published by a major house—even if they don't know a soul remotely connected with publishing—for reasons already indicated.

As for the truth: there's no doubt that it helps to have personal contact with people in a position to make editorial decisions, particularly when your work is good rather than great. The point is not that editors will publish you because you're friendly with them (that would not be a good way for them to keep their jobs); the point is that they will be more likely to take a chance on you if they see you as a known quantity. Editors are as insecure about their own judgments as most other people, and therefore they always find it easier to back a pre-tested, preapproved author. Anything you can do to provide trustworthy testimony to your skills will help reassure editors that by gambling on you they'll be running a fairly small risk.

The idea of a connections approach to publishing shouldn't

repel you, since, in the first place, connections are not necessarily insidious and artificial, and, in the second, most sources of connection to publishing insiders are not only generally accessible but also worthwhile cultivating in their own right.

Think, for example, of writers (including writing teachers), people in publishing (and not only editors) and selected collaborators (including some editorial emigres).

Other Authors

Any way you can associate with writers is bound to be to your advantage.

Michael Chabon, whose first novel, *The Mysteries of Pittsburgh*, sold for $155,000, placed it with the help of his adviser at the University of California at Irvine, the writer Macdonald Harris. And Amy Tan connected with her first publisher via Molly Giles, award-winning writer and teacher. Tan, who met Giles in 1985 at the Squaw Valley Community of Writers, credits her with "the sharpest eye, the keenest ear for false steps, insincere voice, inconsistencies." Through Giles, Tan got to Sandra Dijkstra, the California agent who orchestrated the sale of *The Joy Luck Club*.

Taking a writing course will put you in touch with at least one published author, the teacher (there may be others in the class), whose contacts you may be able to use. Ask your instructor and fellow students for the names of people you should send your work to, and ask if you may use their names in the covering letters.

Readings also provide good ways to get to know writers, so watch your local calendar of events and steel yourself to approach speakers after their presentations. Tell them who you are and what you're working on; they could be valuable links between you and a sympathetic editorial ear.

And then there are writers groups for people at every level of accomplishment. Why not join one or more of those you'll find listed in "Resources"? If you can't get to meetings, you can still benefit from the newsletter and maybe communicate with kindred spirits via computer.

Some writers make it a point to share their contacts—"I know an editor at the *Atlantic*; I'll write and say you're sending an article in." Others you meet may recommend you for assignments they hear about but don't want for themselves.

One of the best ways to meet writers is by going to one or more of the hundreds of conferences and weekend workshops organized each year (see "Resources" for help in finding those nearby). When professional writers and editors and would-be writers gather to share marketing tips and critical evaluations, exciting developments sometimes occur.

This is most often the case for writers who come to conferences with manuscripts in hand. Anne Rice, for instance, brought the manuscript of her first novel to a writers' conference. An editor from Knopf who was there to lecture read it and was impressed enough to bring it back to New York for consideration. Rice's *Interview with the Vampire*, subsequently published by Knopf, launched her phenomenal career.

To forge a valuable connection at a conference, you may have to do more than plant yourself on fertile ground and hope to be discovered. You may have to boldly bring your work to the attention of others. Christina Baldwin's story illustrates the snowball effect that one step of initiative—taken in a mood of nothing lost, nothing gained—can have.

When I saw an announcement of the Second Annual Women in Writing Conference, on women's personal writings, I wrote the director, Hannelore Hahn, of my work teaching and my intention to write a book, and she invited me to be a panelist at the conference. I headed for it in early August with my third-draft manuscript, and a twenty-minute presentation entitled "The Rituals of Journal Writing." After that everything felt like a hurricane. I gave my presentation, and was astounded and delighted with the energy and response it generated. I was asked to do a mini-workshop later in the afternoon and agreed to invite anyone interested. Fifty women crowded into that space, journals in hand, and we shared avidly all we could for the next three hours. Published authors came up to me with advice and referrals for breaking into the New York publishing world. The next day someone introduced me to Meredith Bernstein and told me she was a book agent.

Monday, August 9, Meredith and I had lunch, discovered we liked and trusted each other. I gave her my manuscript copy of *One to One*. She read it that night and called me the next morning saying she loved it, and I agreed to have her handle it. That afternoon she hand-carried it to Herb Katz at M. Evans, who promised that he would read it Tuesday night. Wednesday morning he called Meredith, said Evans was highly interested in it, and he wanted some other staff people to read it and wanted us to meet him on Thursday afternoon. Thursday I met with Evans and found them supportive and helpful about revision. Only one more week passed before Meredith had negotiated the contract and the advance.

It's possible that all you'll get from a conference is a rudimentary suntan and a dent in your bank balance, but it's also possible that you'll come away having found (1) encouragement from peers and/or professionals; (2) references you can use later in submitting manuscripts or applying for grants or jobs; (3) a demystified view of the publishing business; and (4) proof at first hand that unknown writers do get published. The overwhelming response of many conference-goers is joy, because they discover that the publishing world is not as sealed as they had thought.

Publishing People

If you don't want an agent (or you don't want one now) and if close association with writers doesn't appeal to you, perhaps you'd like to make your connections through people who work in publishing.

First, reach far and wide among your acquaintances to see what leads you can turn up. Maybe your brother-in-law's sister's friend or one of your high school classmates is a production assistant at a national magazine. Well, that one name is enough to get you read by somebody and rejected with a letter signed (if not written) by an editor. The same strategy works for book publishing; Peter Tauber, for example, got entrée to an editor's office for his first book, *The Sunshine Soldiers*, through an introduction from a mutual friend who'd worked with Tauber on a newspaper.

Another effective strategy involves turning a rejection from an end into a new beginning. Call the editor who returned your manuscript with an admiring note to ask politely for suggestions about colleagues at other companies who might like your work. A covering letter mentioning one editor's opinion sends powerful signals to the other editors who read it.

A third promising approach lies in making friends with a sales representative. Reps from book publishing houses travel the country constantly. You can find out from your local bookstore manager which ones will be in your area when, and then you can arrange to meet some of them. It would do you no harm to learn as much as you can about their work in general, and if you find that one of them likes what you've written, you've gotten yourself an influential sponsor. (Since acquiring salable books is at least as important to marketing people as it is to editors, sales reps will be as pleased to "discover" you as you will be to have made contact with them.)

In case none of these methods attracts you, there's a still more direct way of building publishing connections: go to work in the field, either informally—by offering editors reliable assistance with clerical chores during your free time; or formally—by getting a job.

Obviously, there's no point undertaking a job hunt in a crowded (and poorly paid) field just to gain connections. But if you're genuinely interested in becoming an assistant editor, say, or a publicity department trainee, and if you manage to get yourself hired, you'll find making connections among the fringe benefits of your work. Lisa Smith explains why:

> At college I told every teacher and student I knew that I wanted to go into magazines and that I was interested in finding out about an internship program so I could see what magazines were like without the pressure and commitment of a permanent job. A teacher told me about the American Society of Magazine Editors internship program

and I applied and was accepted. During my internship I made extremely good contacts. In addition to the people I met at the two magazines I worked on during the summer, I got to meet editors from other magazines who came each week to participate in discussions at the ASME offices. A lot of the editors I met face to face were editors I later submitted story ideas to.

After graduation I was offered a job at *Mademoiselle*, where I worked for two years. Because of my work there, I know how to shape ideas and who to direct them to. I know why manuscripts are accepted or rejected because I've been on the other side of the desk. As far as I'm concerned, going into magazine work is one of the best ways to prepare the ground for a writing career.

The same encomiums can be applied to jobs in book publishing, no matter how lowly they may be to begin with. Crossovers from editing to writing are frequent (Toni Morrison, Michael Korda, Peter Gethers and James D. Landis are current examples of the phenomenon), and all knowledge gained on one side of the spectrum is clearly relevant to success on the other.

Collaborators

Connecting yourself to people with good connections is a fine way to win readers and influence editors. You might try quick canvasses of celebrities on assorted subjects (What's the most terrifying event in your past? How do you think we should deal with the federal deficit?). And deeper patterns of collaboration may ease entrée to publishing houses too.

Consider, for example, the experience of Victoria Y. Pellegrino, a freelance writer and career consultant who had been depressed for some time without fully understanding why. Realizing that lots of other women were feeling the same way, she decided that an analysis of the problem could help them all, and she began to read with an eye to finding an expert who might be interested in collaborating with her on a book.

Research done by Dr. Helen DeRosis, a psychoanalyst and psychotherapist, best addressed Pellegrino's concerns, she discovered, and so it was DeRosis she approached with her idea. "The important thing about collaboration," Pellegrino reported, "is to find someone whose work you respect and whom you personally like and trust." In an atmosphere of mutual admiration, the writer and the doctor decided to work together on a manuscript about overcoming depression, and with the benefit of DeRosis's professional credentials, Pellegrino found a publisher fairly quickly.

The expert collaborator category also includes people who can help you make material marketable. As publishing houses "downsize," accomplished editors increasingly decide to go into business for themselves. Known in the press as "book doctors," they work with writers to create strong proposals and polished manuscipts. Fees for this sort of editorial assistance may be fixed or flexible—several thousand dollars payable in installments, perhaps, or a relatively small payment at first in exchange for a cut of the advance and eventual royalties. When editors opt for a piece of a book's action, they'll want to use their connections to help the book sell, and they're very likely to put their contacts at its service in any event.

Collaboration agreements—with a scholar, a doctor, an editor or anyone else—should be in writing and signed. Consult a literary property lawyer and/or the legal guides mentioned throughout "Resources" for help in drawing up a contract or responding to the one your colleague proposes.

Endnote on Priorities

Regardless of who its members are, an acquaintanceship chain in publishing (as in any other industry) simply greases the wheels. The final verdict on your manuscript will be determined by its perceptible merits. For guidance in making those merits show to best advantage, please move on through the next three chapters.

Subject Matter Matters

THE MAIN TROUBLE with writing for a market is that editors can't know for sure what they want until they've read it. They know what they wanted in the past, of course (and so will you if you study back issues of magazines at the library or this year's book catalogs in *Publishers Trade List Annual* at your local bookstore). And they may think they know enough about what they will want in the future to fill out the questionnaires sent by annual marketing guides (though the statement that a magazine is looking for fiction "on contemporary life and its problems" is not likely to help you much, no matter how accurate it is). But what editors really want is something they can't describe because it doesn't exist yet—the untold story, the fresh perspective, the new idea.

Editors spend a great deal of time trying to think up article and book topics. Once they finally agree on a subject, they spend still more time talking about how to narrow it, how to focus it, what facts to go after and what purpose to serve. After that they'll confer about which writers might handle the project effectively. And when they eventually find a writer willing and able to do the article or the nonfiction book they've been discussing, as often as not the project fizzles (obviously, good fiction cannot result from this process, though popular fiction sometimes does). Bearing in mind that this is what frequently happens when professionals try to create prose that will sell, you may be inclined to abandon the effort yourself. If men and women who are not only intimately familiar with the character and needs of their own publications but also knowledgeable about marketing trends and literary talents can't get it right, what's a writer supposed to do?

Quite simply, follow where your enthusiasms lead. When the individual who's excited by an idea is the same individual who develops that idea for publication, the chances of pleasing an audience (including an audience of editors) shoot way up.

Thus, if you're a lawyer who's eager to propose a new legal status for couples who live together but are not married, or a commercial fishing boat captain who longs to write a novel exposing the corruption in the industry, or a corporate vice-president who's desperate to know whether other highly paid executives feel useless too, you don't have to go looking for a strong subject. All you have to do is write up the one you care about and then figure out how and where to get it into print.

Suppose, however, that your trade is not law or fishing or business, but writing, that you continually need new ideas and angles for periodical pieces or books, and that you find yourself fresh out of enthusiasm from time to time. It may look as though you have a serious problem. For enthusiasm clearly can't be created by fiat, no matter how strong your willpower.

Fortunately, however, it can be grown at home. Just provide an environment that lets your natural passions reveal themselves. One good way to do this is by beginning a program of clipping and filing, as outlined in "Basics." And another is by developing an awareness of readers' motivations and your relationship to them. (What needs could you fill for the reading public that nobody else has filled yet? What needs could you fill that nobody else could fill better?)

Why people read what they read is an endlessly interesting question with plenty of sensible answers. If you keep a list of theories in the back of your mind as you examine events occurring around and within you, you should soon find your energies engaged by an idea for a story or a book.

From the multiplicity of readers' motives, here's a selection to get things started.

Readers Want to Learn . . .

Everyone has some knowledge that would be useful to other people. Perhaps, for example, you could write a manual about financial planning or cooking Lithuanian delicacies or even getting published. Eric L. Reiss had always been interested in old phonographs and "thought that maybe it was time someone wrote a book about them" so he tried the idea out on a small publishing house that "specializes in books for oddball collectors." Reiss's *The Compleat Talking Machine* not only got great reviews, he reports; it sold about 3,000 copies in less than a year, which necessitated a second printing and led the publisher to ask for a sequel.

Or perhaps what you know—and ought to transmit knowledge of—should serve as the basis of what's called a service piece. Can you explain how to find your way through a complicated morass of information? Could you prepare a *Complete Guide to Home-Swapping Programs* or *A Directory of Occupational Diseases*, for example? Have you discovered a scientist whose studies of genetic engineering excite your interest or a musician who's created a startling new system of notation? By all means, consider making valuable technical data accessible to the general public, and explore collaborating with an expert so that new findings that otherwise would be couched in trade jargon and buried in the voluminous literature of a specialized discipline can reach a wider audience.

To find current research that may be grist for a story, make it a habit to browse through special-interest and academic journals in your library. If a title intrigues you, read the article, and if the article meets your expectations, consider writing the author (in care of the magazine) to ask about other good material on the subject; later perhaps you can interview the author/expert.

Interviews offer a good form for communication between experts and the rest of us because Americans today are coming more and more to value the authentic personal voice, the individual mode of expression, the first-hand, eyewitness testimony. But traditional narrative and expository approaches are fine too.

The most complicated kind of knowledge you can relay to an audience involves not just knowing something but knowing what that something signifies. With practice, you can develop the perspicacity and skill necessary for asking revealing questions about apparently commonplace events. What's behind the resurgence of affection for the smell and taste of homemade pasta, for instance? Economics? A recommitment to family life and the home? A diabolical plot by a handful of women's magazines and food manufacturers? The answers may provide fresh material that concerned Americans will value.

. . . to Amass Experiences

Most of us are avid consumers of experience. What we can't do in fact we're usually eager to do vicariously, so that reading matter which can serve either as a trial run or as a substitute for activity has definite attractions.

Thus if you can reveal what it's like to cross the Alps on a bicycle, to experiment with a new method of quality control or to serve on the jury in a murder trial, you have an excellent foundation for the kind of I-was-there-and-this-is-how-it-really-was kind of piece that the media are fond of nowadays.

And if you haven't already had an experience worth sharing, you can set one up. Twenty-two-year-old Mark Rasmussen, for instance, deliberately got himself seduced into attending one of the Reverend Sun Myung Moon's Divine Principle three-day workshops; Rasmussen's edited diary entries appeared in two national magazines. And anthropologist David K. Reynolds arranged to be committed to a veterans hospital as a potential suicide. Reynolds spent two weeks as a mental patient and then wrote a book with suicidologist Norman Farbow about what happened to him and how his experiences jibed with current research findings.

Even when they don't involve this degree of subterfuge and risk, inside stories always appeal to readers' natural curiosity, and there's nothing to stop you from using the form. If you're not an insider by right, you can make yourself one.

. . . to Read about Themselves

It's always exciting to see a movie made in your neighborhood; somehow your own life takes on luster after that and you feel almost as if you'd been featured in that film yourself. A similar pattern of identification probably lies behind the substantial sales of written work with a local focus.

What with diaries and oral histories and natural wonders and the unnatural acts of the couple next door, enough raw materials exist in everybody's town or region to create innumerable poems, novels and works of nonfiction. If you become fascinated by a subject of local interest, you're in luck. The anecdotes and facts that make for a lively manuscript are available nearby, and selling your work will be relatively easy because editors are well aware that Americans love to read about where they live (or where, in this rootless age, they used to live in younger days).

Just as we flock to read about our neighbors because proximity makes us identify with them, we reach eagerly for material about people we recognize as psychological kin. The widening stream of feminist literature results in part from the fact that most women identify to some extent with all women, and therefore feel personally drawn to any discussion of the sex in print. So if you can write as a member of any clearcut group, you can expect other members to form a readership.

. . . to Be Up on the Latest

Check the shelves of your supermarket if you doubt the attraction of the *new* for the American public. Where books are concerned, though, being new means living a year or two in the future because it will take roughly that period to get a manuscript from the idea stage to the bookseller. Since even periodicals usually have lead times of several months, bestseller lists and other conventional hit-parade compilations aren't much use as tools for keeping up with the times; though they seem to reflect the present, they actually portray phenomena that will be in the past by the time you get your manuscript out.

A crystal ball of sorts does exist, however, in the bible of the book trade, *Publishers Weekly* (unfortunately, although there are periodicals about periodicals, *PW* has no counterpart as a channel of communication among editors and publishers of newspapers and magazines). *PW*'s circulation may be small but its influence is enormous; almost everyone involved with book publishing reads it and reacts to it, so that when the magazine repeatedly covers books about money, for example, you can bet (a) that books about money are a big item on current publishers' lists, and (b) that they'll continue to be welcomed by editors, who naturally like manuscripts apt to interest an influential journal.

The pleasure of glimpsing such motives behind the dignified façade of publishing is one of the auxiliary benefits of reading *Publishers Weekly*. As you skim through the magazine, you can begin to feel yourself a member of the gossipy publishing community, listening as hard as the next person for the first sound of a new bandwagon getting ready to roll.

Like its treatment of publishing trends—which it covers in reportorial articles as well as through information tidbits—*PW*'s coverage of forthcoming books provides an outstanding resource for keeping current. Its Announcement issues and roundups present annotated lists of upcoming titles at intervals throughout the year and the magazine often prints items about manuscripts that are still somewhere in the idea or rough-draft stage; books, in other words, that will be published a year or more later. If you can discern a pattern among the new titles, you're on to something that will be hot just when you get your discussion of it off the presses. Similarly, conclusions you can draw from studying *Small Press* magazine or the *Utne Reader* (see "Resources") are likely to foretell subjects that will keep readers up to date in the near future.

To capitalize on current trends in publications more transient than books, you can begin by noting what's selling on the newsstands. Look at the cover lines on view at a variety of locations over a period of several weeks, and see if you can get newsstand dealers to talk with you about what's selling and why. Then, if one of the subjects now drawing customers captures your interest, you can do a piece about it for a periodical that has a very short lead time—a daily paper, perhaps, or possibly a weekly.

. . . to Be Prepared for the Future

If you have to look a couple of years ahead to see the publishing present, it follows that you will have to be even more farsighted to spy its future. Confusing though this seems, it is worth puzzling out because the demand for previews of what's coming next is huge. Looking hard for handholds in a maelstrom of accelerating change, people today are greedy—and will be grateful—for anything that helps them predict, and therefore prepare for, tomorrow.

The trick can be done by anyone who realizes that, in fact, cultural, political and intellectual movements of note almost always start small—with one ardent individual or a small group of impassioned people. At first these initiators are unknown to the rest of us. As they begin to focus attention on themselves, we may well regard them as nuts. But gradually the ideas they've championed catch on, often becoming so widely accepted after a time that new small groups form in rebellion against them.

It's through little observations, which anyone can make, that large changes first become visible. When Mary McLaughlin edited the "Right Now" department of *McCall's*, she spotted a new attitude toward children among a sizable group of parents before it came to national attention as one friend and then another confided in her that, if they had their lives to live over, they'd stay childless.

And it's through small, specialized publishing companies that seminal thinkers and doers are usually first able to address an audience. You can get a leg up on embryonic movements by reading special-interest periodicals and books in fields you care about. Check *The International Directory of Little Magazines and Small Presses* to see which publishing companies specialize in them. Then skim any titles of theirs that your library carries and/or send for their book catalogs or for sample copies of their magazines.

As you study special-interest material, you may develop an ability to sight coming movements long before the general public has any inkling of them. Then you can be the one who introduces evidence for the rebirth of isolationism or schemes for redesigning our schools to the wider world as soon as the time is ripe.

Two caveats:

* Gauging the moment of ripeness is far from easy, because if the future you're describing is too far off, most audiences will see you less as a forecaster than as a fool. Perhaps, like Margaret Kavanagh-Smith, a Waynesville, North Carolina, writer, you'll decide to do a piece whenever you come upon a portentous subject and then put what you've written away in a drawer until you can see indications of a general readiness to accept its content. (For more on timing, read "Openings.")

* While it's true that what's seminal is small, it is not equally true that what's small must be seminal. Again, your own passions are probably your best guide; what you feel strongly about, other people may respond to as well, or at least they may respond to it once you have explained it to them. That way, you'll not only have helped prepare for the future, you'll also have helped create it.

Development

Have faith. Let's assume that one stimulus or another or several in combination have triggered the degree of excitement necessary to launch you on a writing project. As you begin to flesh your subject out, use the following suggestions to help ensure that your readers will respond with enthusiasm as keen as your own.

* If you're writing nonfiction, start by conducting a small, informal survey among your acquaintances to see which other people really would like to know what you're planning to tell, and what their general level of ignorance is. It's as important to avoid boring readers by dishing up background they already have as it is to avoid confusing them by beginning your discussion on too advanced a plane.

* Unless you think you're the sort who'd make talking a substitute for writing, tell all sorts of people about your project. You may be surprised to see how many of your friends and associates will present you with valuable ideas or data. Moreover, you'll make new discoveries about your own ideas as you listen to yourself talk.

* Figure out what special sources might exist for the information you need by following the practice Alden Todd outlined in his masterful *Finding Facts Fast*: on any given matter, ask yourself (a) who would know, (b) who would care and (c) who would care enough to have put it in print.

* Keep tugging on the informational chain. You might want a map as background for a short story, or an example to liven up a piece of social criticism, or some word on who could help you understand black holes in space, but whatever you seek you should find if you press each person you talk with for the names of others who could help you end your search.

* Refer back to "Basics" in the "Getting the Words Right" section, and consider using some of its "Resources."

* Narrow your focus. "Prison Reform" won't work as a subject, but "Why Halfway Houses Are the Best Hope for Prison Reform" probably would. If you can't phrase a good working title, chances are your subject isn't adequately defined yet.

* Be as graphic as you can. Don't tell if you can show. Because specifics are much more interesting than generalities, round

up generous collections of anecdotes, illustrations, descriptions, dialogue and quotes.

* Don't be afraid to put yourself in the picture. Who you are and why you're writing this and what makes you think anyone should listen to you can be important elements of your story.

* Bring the wisdom of your lifetime to your task. Writing from experience does not, of course, mean transcribing experience. You have a responsibility to sift and shape your material until it makes sense as a unit and until that unit can be fitted into the context of the reader's life.

* Stay flexible, expect changes and setbacks in the normal course of development and abandon all rules—including those propounded here—if ever some combination of gut feeling and dispassionate analysis tells you to try something outlandish. Maybe it's just what the world needs now.

Openings, or Where to Submit Your Manuscript

WRITERS TODAY HAVE thousands of markets for their work. Book publishers are multiplying fast enough to make your head spin (R. R. Bowker's *Books in Print* database now includes titles from more than 40,000 firms, with new publishers joining the ranks every week). And magazines keep springing up too (more than 2,500 were born in the '80s, two for every one that disappeared).

Although some of today's small publishers put out scruffy little periodicals every so often (when time and funds permit) or issue books they themselves write (and then can't figure out how to unload), many run durable, lucrative operations, which experienced writers find increasingly attractive. They like the personal attention small publishers give them; they like the way small publishers keep promoting their books year after year, so that sales curves rise over time; and they like the fact that small, specialized publishers get written work to readers who share the authors' special interests.

Large publishing operations may still offer advantages, of course, especially for prose that's directed to a very sizable general audience. Since everybody's heard of big companies, their imprint on your writing tends to confer prestige; also, they often pay higher advances than small firms (but, please note, a good small firm will probably net you more over the course of a book's life), and they frequently have more clout with general-interest media.

On the other hand, big firms may offer you little or nothing in the way of promotion unless you're a celebrity or about to become one. Furthermore, large companies are often—although by no means always—impersonal, and they have an irritating habit of getting tangled up in red tape.

Fledgling writers are frequently advised to start with small companies and work their way up to big ones, on the theory that competition for editorial space is less keen in the so-called minor markets. And sometimes it's true that sales to small publishers will establish a record of achievement that will persuade one of the giants to want you on its list. No press or periodical is designed to be a steppingstone, of course; each has its own independent dignity of purpose. But evidence that one editor thought your work worth printing can serve to embolden another editor to back you, in much the same way that an endorsement from a mutual acquaintance might strengthen an initially shaky editorial judgment.

One good reason not to invest heavily in the steppingstone theory is the fact that some smaller publishers are every bit as fussy about accepting manuscripts as any larger firm. And another is this: at heart, effective marketing of your work has less to do with choosing between big and little or top and bottom than with finding the particular publishers who are going to want the particular manuscript you're trying to place right now.

In some cases, it will make sense to aim at Simon & Schuster or *The New Yorker*; in others, the best targets may be Pelican Publishing or *Entrepreneur*; under a third set of circumstances you might consider trying a special-interest quarterly first and then using a clip of your piece as it appeared there to boost your chances at a slick mass-market magazine.

Because the paths to publication are so numerous, you can probably discover a variety of promising markets for every manuscript you have to place. For best results, keep reminding yourself that tens of thousands of outlets exist. Then, fully aware of your enormous range of options, use the tools in "Resources" and the pointers in this chapter to narrow it sensibly, so that you end up sending what you write to the particular publishers and editors who figure to be receptive to it and enthusiastic about it.

The Affection Approach

"An editor's enthusiasm is the fuel that makes the project go," says Kate Medina, vice-president and executive editor at Random House. "Unless you have somebody who's nuts about a book you don't get a fire lit under it." It's a view most book and magazine editors would endorse. Despite moanings and groanings in the press about how bottom-line managers are running the publishing show, editors still base acquisition decisions more on excitement than on sales forecasts. In fact, Herman Gollob—who's held senior editorial positions at Atheneum, Doubleday, Simon & Schuster and the Literary Guild—has predicted "an unending chain of disasters, financial as well as psychological, for houses that publish books no editor feels strongly about."

The emphasis is undeniably attractive. Unlike the outdoor grill manufacturer or the automobile designer or the orthodontist, an editor can—and should and frequently does—allow passion to rule, at least where acquiring manuscripts is concerned, with the result that publishing doesn't suffer as much from homogenization as most other industries.

Unfortunately, the reverse side of this coin shows a less pleasant picture, partly for reasons to be discussed in "The Sale and Its Sequels," and partly because it's extraordinarily difficult for writers to figure out which editors, among hundreds, are going to respond passionately to them. "Love" is a word even the gruffest editors like to use in high praise—"I loved this story," they'll scribble on the back of its envelope without embarrassment—but, as when boy meets girl, the chemistry is hard to predict and impossible to manufacture.

Fixing yourself up with a promising editorial partner—which is the best possible way to ensure a happy publishing future—is largely a matter of learning a lot about individual editors' tastes (and, at some point—for book authors—about agents' tastes as well). Try one or more of the following tactics.

✱ Compile a data bank, using your computer or plain old index cards, and enter as much information as you can glean about each editor or agent you focus on; perhaps eventually you'll be able to sell a piece about smokers' rights because your files led you to an editor who'd run two pieces on minority power.

One good way to get information about editors and agents without actually meeting them is by reading about them in a publishing memoir (consult the *Subject Guide to Books in Print* for specific titles), and once you've made allowances for bias and for that striving after color which afflicts editors as diarists no less than other people, you can use acquaintanceship through print to facilitate acquaintanceship in person.

Publishing memoirs get published a lot (for obvious reasons), but they're by no means the only things that editors write. Poems, novels and nonfiction by editors appear often, and should prove revealing, so that skimming reviews and ads and biographical notes to find writing by working editors may be worthwhile.

Other good data for your files can come from comments about particular editors and agents that you collect at writers' conferences or from friends; from *PW* items about who sold and bought certain new titles; from dedications and prefatory notes that express gratitude to an editor and/or an agent; and from the assorted across-the-editor's-desk jottings you'll find sprinkled through magazines.

✱ Break through editorial anonymity by investigating personal publishing, which is flourishing today on two fronts. Within the large houses, it's becoming common for editors to acquire and issue lines of books under their own personal imprints. Imprint pioneers like Joan Kahn and Seymour Lawrence have now been joined by many independence-minded editors. Moreover, the number of independent, individualistic publishing operations is growing outside the establishment too.

Brief descriptions of such publishing outfits appear in *Literary*

Market Place and in the *International Directory of Little Magazines and Small Presses.* When one attracts you, write to the head of the firm and ask for a catalog; from the catalog you'll be able to infer a great deal about the publisher's personality and about the way it might mesh with yours.

✳ Discover an editor through a book you feel passionate about. If you're lucky, you'll open the book to the acknowledgments page and find out who edited it; otherwise you'll have to call the publisher's offices. Try the publicity department; people there are used to giving out information. Then, once you have the editor's name, you can write and explain the bond you sense between the book you loved to read and the book you want to write.

Though it takes considerable nerve, this kind of personal approach can get you off to a great start with an editor, or with an agent for that matter. "Sure; I'm interested in your material; send it along," is a frequent response because both editors and agents are impressed by efforts to understand them. And when they learn that you enjoyed a book they helped create, their pleasure may lead them to greet your submission with a small prejudice in its favor.

✳ Advertise. Paid ads may put publishers off, but indirect advertising is worth thinking about, especially since it can be obtained easily and without cost. One method of indirect advertising entails using the biographical notes that run with work you're currently getting published. If you ask the editor who's printing your study of utopian theory to run a line saying, "The author is halfway through a novel called *Bravest New World,* about a messianic cult in Washington State," you may hear from editors and agents who want a chance at the book.

✳ Find a receptive editor by checking the "People" column in *Publishers Weekly.* Editors who have recently changed houses probably had to leave some of "their" authors behind. As they set up shop at new firms, they'll be especially eager to sign up new books and develop new relationships with as many good writers as possible.

Matching Exercises

For a straightforward approach to manuscript placement, nothing beats matching the subject matter of your work with the subject matter that appeals to a particular publisher.

Perhaps, without fully realizing it, you've already formed a mental image of what attracts the editors of magazines you read regularly, in which case you'll know almost instinctively whether your work belongs there. Though your sense of a book publisher's range of interests is likely to be hazier, you can start to bring it into focus by studying the *Publishers' Trade List Annual*, where current catalogs from hundreds of firms are gathered. Lists from small houses and from subsidiaries of large houses and regional or special-interest publishers are easiest to categorize, but even a general-interest publishing giant has a personality of its own, and whatever you can conclude about the likes and dislikes of any size firm will help you with placement.

To supplement impressions formed through study, you can turn to descriptions in *Literary Market Place* (which is commonly referred to as *LMP*; see "Tools" in this section's "Resources" for a full description) or to the other directories you'll find in the "Resources" pages. Moreover, you can read about specific publishers in *Small Press*, peruse the "Call for Manuscripts" notices in *Poets & Writers Magazine* and get hold of the newsletters published by PMA (Publishers Marketing Association) and COSMEP (The International Association of Independent Publishers) to see whether any of the publishing companies they mention are likely to welcome your work (again, see "Tools" in "Resources"). Have you, for instance, written a travel book, an autobiographical poem or a report on a new development in psychology? Not long ago, publishers who belong to COSMEP were looking for just such material.

Furthermore, you can try the *Subject Guide to Books in Print*, a multi-volume directory listing more than 700,000 books under a galaxy of subject headings. Start by looking at the titles under several headings that are relevant to your work. You'll probably discover that certain publishers' imprints appear again and again, and you may be tempted to conclude that the editors there are now surfeited with the subject. That's possible. It's at least as likely, however, that they're still hungry for more. They wouldn't have done a second book on exercise for the elderly, after all, if the first hadn't sold well, and the fact that they issued a third or a fourth indicates that they've tapped a responsive market they'll be eager to supply with new reading matter. Specializing in nonfiction about sports, the outdoors and the environment, Sierra Club Books even branched out into publishing fiction when they got an allegorical novel about fishing, David James Duncan's *The River Why* (which, incidentally, Bantam later reprinted).

Matching your subject to a company's demonstrated strength may be the single best placement strategy, but matching it to a company's obvious weakness can make sense too. Is one national magazine you read short on profiles, when the form is clearly fashionable? Are there no books about the environment in the publisher's catalog you've been studying, even though *PW* has just announced an unprecedented boom in their sales? If so—like the high school student who accused the editor of the local paper of ignoring the kids' point of view and got himself hired to write a column—you've found a gap in need of filling.

Once you've made good matches between your work and publishers' needs, go one step further and try match-making with businesses or other kinds of organizations that publish articles and books of interest to the people they serve, as all sorts of groups— including corporations, associations, governmental bodies, schools and fraternal societies—now do. Look for likely candidates to approach in the *Encyclopedia of Associations*, the *Thomas Register of American Manufacturers* and other directories you'll find in "The Self-Publishing Option Resources."

Tips on Timing

Consider Judy Delton and her Houghton Mifflin Kitty books for children. When she began to do them in the late '70s, she notes in *Publishing Research Quarterly*, she "wrote about growing up Catholic in the forties. *Roots* had just been published. Ethnic cultures were trendy. I thought, now is the time for me to write about my childhood and get away with it. If I'd waited, I'd be out of luck. The market is saturated with growing-up-Catholic books.

"When my husband lost his job (before it was popular to lose jobs) I wrote *My Daddy Lost His Job Today*. When it didn't sell, I changed the title to *My Mother Lost Her Job Today* and it did. This was 1971. Role reversal books like *William's Doll* were just coming into print.

"Timing is important," Delton concludes, and the point is crucial. Because each moment creates and destroys publishing potential, sensitivity about timing is an enormous aid in placement.

If you are alert to passing events you can sometimes hang an already completed manuscript on a news peg to attract editors. A much-rejected book about Big Foot, for example, might suddenly become salable the instant that new evidence of the monster's existence turned up. Similarly, if an article about the unquenchable desire for war has been repeatedly turned down on the grounds of familiarity, a timely new lead might help. Perhaps, for instance, the piece could be sold to a newspaper for the June 6 issue if it began by pointing out that June 6 isn't just the anniversary of D-Day; it's also Korea Memorial Day and the beginning of Superman Celebration in Metropolis, IL (this celebration, along with hordes of others that delight and inform, is listed in *Chase's Annual Events*; see "Tools" in "Resources").

People unprepared with manuscripts can also take advantage of propitious moments for getting published. Was it your town the tornado hit? Your aunt who gave the governor a ticket for jaywalking before the speech at the travel agents' convention? Your college that voted overwhelmingly to reinstate single-sex housing? When you're involved in any way in a newsworthy event, it makes sense to offer an eyewitness report to interested publications that have no representative on the scene. If you can plan ahead for the story, query selected editors about it beforehand (see "Procedures"); otherwise make a few phone calls to see if you can get an expression of interest.

Either way, you might consider parlaying the temporary position of on-the-spot reporter into an ongoing job as a stringer for one of the national newsmagazines or large metropolitan papers that like to keep up with news breaking locally around the country; get in touch with the nearest bureau chiefs (you'll find their names on mastheads) if the prospect appeals to you. Stringers' assignments are sporadic; their copy is generally rewritten beyond recognition; both their by-lines and their pay may be virtually invisible. But think of it this way: magazines like *Time* and *Newsweek* make nice additions to anyone's list of credits, and being even partly responsible for what millions of people get to read has its charms.

Not every story needs, or should have, explicit links with current events, but no manuscript can be sensibly submitted unless targets are selected with timing very much in mind, because every publishing enterprise has a definite position on a temporal spectrum. As noted in "Subject Matter Matters," special-interest publishers tend to congregate near the leading edge, getting to the future way ahead of most mass-market, general-interest publications. Thus a piece that *Medical Self-Care* might like this month probably won't be suitable for *Self* until sometime next year and might not be welcomed at the *Reader's Digest* until long after that (for tips on making several sales with the same story, see "Spin-offs").

Art Harris, a prep-school teacher turned freelance writer, learned his lesson about timing the hard way: Years ago, "having three sons and a wife who was reading all these articles on 'How Safe Are Birth Control Pills?' I had a sterilization operation—the vasectomy. What a great idea for an article, I thought. It even tied in with another subject—zero population growth. 'You're a nice fellow,' the editors said, 'but frankly nobody wants to hear about your operation. Forget it. It's too personal a subject.' So I put the idea aside only to see a whole crop of articles on the subject a year or two later. If I were to approach an editor today with 'My Male Sterilization,' I would get laughed out of the office; the subject has been well covered, thank you."

However painful Harris's education, he learned enough in the end to write a piece called "Timing the Submission" that he sold to *The Writer*. The advantages you'll derive from developing timing skills may not be quite as direct, but they're sure to aid your progress nonetheless.

Easy Access

"We regret that we are unable to consider unsolicited manuscripts" is a sentence that causes a lot of needless anguish. It's true, as enraged would-be authors are quick to point out, that many publishers make it a rule to return unsolicited material unread. But that policy can't debar anybody's work as long as editors respond to queries and proposals with invitations to submit the manuscripts described (see "Procedures"). And besides, no matter what rejection slips may say, the periodical press is increasingly open to contributions from unknowns, as witness the following rundown.

Reader-Participation Departments. Magazines and newspapers of all sizes and sorts are now actively soliciting material from the general public. Like modern physicists and politicians, publishers have discerned that our deepest sense of reality demands some confluence of subject and object, of actor and acted upon. The results of this realization—which is especially powerful because it's not entirely conscious—vary among disciplines, but in publishing it has led editors to try making writers of readers. "The magazine game has tended to look on readers as spectators," editor Tony Jones explained when he sparked the trend with

Harper's Weekly. "We think they should be players, and we're looking for ingenious ways around the limitations on how many can play."

Not long ago, the only place open to readers as players was the "Letters to the Editor" column, but today ordinary folk are cordially urged to contribute to "Viewpoint" in *Glamour,* the "My Turn" column in *Newsweek,* the "Living" section of *The New York Times* and the Op Ed pages of innumerable newspapers, to name a few items on the steadily expanding list of reader-participation departments.

In all these columns, and in the letters column too (which remains a good launching pad for an idea and/or a writing career), short pieces that emphasize specific, significant experience rather than abstract theory are most likely to succeed. Editors can use writers with reputations when they want opinion and analysis; it's for the small wisdoms of everyday life, the personal stories that will resonate in readers' minds and lives, that they have to turn to you.

Book Review Columns. In addition to sections that solicit contributions from readers, a good many periodical departments are entirely open to the public, though they seldom proclaim that fact. One of these, as Robert Cassidy discovered, is the book review section. Cassidy, who got his start with a review, is the author of *What Every Man Should Know About Divorce,* among other books. You can follow his example by checking publishers' catalogs and *PW* for forthcoming titles you'd be able and eager to write about, and then querying editors to see if they'll either let you cover a book you'd like to discuss (mention title, author, publisher and publication date) or try you out on one they have up for grabs. Book review editors' names are listed in *Literary Market Place,* and their preferences as to style and substance can be inferred from the reviews they ordinarily run; try your library for copies. Book reviewing doesn't usually pay much (in fact, the book itself may be your only payment), but the rewards in terms of exposure and contacts and credits and pride of performance can be considerable.

Other editors who are especially receptive to newcomers include those who work on:

Community Newspapers. Applying to a neighborhood weekly for a particular beat is a fine way to begin a career as a published writer; once you've regularly covered dance, say, or profiled local businesses for a small periodical, you've got credentials to present to a big one. And if you've written anything with a local focus, you should find a ready market among community weeklies.

Company Magazines and Newsletters. Both profit and non-profit organizations need people to discern and relay ideas relevant to their concerns. Here again, the pay may be low or nonexistent, but the audience will consist of anything from a couple of hundred employees to thousands of sympathetic members of the general public, so that you can expect high dividends in the form of exposure.

Campus Publications (Including Alumni Magazines). The connection between you—or your subject—and the school will give you an edge here, and though the pay scale varies widely, most editors in this field—like their counterparts on other small publications—are generous with assistance. "We have to scratch harder for good stuff," said Elise Hancock, editor of *Johns Hopkins Magazine.* "So if something has possibilities we'll work on it rather than turn it down because the possibilities weren't quite realized. I once published a piece called 'Bald Is Beautiful,' a magnificent parody on radical manifestoes that maintained (quite rightly) that bald people *are* discriminated against. The author was urging the *Ten Commandments* be refilmed starring Woody Allen. It was a great piece, but *Esquire* had turned it down. I think they just weren't willing to spend the hour required to cut it by two-thirds, which was all it needed. So that's a plus of working with alumni magazines."

Contests. Both book and periodical publishers use assorted competitions to attract new talent and, not incidentally, to generate publicity. Announcements about them appear from time to time in trade journals, in a firm's own publications and in the directories listed in "Resources."

It would be misguided to treat the easy-access openings with less respect than any others; what you've written must be right for the specific publisher you send it to in terms of subject matter, style, tone and timing. But if you submit to the most hospitable editors with the same care you'd use for the most forbidding, you can anticipate better results.

Vanity Presses

With one exception, any publication opportunity you can seize is worth seizing; ever-widening ripples move out from even the smallest splash.

Something more like a self-contained plop is all you're likely to get, however, if you resort to a vanity press. Vanity publishing is not the same as either subsidy publishing or self-publishing, though the terms are often used as if they were synonymous. Subsidy publishing is best defined by its guaranteed audience (see "Front-end Funding"); self-publishing is partly defined by its realistic efforts to find an appropriate audience (see "Managing Sales"); vanity publishing frequently involves no audience at all.

You can recognize a vanity press by its come-hither ads. "An invitation to authors of books," they'll say (or words to that effect). And they'll offer a free (no obligation) manuscript evaluation and a free (no obligation) brochure about the publishing operation. Usually vanity houses wait until you've begun corresponding with them to mention their fee. Be advised, though, that a vanity press is likely to charge you several thousand dollars to handle publication processes that you'd be far better off directing and/or executing yourself. (Please don't decide you lack the necessary skills before you've read "The Self-Publishing Option" chapters.) And don't be dismayed if you recognize vanity as one of your own motives for getting published, as long as it's not the only one you see; virtually every writer is seeking glory to some extent.

Most vanity houses issue impressive-looking pamphlets that explain their operations with varying degrees of candor and detail. These booklets generally fail, however, to stress two crucial points:

* The press has no stake in the success of your book; it takes its money up front by getting you to pay all the costs of editing, typesetting, proofreading, printing, overhead and the like—plus a sum that's pure profit for them; then, if the edition actually earns anything they'll take a cut of the revenues from sales too (and they'll charge you for any copies you buy over and above the allotment mentioned in your contract).

* Distribution efforts by vanity presses can be worse than useless because vanity books bear a stigma. Most libraries, bookstores and book reviewers won't touch them; and while some titles do manage to rack up sales, it's virtually certain that most vanity press successes could have been easily equaled by writers on their own.

Testimonials from happy authors are a regular feature of vanity press catalogs, which don't, of course, print any litanies of complaint. The complaints are a part of the picture, though ("I never realized that binding all the copies in the first printing wasn't included in the deal" commonly heads the list). Anyone who's considering vanity publishing should, first, become familiar with "The Self-Publishing Option," and second, consider having your manuscript bronzed for display on the mantel. That might be a smarter way to spend money on it than coughing up cash to a vanity press.

Procedures, or How to Submit Your Manuscript

A LOT THAT'S WRITTEN about the fine points of submitting a manuscript not only can be disregarded, it should be. Editorial etiquette is mainly a matter of common sense; for obvious reasons, your copy should be neatly typed, free of misspellings and coffee stains, consecutively numbered page by page, clearly labeled with your name, address and telephone number and accompanied by a stamped, self-addressed return envelope. Those rules that have no common-sense basis will only divert your attention to minutiae when it ought to be focused on your primary purpose: getting editors to publish what you write.

Any pieces of paper you send editors—from three-paragraph queries to thirty-page proposals—will persuade them either to move your manuscript one stage closer to publication or to reject it right then, depending on whether they've been led to answer yes or no to the two all-important questions that echo in editors' heads:

* Will this article (story, book), if it's skillfully handled, add to my company's prestige and/or profits (and therefore to mine as well)?
* Can this writer handle it skillfully?

If your idea comes across in the beginning as a half-baked notion jotted down in a spare moment, no editor is likely to take it more seriously than you apparently have. It's best, therefore, not to think of any approach to an editor as a preliminary move designed merely to feel out the situation before you submit your "real" work. Even the shortest introductory note, though it should look effortless, probably ought to be the end result of several drafts.

Essentially, what you're doing when you first make contact with an editor is applying for publication, much as you might apply to college or for a job. And just like a director of admissions or of the personnel department, the editor you apply to will be only the tip of a decision-making iceberg. Almost always, a group rather than an individual has the power to accept or reject, and if your proposal succeeds in winning one editor's vote, that editor in turn will have to convince several colleagues that your project is worth backing.

Queries and proposals generally circulate among editors, with more and more people becoming involved when the risks of commissioning a project are high; some book publishers insist that every manuscript under consideration be reviewed by two or more sizable committees before an editor gets clearance to buy it. No matter how many people participate in the process, however, what you've set down on paper is all they've got to go on.

To give yourself every advantage in approaching editors, you'll need a working knowledge of the forms of communication they've developed over the years. Here's a roundup.

Queries, or Don't Get Stuck in the Slush Pile

On the surface, a query is simply a letter that asks editors whether they'd be interested in work you're planning or have already produced. It's an introductory move, used to pave the way for submitting articles to periodicals and proposals or finished manuscripts to book publishing houses (and to agents too). With magazines, queries may also function as proposals, in the sense that they can earn you an assignment—complete with guaranteed minimum payment (but they're not likely to do that if you're an unknown). And in all cases they obviously make for efficiency; evaluating a letter takes a lot less time than reviewing the entire manuscript it describes, so the winnowing process is speeded up. But the query's most important function is often—and oddly—ignored: a query is a tool for steering your manuscript clear of the slush pile.

Judging from the number of unsolicited submissions that reach editorial offices daily, most writers either don't know this or don't believe it. The fact is, though, that queries get manuscripts solicited status, with benefits all around.

Queries about nonfiction offer editors the opportunity to become involved in shaping your material at the outset. When the subject you've suggested is one they're interested in pursuing, they'll welcome the chance to share thoughts on how the story should be approached, what length it merits and what information should be included. Their suggestions will improve your manuscript, at least for their purposes. And to come closer to what an editor has in mind—as long as doing that doesn't violate the basic premises of what you want to say—is obviously desirable.

With fiction, phrasing a query is more difficult, but if you write an intelligent letter in which you explain what led you to tell your story or why you think its subject is important and timely, you should succeed in building editorial interest in you and your work that will help it over the final decision-making hurdles. In her query about her first novel, a mystery called *Who Buried Sweet William?*, Sharon Villines offered a summary rich in associations: "Environmental foul play, sexual politics and financial greed emerge in a tangled maze." Three editors responded by return mail, asking to see more material.

Whether or not an editor offers specific comments on a query, a go-ahead means that your submission will land in that editor's personal in-basket rather than in the unsolicited-manuscripts bin when it arrives. Expressing interest obligates editors to read, or at least to skim, what you send. That's all it obligates them to do, however, unless they've agreed to commission your forthcoming work; when editors say they'd be delighted to see your manuscript on speculation (or "on spec," to use the common jargon) they mean they think it has promise but they're guaranteeing nothing.

"A beginning magazine writer shouldn't expect to get an assignment the first few times out," Rona Cherry, editor-in-chief at *Longevity*, explains:

> And anyway—at *Longevity*, at least—the only difference between an invitation to submit on speculation and an assignment is that with the latter you get a kill fee (generally a couple of hundred dollars) if the piece doesn't work out. We usually give formal assignments only to writers with good track records who bring us good ideas, but if an editor expresses real interest in your article and would like you to send it on spec, then go ahead and give it everything you've got. That may mean investing two months of your life; still, when you want to be published that damn much, that's what you have to do. If, after all that time and effort, the piece doesn't succeed, at least you'll have impressed the editor by the work you put in. And that means on the next try you'll have a sympathetic, receptive audience.

To get a positive initial response to your query you need to do more, of course, than ask to be invited to submit your manuscript. The question "Would you be interested in my story about snowmobiling being hazardous to health?" can call forth only one reply: "Well, it depends." It depends on what, exactly, your point is and how you're going to express it.

"A query letter is really a sales letter without the hype," says Lisel Eisenheimer, deputy editor of *McCall's*. "It should show that you have our market in mind, indicate the kind of color and life you can bring to your subject, and represent your best writing efforts. That's important even if you already have a relationship with an editor, because that editor probably can't make an assignment unilaterally."

Remembering that a query must do double duty—by selling your idea to the editor it's addressed to and then by helping that editor sell it to colleagues—makes it easier to compose a good one. The following checklist outlines the elements of a good one-

or two-page query letter about a nonfiction manuscript; if you adapt them creatively, they'll serve for fiction as well.

* *Explain why you believe the particular editor you're addressing will be interested in the work you want to place* (because they've edited material on similar subjects or material displaying similar sensibilities; because they come from the place where your story is set; because you know they share your interest in, indignation about, passion for whatever your topic may be).

* *State your specific idea* (as opposed to your general subject). A catchy title and subtitle that convey the essence of your article or book will be useful here; perhaps skimming magazines will help you come up with them.

* *Describe the main point your manuscript makes, the ground it covers and its style,* and offer a brief excerpt by way of illustration.

* *Say where and how you got (or are getting) your raw material* (from interviews? primary sources? personal experience?).

* *Show how what you have to say is fresh and different from specific articles and/or books already in print* (hit the highlights here—you have information such-and-such a piece didn't reveal; you hook your findings to a narrative instead of presenting them in the scholarly tones of such-and-such a book).

* *Estimate length.* A figure that's appropriate to your topic and to the publishing concern you're writing for gives an editor a clue that you do your homework.

* *Provide a tentative delivery date for your manuscript.*

* *Mention your connections and qualifications.* If you have any relevant expertise, let editors know, and tell them, too, about your publishing credits, even if they're minor. A young writer who's worked during the summers on a newspaper or won honorable mention in a high school short-story contest has credentials worth mentioning; in fact, some editors ask their first readers to direct manuscripts from anyone who lists such credits to their personal attention. Include clippings (two at

most) only if they're relevant to the piece you're proposing or if they're outstandingly good samples of your work.

∗ *Convey your enthusiasm for the project.* Enthusiasm is infectious and, as noted above, editors are inclined to encourage writing that obviously has conviction and energy behind it.

It should be needless to say (but experience indicates it's not) that you should direct your query to a specific editor by name, not to The Articles Editor; that you should spell the editor's name correctly; and that you should remember that the editor-in-chief isn't the only one on the staff. Associate editors, assistant editors, department editors and others still lower in the ranks may give your manuscript more personal attention than the higher-ups who get most of the mail.

To find your target editor, consult the directories listed in "Resources" or the most recent issue of the magazine you're aiming at. Then, because editors are notorious job-hoppers, call and find out whether the one you've chosen is still with the company before you write.

Some writers shy away from queries for fear that editors will steal their ideas. Well, in the first place, they probably won't. In the second place, they may well get similar stories from other writers, so if it looks as if they stole something of yours they probably didn't. And in the third place, what alternative does an author have? You can't sell your work without describing it. So conquer your paranoid tendencies. The grain of truth that may lurk behind them in this instance is a rotten reason to give up one of the best door-opening tools you have.

Person-to-Person: Calling Up and Calling On

Occasionally, telephone calls or personal visits to editors will provide the best way to acquaint them with your idea for a piece. Long before she wrote *How to Eat Like a Child*, for instance, Delia Ephron dropped in unannounced on the editor of the magazine supplement of the Providence *Journal* to propose writing about sports from a woman's point of view. He said sure, on spec, and bought the first piece she did. Ephron then used that clip to get an assignment from a national magazine.

Once you've got an editor listening, you're in a make-it-or-break-it situation, so be 100 percent sure that you've formulated what you have to say in the best way possible. Boiling your story down to three or four sentences or coming up with a descriptive title beforehand will help you arouse an editor's interest during the few minutes of time you've requested.

Perhaps, following the lead of successful freelancers, you'll want to equip yourself with three or four well-developed story ideas before you enter conversations with editors. Then if all those fail, two other tactics will remain to be tried. You can turn the tables and ask editors whether there are any weak spots on their lists of upcoming titles that they'd like you to work on; maybe after they tell you their editorial problems you can mull them over and return in a week or so with a list of ways in which you might help solve them. Or you can see if editors will suggest other markets or other topics that might work for you.

Like the written query, a well-planned phone call or visit gives receptive editors the chance to help shape your idea and ensures personal attention to your manuscript once they've encouraged you to send it in. Established writers approach editors in person all the time; and for beginners who are effective in one-to-one situations, it offers an exceptionally good means of entrée.

Book Proposals, or Sell It Now, Write It Later

In essence, what you're asking when you send a query to a magazine editor is, Will you buy my manuscript or at least tell me you think it sounds promising and ask to read it? When you send a query to a book editor, though, what you want to know is, Will you look at my book proposal? (See below for a checklist of what a proposal should contain.)

It then becomes the book proposal's job to give editors the

information they need to answer the harder question, Will you buy this book or at least ask to read it?

Editors routinely bid for nonfiction books on the strength of a proposal alone (the payments can be made half on signing, half on delivery of a satisfactory manuscript or in thirds or even quarters), and although it may be hard to convince them to buy a first novel if they haven't seen the whole thing, it's by no means impossible. With second and subsequent novels, the proposal becomes a more powerful selling tool. If publishers are to advance money for books, however, they must generally be convinced that the book they're buying will be a book they can sell.

Book proposals can be submitted to agents (who will take you on—or not—having read them) as well as directly to editors, and the basic principles that contribute to the success of a query apply to proposals too: because it's much shorter than a full manuscript, a proposal can be considered more quickly and easily, and because it represents raw possibilities, it has the power to ignite editors' imaginations and get them involved in what you're trying to do.

Editors commonly define a book proposal as "an outline and a sample chapter," but what they really want is anything on paper that will give them some sense of how you write (which several unrelated passages may demonstrate better than a chapter in a book's early stages) and some reason to believe that your subject, when developed, will interest a large group of readers (which no rigid I, II, III, A, B, C outline of contents is likely to convey).

The following checklist for organizing a complete and effective proposal will keep you from omitting elements of importance to editors, but it won't serve as a guide to phrasing or arranging your presentation. Only you can figure out how to mesh your proposal and your earlier query so that together they do justice to the book you hope to write.

✳ *Link the work you're submitting to the editor you're approaching.* Having chosen your targets with care, you want to make sure they understand what aspects of their professional or personal lives led you to them. The stronger the connection, the more receptive they'll be.

✱ *Describe your book* well enough so that editors can say to their colleagues, "I have a great proposal here for a book that picks up where all the other guides to looking good leave off." Later, this same pithy description will be useful in acquainting sales people with the book, an eventuality the editor already has in mind. Your title, if it's catchy or compelling, can be a strong selling point.

✱ *Give at least one anecdote or example that illustrates your theme and its significance.* Take whatever space you need for this—a paragraph, a page or more.

Ralph Keyes, for instance, used the following paragraph in the proposal that won him a contract for a book called *Timelock: How Life Got So Hectic and What You Can Do About It*: "We all notice life's quickening pace in different ways. During two decades of writing for magazines, I've watched the preferred length of articles halve, even quarter. A Florida court reporter says today's witnesses speak 20 to 40 words a minute faster on the average than they did in the 1950s. Coffee merchants attribute their sagging fortunes to a generation which finds even instant coffee too time-consuming and would rather pop open a can of soda for breakfast. 'All hot drinks are going down,' says market analyst John Maxwell of Lehman Brothers. 'People today are in a hurry. They want to slug something down and move on.' "

✱ *Identify the audience to whom the book is addressed* (coin collectors; people in rebellion against impersonal bureaucracies; everyone who loved *Parliament of Whores*). Sometimes you can direct editors' attention to several possible markets and thus inspire them to think of still others.

Since salability is a vital consideration for most editors, it's a good idea not only to identify your markets but also to suggest ways of reaching them. If you're planning to write about St. Louis architecture, for instance, you might mention that you're game to approach architects about your book at their upcoming convention and that you're planning to write some articles for publication in their professional journals around the time the book comes out.

✱ *Talk realistically about the competition and how your book is different,* so that both editors and sales reps will understand why it needs to be written, why it will be read and how to distinguish it quickly when booksellers say, "But we already carry six titles on that very subject."

✱ *Show how you plan to develop your book.* Indicate the breakdown by chapters and sketch your primary sources of information (where will you go; whom will you talk with; what facts and figures will you gather?).

✱ *Explain your credentials.* Cite publishing credits as evidence of your ability to write, and any experience or training that qualifies you especially well for this project.

✱ *Enclose a sample of your text* (there is no normal length for text samples but many run between twenty and forty pages). Send whatever chapter or excerpts will reflect your book's content and style most accurately and most favorably.

✱ *Express any passion and excitement you may feel about the project.*

"I decided that, no matter what it took, my students would write simple, honest, readable prose that showed they were in some way connected to the words they wrote," Elaine Hughes said with some gusto on the first page of her proposal for *Writing from the Source.*

Hughes wanted to put the exercises she'd developed as a teacher into a book for writers outside the classroom. Having queried Carol Cohen at HarperCollins and been invited to submit her proposal late in 1988, she used the proposal checklist to create a 40-page package divided into many short sections ("The Basic Premise and Theme of the Book," "The Audience," "The Competition," "My Credentials," "Book Plan," "Student Comments") and included a handful of very brief excerpts and exercises.

"I consider both the title and the current draft of the manuscript only a work in progress at this point," Hughes explained, taking note of a phenomenon editors know well: Books always change in the writing. "The breakdown of chapters will go something like this," she continued in the same vein; "I expect that each category will have 6-8 different exercises"; "I think this chapter will include suggestions for clustering the exercises."

Writing another book, Hughes would probably have structured her proposal differently and used a different tone. Indeed, every book demands its own distinctive document. It's a pleasure to report, though, that this approach worked for this project. Cohen liked what she saw enough to offer a contract, and Hughes's "writing and meditation exercises that free your creativity, inspire your imagination and help you overcome writer's block" came out in early '91, retitled *Writing from the Inner Self*.

Poetry

Certain guidelines will serve you well no matter what kind of manuscript you're trying to place. It's always a good idea, for example, to address an editor by name and to triple check for typos. But what makes sense for poetry submissions does differ in some respects from what makes sense for prose.

In the first place, poets don't need to use query letters since the material they submit won't run to dozens or hundreds of pages. Instead, it's best to start by sending roughly half a dozen poems ("five has always felt comfortable to me as an editor," said Diane Kruchkow, editor of *Small Press News*), along with a brief covering letter that shows you're familiar with each publisher you approach and tells publishers about your credits if you have them.

Poets often aim their work at magazines first because, as Alice Quinn has noted, "In general, poets enjoy and require the reinforcement magazine publication provides." Quinn, a poetry editor for Knopf and a fiction editor for *The New Yorker*, has observed that some poets use a lazy-susan system. Instead of agonizing when something is returned, they send it right out again; "the three poems *Grand Street* turned down go straight to the *Atlantic*; the two that *Poetry* didn't want go straight to *Southwest Review*."

A lazy-susan system can, of course, also cover magazines that aren't devoted to poetry. The poet Judson Jerome found that "specialized publications are a wonderland for those of us swamped in the miasmic plains of literary magazines." Jerome was particularly taken with the notion of submitting some poems about horses to *Arabian Horse* in Waseca, Minnesota at $10 to $75 apiece, and to *Toys "R" Us Magazine* for pay that could be called handsome—$200 to $700.

Going to the other extreme, certain literary magazines have lately begun to demand payment from poets by charging what they call "reading fees" for considering submissions. The practice is common, and conceivably defensible, for contests. But the consensus among poetry editors is that no self-respecting magazine charges to screen manuscripts for publication, so steer clear of those that do; credits from them aren't likely to count for much.

Having poems appear in reputable magazines gives you credibility with book publishers, as Jonathan Galassi points out. Galassi, editor-in-chief at Farrar, Straus & Giroux, thinks magazine credits are a poet's most important credential when the time comes to try for a book.

Should that time come for you, consult the preceding section on book proposals, and bear in mind that "in almost all instances it is better for poets to publish with a smaller house, if only because the smaller house will keep their work in print longer." That advice comes from Scott Walker, head of the distinguished Graywolf Press, who adds that a small house is more likely than a large one to "consider poetry books as its meat and potatoes, so it will give them more attention and more marketing energy."

Children's Book Channels

The main difference between children's books and adults' books in terms of procedures is that you can sometimes make your first move with an entire manuscript. If you're working on a lengthy book for older kids, you should still approach editors first with a query letter, but if what you've done is a picture book, you should know that "at Greenwillow, any unsolicited children's book manuscript will be looked at," according to the editor-in-chief, Susan Hirschman, and editors elsewhere are equally welcoming.

To target editors and publishing houses that will want your work for kids, browse through the children's books sections in nearby bookstores (they're increasingly popular nowadays). Study the children's books on your library's shelves (although they don't dominate the market the way they used to, libraries are still big buyers). And if you're in New York, familiarize yourself with The Children's Book Council collection (see "People, Places and Programs" in this section's "Resources"). Then use any applicable "Foot in the Door" tactics to make your approach.

Unless you want to illustrate your book yourself and you're as good an artist as you are a writer, do not send illustrations along with your manuscript. "Children's book editors are trained to see the illustrative possibilities in text," Elizabeth Gordon explains, and editors spend a lot of time looking at artists' portfolios. Gordon, VP and publisher of Hyperion Books for Children and Disney Press, sees choosing the right artwork as "one of the value-added pieces of expertise a publisher brings" to a book project. "Sometimes," she adds, "we can do things that are unusual, like matching a well-known illustrator with an unknown writer."

Covering Letters

Several marketing manuals suggest dispensing with a covering letter when you mail your manuscript, on the theory that if the thing's going to sell, it will sell on its own merits and that a letter saying simply "Here is my manuscript" only wastes an editor's time. There is, however, more than that to say.

You can use your covering letter to reestablish personal contact with editors by reminding them of previous exchanges between you (or to establish personal contact if you've decided a query won't convey the strengths of your short story and opted for just mailing it in). You can use it to convey thoughts or information of the sort that might have appeared in your original query but didn't. And you can use it to indicate that you're eager to improve your work even now, after you've tried hard to do your best.

Listen to an editor vacillating about a submission: "A very interesting idea, I think—'romanticizing the Holocaust.' It's good. But he is heavy-footed, repetitive and clumsy in places. Excessively wordy. It could be helped by a few passages of quotations, to refresh our memories if not to make the point. Is it worth sending back for fixing?"

In a case like this, the fact that your covering letter proclaims an openness to criticism and a willingness to make changes might be enough to keep rejection at bay. Although major revision is a headache and a gamble for both editor and writer, it is also a much-traveled route to publication.

Authors of magazine pieces are regularly asked to revise on speculation, but most book editors say they wouldn't think of requesting that a writer make substantial changes without offering to pay for the labor, and without fully intending to buy the improved version of the work. Since one editor's idea of an improvement may be another editor's idea of a change for the worse, you'll have to assess your own position carefully before you decide whether the risk/reward ratio is reasonable enough for you to proceed.

The Question of Multiple Submissions

Only a few years ago, writers who sent out queries, proposals or full manuscripts could anticipate one of two fates. Either they'd wait several weeks—or months—and then be rejected, in which case they'd have to start all over again. Or they'd wait several weeks—or months—and be accepted, in which case they could take whatever terms they'd been offered (perhaps with minor modifications) or start all over again. Now, however, thanks in large part to innovative agents, all that has changed, and the vehicle of change has been the so-called multiple submission.

In book publishing, where long periods usually go by between the time you present your work and the time you get a response to it, multiple submissions are now standard operating procedure, and anyone who receives positive responses from more than one publisher may be able to play them off against each other a bit before picking the one that's best. (See "Getting What's Coming to You" for a further discussion of choosing among offers.) For periodicals, one submission at a time is still common, but by no means the rule. The fact that magazine editors respond more quickly than book editors makes multiple submissions less necessary and less usual where they're concerned.

Follow-Up

Queries normally elicit a response within a few weeks; book proposals can have you checking the mail for months. It's a good idea, therefore, to keep records of everything you've sent out and to follow up on magazine pieces after about six weeks and on book outlines after roughly twelve. Editors do get bogged down, go on vacations and sometimes even lose manuscripts (this is as good a place as any to remind you always, *always* to keep a copy). Furthermore, delays may result when a project hovers on the borderline between acceptance and rejection. A polite letter of inquiry is a reasonable and perfectly proper way to find out what's holding things up.

If and when you do get a positive response from an editor, acknowledge it with thanks and with some word on when you expect to deliver your finished manuscript. Be as realistic as you can about the due date; then if you find it impossible to stay on schedule, let your editor know.

Any rapport that you establish with particular editors obviously works to your advantage, and can be strengthened by simple gestures of courtesy—saying thank you for comments, for example, or expressing gratitude for encouragement offered along with rejection.

And speaking of rejections—well, everyone gets them, even the best of writers. And everyone feels the same way; rotten and hurt. But bear in mind that it's probably true if editors say that they really liked your piece even though colleagues didn't, or that everybody liked it except the editor-in-chief (whose no means no). And remember, too, that the roots of rejection are infinite: an editor who had a marital spat last night bristles at your piece about how to achieve a blissful relationship through yoga; a story like yours just came in from a house author and, while it isn't any better than the one you wrote, it isn't any worse either; your book just doesn't strike the sales manager as a good bet; or your article sounds too much like one that just came out in *Business Week*.

What this variety of causes signifies is that one editor's rejection may be another's acceptance, so continue to circulate your material. If you've followed the advice in these chapters without garnering a single encouraging word from the forty-six editors who've considered your manuscript, then it's time to take stock. Perhaps your logic is not as sound as you first thought, or your point is not so fresh and crisp after all. Sigh one sigh, file the manuscript away, and get on with something new. (Unless you're still convinced of its merit, in which case you might consider publishing it yourself; see "The Self-Publishing Option.")

If, heaven forbid, you receive nothing but printed rejection slips without so much as a personal note scribbled at the bottom, go back to the beginning of this section and start rereading.

A Note on Improving Your Vision

The next two sections present complementary perspectives on the same set of processes. "The Sale and Its Sequels"—which approaches publishing from the point of view of authors who want someone else to take charge of producing and selling their work while they assist—should provide self-publishers with valuable information on the standard operating procedures that have helped conventional firms succeed over the years. And "The Self-Publishing Option"—which approaches publishing from the point of view of authors who want other people to assist in producing and selling their work while they take charge—will prove a good source of innovative ideas for conventionally published writers.

Therefore, whatever role you want to play, please read both.

The Sale and
Its Sequels

* * *

Getting What's Coming to You

RECEIVING WORD THAT a publisher is interested in buying your work is just cause for celebration. What follows, however—the business of talking money and rights—can be (and usually is) an ordeal, especially where books are concerned, because although you and your publisher share many goals, your aims diverge on the division of profits and risks.

With magazine pieces, areas of contention are relatively minor. You can ask to be paid on acceptance rather than on publication; you can ask for a kill fee; you can ask to be reimbursed for expenses; you can ask to retain everything but first serial rights. Your publisher can then refuse any or all of these requests. If your wishes are largely ignored, though, it may not matter much, and in any case, writer/publisher relations are likely to be amiable.

The situation is quite different with books, as a quick glance at the average contract will convince you. Book publishers, who must sink substantial sums of money into each title they issue, have developed complex, formal mechanisms for minimizing their losses and maximizing their gains, which tend to put burdens on—and take rewards away from—authors.

Authors, understandably, resent this, and many of them are tempted to vent their anger on their editors, whose earlier support may now seem suspect. You'll be better off, though, if you can manage to treat yours with kindness. After all, the editor has just assumed the unenviable role of mediator between you and all the publishing people who will be handling aspects of your book; and besides, you'll probably never have a better friend at a large house. With everyone else there, you might as well gird yourself for an adversary relationship; expect the worst and be prepared to fight for the best.

Comparing Offers

If, having made multiple submissions, you've attracted two or more interested buyers with your book proposal, your first task is to consult with your agent or your literary property lawyer and decide which one to accept. The house that offers the most money? Maybe not. Although the size of an advance does provide a tangible index to the publisher's level of commitment, as well as an all-but-guaranteed income, you should investigate each publisher's abilities to prepare and sell your book in addition to each one's proposed down payment on it before you make a decision. These are the areas to explore:

* *Distribution* (i.e., sales to booksellers). Does the house have its own sales force? How large is it? What territories does it cover and how often does a sales rep visit each one?

  Houses that can't afford to maintain their own sales departments depend either on sales reps from larger firms (who handle books from a number of houses besides their own), on commissioned sales representatives (who sell books for lots of different publishers) or on independent distributors (whose interest in selling books is likely to coincide neatly with that of their clients, so that they may do as good a job for the titles they represent as any salaried, in-house sales force could).

* *Backlist policy*. Many houses actively market brand-new books only, paying no attention to older titles—a.k.a. backlist— which means that books they issue usually die fast. As a number of small publishers regularly prove, however, there is an alternative. Continual promotion, updating and/or re-

packaging can give a book not just a long life but an increasingly profitable one. So ask about predictions for—and commitment to—your book over time.

* *Subsidiary (a.k.a. Sub) Rights.* As publishing (like other industries) becomes increasingly international and book format distinctions become increasingly blurred, many houses push harder for more rights. Instead of buying the right to issue a book in hardcover *or* in paperback, they'll try to buy "hard-soft." Instead of buying English-language rights, they'll say they want world rights. Such demands can occasion some horse-trading.

  Maybe you and your representative will decide to swap some rights for a bigger advance, a better royalty schedule or a higher discount on copies you buy. Maybe, if your book figures to sell outside the U.S. and the publisher wants world rights, you'll grant them conditionally ("I'll be happy whoever sells to publishers overseas," a first-book author told his editor, "but any foreign rights you haven't sold after six months should revert to me." "We can work with that," the editor said). And maybe, if people would like audio tapes of your book, video tapes derived from the book, toys or clothing inspired by characters in the book or other related products, you'll bargain to keep control of them (provided, of course, that you're as well equipped or better equipped to market them).

  In any event, though, it's important that authors, agents and publishers all think hard about what sub rights to give up and what to seek in exchange.

* *Library sales.* Since libraries account for big chunks of book sales in many categories—including children's books, mysteries and other adult trade titles—an active library promotion department or, at the least, a dynamic library sales specialist is an important asset.

* *Mail-order sales.* Authors who have concluded that their books can be sold easily through the mail should find out which editors agree, which houses have mail-order departments and what freedom they'll have to sell through the mail themselves.

✱ *Special sales.* If you've written a book about cross-country skiing, perhaps sporting goods stores would do a good job selling it. Ask publishers whether they use "non-traditional" sales channels and, if so, which ones and with what results.

✱ *Pecking order.* The importance of your book in relation to others on a publisher's list is significant because you will be competing with every other current title for the time and money budgeted to all departments in the house. Perhaps your book would not be considered a "big book" by any publisher, but even second-rank titles get appreciably better treatment than those on the bottom of the heap, so try to feel editors out about their expectations for yours; most will be quite frank about the prospects.

✱ *Personal compatibility.* Don't be ashamed to ask a lot of questions; naïveté coupled with an eagerness to learn may prompt an editor to talk with you at length, and the longer you converse, the stronger will be your sense of how well the two of you would work together.

Contracts, or the Agent's Hour

Because a book publishing contract is a complicated legal agreement in which the commitments of both author and publisher are defined (by the publisher) and the financial terms of the partnership are set forth (by the publisher), an agent or a literary property lawyer should be on board to represent your interests when you get an offer for your manuscript, if not before (once more, a warning: don't agree to any dollar figures until your representative is in there fighting for you).

If you hope your first book will be only the beginning of a long writing career, an agent will probably serve you best (remember, once you have an offer from a publisher, you're a desirable client, one who guarantees the agent a commission). If writing isn't on your agenda for the future, however, then consider a lawyer with expertise in publishing who will negotiate your contract, bill you and be gone.

There's only one case in which you'd be wise to proceed without the help of either an agent or a lawyer who's familiar with publishing, and that's when you're signing up with a small house that uses a simple, straightforward contract to buy rights that are strictly—and appropriately—limited. If all they have to deal with is a short memorandum of agreement and a one-person publishing operation, assertive authors can probably handle negotiations themselves by using one or more of the relevant guides in "Resources."

Authors who are represented are obviously not relieved of all responsibility for shaping a contract that's acceptable to both sides; at the least, you should be familiar enough with your publisher's contract form to know what changes you'd like to make. You'll have to read the thing, therefore, and probably more than once.

Much of it, you'll find, is intelligible, and what you don't understand you can ask about (consult your editor and/or your lawyer and see Levine, The Authors' Guild and other entries in this section's "Resources.").

But comprehension of a contract's basic provisions is about all writers can hope to achieve on their own. For common sense (which this book has touted before and will encourage again by and by) has only a minor role in the highly stylized negotiations of the usual contract quadrille. And that's where the agent's or the lawyer's expertise comes into play. Almost as if there were annotations throughout the contract that were visible to authors' representatives but invisible to authors themselves, your champion will X out and add in and modify clauses, acting a part that's as predetermined as the patterned figures of a dance.

Each house has a different contract—Simon & Schuster breaks the record at over sixteen pages—so that standard changes vary a bit, but both sides always know which moves are about to be made; in fact, even your editor will know (and might tell you in advance if you ask) roughly what terms the whole maneuver will produce in the end.

Why, you may well wonder, go through the motions? If every expert is aware that an author with clout can get the paperback split changed from 50-50 to 60-40 (author's favor) this year, and that clauses D, H and Z are always deleted by authors' representatives, who regularly add identical riders to paragraphs 3, 7 and 12, wouldn't it make sense to amend the forms before issuing them and skip the back-and-forth that comes afterward?

Well, arguably, no. For one thing, although the initial round of demands and counterdemands about changes in a publisher's standard contract is pretty well determined by custom, its outcome and the outcome of all subsequent rounds can be influenced to some extent by an astute and aggressive bargainer. For another thing, no matter how generous the form contracts were, authors would always want more. And for a third, publishers still scent the possibility that unrepresented writers may swallow the package as printed.

Don't do it. If you're forced to conduct contract negotiations yourself, consult relevant guides listed in "Resources" and see if you qualify for membership in the Authors Guild ("Resources" gives the group's address and phone number) so you can get a copy of its recommended trade-book contract. It's an excellent document, designed—with full knowledge of the contract quadrille's choreography—to get every author a decent deal, and even writers who are represented can use it to assist their agents in arranging for the best possible terms.

Payments

Controlling payments from periodicals is fairly simple, the idea being to collect once, for a single use of your material by a magazine or newspaper, and then, if any other use of your article, story or poem occurs, to get paid again by the second user. Thus, you have only two things to watch out for:

* *Get the going rate.* To learn what a magazine or paper normally pays its contributors, read its guidelines sheet (if it has one) and check to see if it's listed in *Writer's Market*; then multiply any figures you find by roughly 150 or 200 percent (because

they're directed to neophytes, published prices almost always fall at the low end of a periodical's payment scale).

* *Don't sell more than you must.* When you receive a check from a periodical, be sure to examine it front and back for fine print before you endorse it. Otherwise, you may sign away all rights to your piece, with the result that the periodical will get the fee if it's reprinted in an anthology, say, or sold for use on TV, and you won't.

Periodical publishers don't usually try to buy all rights from anyone with an agent or from any writers who can be presumed to know their business as well as their craft, mostly because the publishers realize they'd never get away with it. They shouldn't get away with it where you're concerned, either. Speak with your editor and see if management will issue you the same voucher they use for sophisticates. If that fails and the magazine insists on purchasing all rights, then you should insist right back that they agree to return some of those rights to you later on (you may well need them if you plan to reuse the material in other ways). Do this even if you have no plans at the moment to reissue your material in various ways.

Payments for book manuscripts are, predictably, far more complicated, and consequently far more likely to provoke and prolong aggravation.

The first money you get for a book will probably be your advance; as much as a half or as little as a fifth of that may be paid when you sign your contract, with the remaining payments coming due per contract specifications, usually on delivery of satisfactory sections of your manuscript. Occasionally, a publisher can be persuaded to pay the entire sum up front (this is worth angling for if you need the money to pay back bills or to keep a roof over your head while you write). Sometimes, in the case of a very small publisher perhaps, no advance at all will be forthcoming. And all too often, collecting turns out to be a chore because of sloppy bookkeeping on your publisher's part.

Payments that are slow in arriving are no rarity in modern publishing circles. Payments that must in the end be returned are a somewhat less frequent phenomenon, but if you fail to deliver a manuscript that's satisfactory to your publisher (or if you fail to deliver any manuscript at all), you may be obliged to repay any advance you've received.

Nowadays, partly because advances have escalated into five, six, and even seven figures and partly because some publishing houses are being pounded into financial shape by new corporate owners, it's increasingly common to find a publisher demanding its money back when a book project doesn't pan out. If your advance was relatively small and if you tried your best to write a good book and if you're poor and starving anyway, your publisher probably won't pull out all the stops to try to get money back from you. But don't count on it.

Assuming that you turn your manuscript in on time, or nearly so (editors grant extensions on due dates much as professors do, although here too they are getting stricter), and assuming further that it's found acceptable and subsequently published, the next money due you will be paid after your advance has been earned out, and it will come in the form of royalties.

If you have an agent, your contract probably takes some subsidiary rights out of the publisher's hands and puts them in yours; among them, you'll usually see first serial rights (for excerpts in magazines and newspapers before book publication) and motion picture rights, but you'll almost never see reprint or book club rights, which are too lucrative for publishers to part with.

All monies from subsidiary sales effected by agents go directly to them; they subtract their commission and forward the rest to their clients. When writers are not represented by agents, their publishers can sell all subsidiary rights and will keep the monies received until they've been reimbursed for whatever advance they paid. Thus, if *Sports Illustrated* bought an excerpt from your book for $3,000, $300 would go to your agent, if you had one who charged 10 percent, and $2,700 would go to you; if you had no agent and were represented by your publisher, approximately 10 percent would go to your publisher no matter what and the remaining 90 percent would go to the publisher until such time as your advance had been earned out, unless your contract specified otherwise.

The sooner your advance has been earned out through one sort of sale or another, the sooner you begin earning royalties. For a typical hardcover, you'll get 10 percent of the retail price on the first 5,000 copies sold, 12½ percent on the next 5,000 and 15 percent on all copies sold thereafter (*n.b.*: a percentage of list price is still standard for trade book contracts; tying the percentage to wholesale price or publisher's net receipts will yield substantially lower dollar figures). Royalty rates may differ a good deal from the ones mentioned here, depending on the book's format, the publisher's financial situation and the author's clout.

Essentially, royalty figures represent your cut of the money a customer pays for your book. But if you get $2 per copy on the first 5,000 sales of a $20 book, where does the other $18 go? One big chunk is for bookstores and wholesalers, who will buy your book at a discount of roughly 45 percent, which gives them their margin of profit and means that all they actually remit to the publisher is $11. After your $2 has been subtracted, the $9 balance must stretch to cover the costs of editing, manufacturing, advertising, selling, shipping, warehousing and, of course, the publisher's normal overhead (rent, utilities and payroll).

Taking all this into consideration, it's easy to see why large publishing houses maintain that they must sell thousands of copies of a book just to break even, and why they may sometimes engage in a variety of shenanigans to hang on to whatever money finally comes in. One author who suspected that his publisher was keeping cash it owed him was lucky enough to discover an interview in which his editor bragged about sales of his book. Since sales figures quoted in the interview far exceeded those indicated on his royalty statements, the author called at once to discuss the matter; it was then settled in his favor.

The point of this story is not that all publishers will try to cheat you or that if you read widely enough you will catch the ones who do; instead, it's that you may need to take the offensive not only to get the money you're entitled to, but also to find out how much it is. Royalty statements don't divulge a great deal (few note, for example, how many copies have been printed and how many are still on hand), and the way in which they're issued makes the data that do appear hard to grasp.

Twice a year the income generated over the preceding six-month period is supposed to be reported in a royalty statement. Usually, there's a lapse of three to four months between the closing date of the royalty period and your receipt of that period's statement, which means that money for a serial sale consummated in February will show up not on the statement you get in April but on the one you get the following October, some eight months from the date of sale. To make matters worse, money earned just before a given closing date is sometimes not included in the statement where it belongs; instead, it's held for the next statement because a publisher "forgot" to list it (and thus gave itself an interest-free loan at your expense).

How do you figure out whether what you're being paid is what you should be being paid? Two new programs offer help. The Book Industry Study Group has come up with a standard format for royalty statements that it will continue to develop and disseminate (see "Resources"), and the Authors Guild is now doing spot audits which may encourage better accounting by publishers.

The main responsibility, though, still falls to the author. "You have to understand the structure of your royalty statement and keep track of your royalties yourself," Stephanie Winston explains. Because she had been in book publishing, Winston, the author of *Getting Organized*, knew that the financial information she'd be getting as a writer wouldn't be the financial information she needed.

Since she also knew that agents can be flummoxed by royalty figures, she developed her own personal auditing system. She identifies someone on her publisher's staff who can explain the company's royalty policies and practices—the chief financial officer's assistant, perhaps; she gets a copy of the publisher's basic royalty statement, and she calls her editor's assistant every so often to find out about new printings (though it would make an author's day, editors rarely share the news that a book is going back to press).

With the information she gathers, Winston can see right away whether a royalty statement's figures are reasonable. Then, if gross discrepancies appear, she calls her contact in the publisher's financial department to say that something's wrong.

Catching errors and oddities is more than half the battle (publishers can usually find the problem and fix it) and well worth the effort. By flagging mistakes on a short succession of royalty statements, one astute author brought in an extra $50,000.

Fringe Benefits

Authors who know the ropes routinely ask their publishers for a host of extras that no contract will ever stipulate. As long as you're not greedy in your requests and not churlish if they're refused, you may well follow suit. What you have to gain, among other things, are the following benefits.

Office Space. Occasionally, you can arrange to use an empty editorial office, and sometimes you can manage to get access to a word processor, a telephone and a variety of office supplies as well.

If you regularly spend time in your publisher's quarters, perhaps you'll meet and make friends with employees who'll get interested enough in your project to give it special attention.

And even if you show up only occasionally, you may gain the privilege of using the company's copying machine.

Expenses. Particularly in the case of a nonfiction book that involves extensive research, it's worth asking for a supplement to your advance to cover the costs of travel, interviews, postage, copying and research materials. Unlike advances, expense allowances don't need to be earned out before you can collect royalties.

Free Books. The most obvious fringe benefit for writers under contract to publishing firms comes in the form of reading matter. Don't expect to stock your library from your publisher's warehouse, but if you see a book you'd love to have, go ahead and ask for a copy of it.

Power Plays

The self-fulfilling prophecy has doomed many a book. Here's what happens: Your editor views your manuscript as nice but minor; if it breaks even on sales, everyone figures to be satisfied. Because it seems minor, the editor won't lean on anyone in marketing or publicity to produce special sales strategies or promotion campaigns to attract the attention of the buying public. And because no special efforts will be made to publicize and distribute your book, it will end up nice but minor; if it breaks even on sales, everyone will be satisfied. Except, of course, you.

This scenario—a common after-the-fact explanation of why-my-book-was-remaindered-after-three-months-and-I-never-got-a-penny-more-than-my-advance—can seem inflexible enough to convince writers that their books' failures were preordained. Feeling helpless and anguished at this realization, they'll turn on their publishers, who will respond to shrieks of outrage and demands for bigger advertising budgets with veiled (or possibly not so veiled) anger, and nothing else.

But there's no need for writers to place their books at the mercy of editors and marketing directors until it's too late to do anything about plans for them but scream. With determination, tact and knowledge, you ought to be able to steer clear of the minor-category catch. (The analogous exercise for magazine pieces would consist of working to make yours the cover story, the lead or one of the articles in the "well," or center, rather than one of those in the front or back of the book. As with contracts and payments, however, positioning is relatively unimportant for periodicals and relatively simple to fight for if you're inclined to argue.)

The first step in positioning a book with a publisher is to grasp the fact that it will be categorized very early, either in some formal way, on paper, or informally, in the minds of editorial and marketing people. One popular system involves an *A, B, C* scale designed to help publishers allocate their limited supplies of staff and money. All publishers obviously want the maximum return on their efforts, so when half a dozen books on a forthcoming list seem likely to bring the house a profit if they're heavily promoted, those titles will be designated *A* books and slated to get the bulk of the promotion budget. The *B*s and the *C*s will have to compete for what's left over (which may not be much), and it's more than likely that the *C*s will end up with no budget whatsoever. Authors today are more and more apt to ask for promotion provisions in their contracts, but since publishers aren't eager to grant such requests, most writers still have to rely on plumping for position. And the optimal time to begin doing that is immediately after you sign your contract. Normally this is the very moment when writers are most anxious to get out of business hassles and back to the business of writing. But the hours you put in now planting seeds for the full campaign to come (see "Why and How to Be Your Own Best Sales Force") can mean the difference between a book that is ignored or mishandled and one that is granted the most favorable treatment possible.

Your primary goal between the day your manuscript is accepted and the day it's published should be to get everyone—from your editor to the publicity director to the people handling all sorts of sales—involved with (and, if you can manage it, excited about) the future of your book. To make them envision that future the way you want it to happen, you'll have to reinforce and supplement the marketing suggestions you made in your original proposal through occasional short, informal notes to your editor.

Since most editors have numerous authors to deal with, an outpouring of "me first" epistles is not recommended. Just write in an enthusiastic, contributory spirit. "It's occurred to me that it might be a good idea to play up the self-improvement angle in promotions throughout California" may make an effective approach. And suggestive tones—*coulds* rather than *shoulds*; *we might* rather than *you'd better*—will make it clear that you're willing not only to fire off suggestions but also to do the work entailed in executing them. Each of your letters, if it's well worded, will encourage your editor to think about a new dimension of your book and provide at least one viable idea the editor can pass along to sales and publicity people. Keep copies; as publication date nears and promotion plans are firmed up, you'll want to refer back to these early memos.

Among your efforts to gain momentum for your book in its early stages, you might include the following:

* If there's anything in the news that's relevant to your book's contents, write a short piece for newspaper Op Ed pages or letters columns or for a magazine's opinion department; include a biographical note mentioning that your material comes from a book you're working on; and use clips of published pieces as evidence to convince your publisher that you're dealing with a timely and important subject.

* If your book requires that you do research, ask for data by running an author's query in the pages of *The New York Times Book Review*. Publicly seeking information will not only help you get it but will also start people talking about your book, and it may lead to invitations to speak before groups or at conferences, which will add further to your fame and thus to your developing good fortunes.

* Keep your eyes open for gatherings relevant to your subject; volunteer to be on a panel or to participate in a series of readings. Ask for, or collect, a list of names and addresses of attendees to whom you can send notices and order forms when your book is published, and after a successful speaking engagement drop a note to your editor about the event and the enthusiastic response you met at it.

* Once you develop the habit of thinking in terms of positioning, you'll be visited by enticing ideas at all sorts of odd

moments. To keep them where you'll be able to find them, start a file that will include:

Names (and addresses if possible) of writers, critics, broadcasters and anyone else who's famous and who, because of their interest in your subject or their ideological bent, might give your book favorable advance comments for use in cover blurbs and press releases.

Names of magazines and newspapers that would have good reason to run excerpts from your book or to review it or to plug it in one of their regular columns.

Potential sales pitches. "This book is for people who . . . and we can reach them by . . ."

Titles. Improvements in your working title are likely to occur to you as you write, and if you keep a record of them all—even those that don't quite make it in your mind—you may eventually come up with one that works beautifully.

All of these steps, along with others to be discussed in the chapters that follow and still others that you'll think of on your own, will help give your book its best chance. But that's not all the good they'll do: when you're so stymied in the actual writing that you've begun to think nothing will ever be published at all, they'll give you a psychological boost. Even (and sometimes especially) when you're disgruntled, it's just plain fun to work on ways of making your book the biggest deal it can legitimately be.

Editing, Copy-editing, Design, Production and Part-and-Parcel Advertising

T HE IDEAL AUTHOR, from the point of view of practically everyone in a large publishing operation, will speak not at all (except possibly to say thank you) as a manuscript moves through the editing and production stages. Even the editor who loved a book from the start won't be eager to hear protests about the changes that seem indicated now, while the copy editor, the designer and the production manager (all of whom are trained in technical fields) are apt to bridle if a writer tries to tell them their business, on the entirely plausible grounds that an amateur's mistakes will cost dearly in money and time.

Partly because they are less compartmentalized and partly because their general approach assumes a partnership, people in smaller firms are far more likely to welcome an author's participation. Writers for small houses are freer to contribute ideas, to challenge preconceived plans and to involve themselves in production, sometimes by submitting their work on computer disks and helping to process it electronically.

Large trade houses have been slower to use writers' computerized copy. "Authors are light years ahead of editors in terms of word-processing skills," in the words of Simon & Schuster's Jack McKeown, who believes "it is the mission of publishers to find a way [to] upgrade their capabilities in house, educate their staff to be able to work with disks, and cut out unnecessary production costs." Sooner or later, you can count on them to complete that mission. It's less clear, though, how much—if any—of the money that they'll save will find its way into authors' pockets.

But if the tone of the proceedings differs between larger and smaller publishers, the steps are the same, and it's important for every author (a) to have control over them and (b) to exercise that control for the good.

Groundwork

The best preparation for smooth passage through editing and production shoals is a thorough dry run through your manuscript. After it's been accepted and before editing begins, get the typescript back and go over it, marking every textual and stylistic point you care deeply about. Is it important to you that a particular example not be cut; that footnotes appear at the back of the book instead of on the bottom of each page; that section headings seem twice as powerful as chapter headings; that dialogue be punctuated exactly as you've indicated? Expressing preferences of this sort may not get you everything you want (and perhaps you'll eventually be glad if it doesn't), but it will help you avoid some conflicts, and it will maximize your influence on the outcome of others.

It's intelligent also to state clearly and in writing—before work starts—whether you want the right of approval for any or all of the following (and to insist on reviewing at least the first three):

The edited manuscript.
The copy-edited manuscript.
The title and the subtitle if there is one.
The index.
The typeface(s) and layout.
The illustrations (if there are any) and their captions.
The book cover design and copy, or the magazine cover line.
The catalog copy.

You needn't—in fact, you shouldn't—be strident or combative when you make your request. A friendly, informal note to your editor explaining that you want to be involved (and that you don't intend to be obstructive) should serve you well. Backstop the note, though, by becoming familiar with your manuscript's timetable. The anti-snafu checklist that follows will let you identify key opportunities for input.

Here's what you need to find out:

* When will editing and copyediting be done? The edited, copy-edited manuscript should go to you before it goes anywhere else. After you've gone over it, consider making copies to send out with requests for early blurbs that you can use on your cover.

* What's the designer's deadline for sample pages and layout?

* When will the manuscript go to the typesetter? Any changes you want to make should be on record before that date.

* What's the schedule for preparing the index?

* When will you be getting your author's questionnaire and how much time will you have to fill it out? (Remember: your editor may use material from the questionnaire in writing promotional copy.)

* Which catalog(s) will your book be in and when is copy due? Overworked editors may be glad if you offer to draft catalog copy, and you'll want to check it before it goes into print anyway to make sure that your name is spelled right, that your new, improved subtitle is included, and that your bio credits you with the degrees you really earned.

* Which sales conference will cover your book. Once you have the dates, prepare materials that display your work's strengths and give them to your editor at least three weeks before the sales conference begins (see "Why and How to Be Your Own Best Sales Force").

* When will the cover design be ready? Again, you'll need to see it to check for accuracy.

* When is cover copy due? It's wise to ask to OK final front and back cover copy and flap copy, if any, and fine to offer to draft

the copy if you're good at promotional prose. Blurbs on hand should be included, of course.

✱ What day does the cover go to press?

✱ When will proofs come from the typesetter, how fast will you have to proofread them and how many sets of bound galleys will be available for people who might provide blurbs?

✱ What's the timing of the press release? As with the catalog copy, consider drafting or ask for a chance to check the publicity department's draft.

✱ When are bound galleys due? Sets should go not only to potential blurb writers but to reviewers like *Publishers Weekly* and Kirkus that need materials well before publication and to periodicals that publish once a month or less often and that may review your book or buy serial rights. This is SOP but glitches do occur.

✱ When will finished books be ready? That's the time to check on copies for reviewers and serial rights buyers at weeklies and dailies and in radio and TV.

✱ What's the official publication date? After that, you can start collecting reviews and comments to add to cover copy if your book goes back to press.

Editing

Editors come in two varieties at some giant firms: acquiring and line. Acquiring editors scout for material, take authors and potential authors out for lunch or drinks to discuss projects, and herd manuscripts through the acceptance stages. Line editors edit. Most companies, big and little, are set up so that every editor is an idea person and a blue-pencil person, but if your publisher divides the functions—or if your editor turns editing jobs over to junior colleagues—try to arrange to deal face to face with the editor who's actually working on your manuscript as well as with the one who was in charge of it to start with.

How much editing that person will do depends on how much

your work needs, on individual style, on time pressures and, obviously, on ability. Ideally, an editor will clarify what you have to say, suggest cuts and additions to strengthen the impact of your work and change nothing unless change means improvement.

In fact, some editors habitually change a great deal; tackling a manuscript with scissors and stapler as well as pencil, they cut, rearrange and reword until they think they've got the material in its most effective shape. Others make virtually no alterations, sometimes because they simply don't have time to rework the text. Occupying a very large middle ground between those who over-edit and those who hardly edit at all are editors who vary their activities markedly with each manuscript they handle, deleting large chunks of the flabby ones, moving sections around in the disorganized ones or making detailed suggestions about revisions to authors who seem capable of fixing their own text, given guidance.

If your manuscript hasn't changed much in appearance by the time an editor is through with it, you can be sure it's been edited lightly. If it's heavily pencil-marked, you're an average editee. And if it's clean, fresh copy, the editor probably rewrote the whole thing, and you probably had to wait quite some time for the results. It takes most editors a week or so to edit an average book and roughly a day to do a normal magazine piece, but with heavy rewrites these figures can easily triple.

Despite individual differences of style and speed, editors generally agree on what to do to a given manuscript (the opening should build up momentum more quickly; the mother's speech in the confrontation scene should be foreshadowed; readers ought to be told the basis for the findings in paragraph 4). And they tend to agree, too, about what not to do. Editors remind themselves and their assistants—often and with conviction—to refrain from superimposing ideas on or changing characters in an author's work. Editors are supposed to realize your story's potential; if they have tales they themselves want to tell, they should tell them on their own time.

Good editors take pains to treat authors as carefully as they treat manuscripts. In fact, some editors are so solicitous of writers' egos that they've developed a special diction for suggesting revisions. "That's a marvelous lead," they'll say; "compelling and thoroughly apt. And your conclusion works beautifully. But I wonder whether the middle section might, perhaps, benefit from just a bit of tightening. If you don't object, I'd like to try tinkering with it a bit, being careful, of course, not to injure your style or your point in any way."

Roughly translated, this means: "I genuinely admire what you've written; I know how hard it was to write; and I don't want you to feel hurt because the final product is less than perfect. What you don't know and I do, however, is that every manuscript has notable weaknesses; for your own good, I want to correct the flaws in yours. The midsection is verbose and confusing and needs to be cut by a third."

To forestall the defensive reaction that may arise when editors come along and tell you, tactfully or not, that they can make your manuscript better than you've made it, think about these contrasts:

* Editors don't have to cope with a blank piece of paper or a blank screen. You've originated a story or a line of argument that's worth transmitting to readers; all they have to do is fine-tune the signals.

* Editors are intimately familiar with a wide range of literary techniques because they've worked with dozens of writers, while you've got only your own experience and learning to draw upon.

* Editors know their audiences. Sometimes, by using their hard-won knowledge of readers' predilections, they can reshape a manuscript so that it will draw a bigger and more receptive crowd.

* Your editor isn't sick of the whole damn thing. After endless rewriting, both your words and your concepts may blur and grow stale in your mind, but the material is new to the editor, who can therefore come to it clear-eyed and energetic.

In spite of everything writers can do to persuade themselves to adopt a professional attitude toward being edited, some find it impossible not to bristle. If you're in this group, read your revised manuscript through once, fast, and take a breather. Go run around the lake or play a couple of sets of tennis before you look at your copy again, and then try to read it as if it were the work of a total stranger and to imagine as you read what your publisher's problems with it may have been (does the magazine have a particular tone of voice to maintain; are cuts of twenty-three pages necessary to keep your book's cost down to the point where bookstores will stock it; did that lovely descriptive section you struggled with for weeks destroy the story's pace?)

Whatever complaints survive a dispassionate reading should be taken up—calmly—with your editor. Don't squabble if you can avoid it, because you and the editor are jointly responsible for creating and nurturing a piece of writing, and creative, nurturing tasks are best performed by teammates who focus on the good of the offspring rather than on failings in each other.

Copy-editing

A mutually satisfactory working relationship with your editor is at least as important after editing is finished as it was before and during the editing phase, since from now on you'll have to rely on the editor to help settle disputes with everybody else. The odds-on favorite for most-likely-to-be-disputed-with is the individual who gets your manuscript next: the copy editor. (On many newspapers the editor who's called the copy editor will have general, high-level responsibilities, but you're not likely to have much direct contact with people of this stripe.)

Copy editors have a lot to put up with. Their status is low, as is their pay, and their job—which tends to be literally thankless—demands a peculiar, contradictory blend of character traits: copy editors must be highly intelligent, dazzlingly knowledgeable, keenly alert nitpickers.

To copy-edit is to be responsible for making a manuscript correct in all its details. Authors are generally uninterested when a copy editor conforms their work to house style ("theater," not "theatre"; *The New York Times,* not the *New York Times* or the New York *Times*) and they're grateful, on the whole, when copy editors catch and correct their mistakes, by supplying appropriate double consonants in "accommodate" or "desiccate," for instance, by taking San Antonio away from the Pecos River and placing it on the banks of the San Antonio River or even by pointing out that the action in a particular story couldn't happen (take the tender scene in a leading novelist's work in which a father tiptoes in to place a goodnight kiss on the cheek of his child as she lies asleep in her crib; Listen, said the copy editor, you can't kiss a kid in a crib unless you balance on your stomach over the railing; God, how embarrassing, said the novelist; thanks very much).

It's when the copy editor presses for documentation or defines as a correction something the author sees as a distortion that trouble starts.

More and more, documentation is the author's job because fewer and fewer publishing concerns can afford to have a fact checker on the staff nowadays. To protect against lawsuits and to ensure accuracy, the copy editor must often call upon writers to cite (and perhaps to produce) their sources. Writers who have kept careful notes will naturally find the task less onerous than writers who haven't, but even the most rigorous recordkeepers may have to exert themselves considerably, because copy editors know—from long and sad experience—that what you read in print is not necessarily so.

Satisfying their rule of thumb—when two out of three authorities agree, that's good enough—generally calls for additional research, which few authors undertake without grumbling.

The grumbling turns to groans, or even screeches, when writers come up against copy editors who have a context to contend with (is yours the second piece in this issue to use the Mad Hatter's tea party as a metaphor? If so, you'll probably find the allusion has been cut) or whose ideas of correctness don't jibe with their own. Robert Pilpel, who repeatedly referred to Churchill as Winston throughout his "affectionate portrait," *Churchill in America*, was furious to discover that a copy editor had laboriously changed all his "Winstons" to "Mr. Churchill," "Churchill," or "the PM" on the grounds that "Winston" sounded disrespectful. Pilpel thought it conveyed just the tone he wanted. He won the point.

You can win similar arguments with copy editors if you treat them with kindness and respect. In fact, you can probably have your way on most editing and copy-editing questions; after all, it's your story. It's important that you not make an issue out of everything, however, and it's vitally important that if you're going to take a stand, you take it early. After the copy-editing stage, it's most costly to fuss with the text. (For more about copy-editing, see the Starter Kit in "The Self-Publishing Option.")

Indexing

All too often, an author assumes that providing an index is part of the publisher's job, while the publisher assumes that an author who doesn't ask for an index doesn't want one. Since a nonfiction book with an index will sell many more copies than the same book without it, you should check your contract on this subject and take appropriate steps in good time.

Design and Production

When you and your editor and your copy editor have finished with your manuscript, it is sent off to the typesetter with a full set of specifications for typefaces, column widths, spacing and the like. The person who chooses specs is a designer; the person who supervises their execution is a production manager. The smaller the firm, the more likely it is that the designer and the production manager will be one and the same; in every firm, their functions are intimately related.

To get a firm grasp on design and production, you can turn to books listed in "Resources"; to learn enough about these operations so that you'll know what their effects are, read on.

At its simplest level, design has to do with how a manuscript should look in print. Given the available space, a range of type options and possibly a budget for artwork, a designer will select one or more sizes and styles of type for text and several others for headings; the designer will also devise a format and perhaps commission or secure drawings or photographs—all this with two goals in mind: making your work readable and visually reinforcing its message without overspending. Once the basic choices are made, the designer combines text and titles and pictures to create an effective array of pages. Because most writers know little or nothing about layout and type, and because many book and periodical designers have a strictly limited range of options, there's not much an author can contribute at this stage; in fact, you should feel freer now to ignore your manuscript than you've been before or will ever be again.

With intermittent breaks for required activities, your recess period should last all through production—which consists of purchasing materials and services, scheduling and routing the manuscript, coordinating printing and binding with distribution and keeping everything straight and moving along with the help of detailed written records. A production cycle lasts several weeks at most magazines and six months to a year or more for books, and unless you're responsible for coding and correcting your manuscript on your computer, you can safely leave it to the specialists. Do read your galleys and/or page proofs, though, to catch any mistakes you and the copy editor missed and any a typesetter may have made; and return them on time because deadlines matter more now.

As publication date approaches, your manuscript's schedule gets increasingly inflexible and changes get more and more complicated and costly. There's a little bit of give at every point of every production timetable (despite what you'll hear to the contrary from people who don't trust you to meet a real deadline), but by the time page proofs are pulled, things are generally moving so fast that only minor and absolutely essential corrections can be made.

Authors don't see page proofs as a rule, so if you want to have some effect on layout and illustrations, don't wait; get involved while rough sketches are in the works. Be prepared, even that early, to meet resistance; editors and designers are apt to have sharp preferences of their own about how your manuscript should look in print.

Part-and-Parcel Advertising

After a book or article is published, its author should find a variety of ways to let people know it exists and to make them want to read it ("Why and How to Be Your Own Best Sales Force" and "Managing Sales" will elaborate). There's one piece of advertising, however, that's conceived and executed well before publication because it's an integral part of your work. For a book, it's the cover; for an article or a story, it's the cover line (only a few items from a magazine's table of contents get listed on its cover; if you can come up with a phrase that will attract buyers to yours, perhaps it will be one of those that's featured).

Like coming-next-issue squibs and headnotes, magazine cover lines are presented as the publisher's work rather than the writer's. That being the case, editors frequently feel no obligation to check them with authors, and authors usually don't mind.

Almost always, however, writers want to preview their book covers and, unfortunately, almost always, they don't know how to evaluate what they see. Controversy in this area erupts when publishers define covers as point-of-purchase ads, while authors assume they should be works of art. Since the first point of view is demonstrably healthier for sales, you'd be wise to adopt it and, having adopted it, to decide then what ideas and/or sketches and/or leads to picture sources you might usefully contribute.

Out of politeness, publishing people may pay lip service to your suggestions, no matter how off-base they think you are. But if you want them to heed as well as to listen once you get into the conflict-ridden area of publicity, advertising and sales, you will have to convince them that you don't fit the conventional writer's mold. For a writer, as pictured in publishing's collective unconscious, is a babe in the business woods, an impractical type who's understandably eager to succeed and infuriatingly misinformed about how success is achieved. Because this mental image has a substantial foundation in fact, overcoming it means absorbing knowledge and terminology. You can start by realizing that your book's cover may be the only ad it ever gets, and by the time you've read the next chapter you'll have learned enough to position yourself verbally and intellectually on your publisher's wavelength. Then you can really start to fiddle with the controls.

Why and How to Be Your Own Best Sales Force

CALL IT THE curse of abundance; with roughly 40,000 new books each year, and periodicals starting up all the time, only a small percentage of what's published catches the attention of the public. This reality comes as a shock to most writers, and as an especially severe shock to authors of first books, whose expectations about sales and reviews always escalate as publication day approaches.

To help cushion the inevitable blow, many editors deliver a standard prepublication speech. At small houses, the gist of it is, We hope to rack up sales over the years, but making a big splash now just isn't in the cards. And at large houses, an editor may say, in effect, Don't expect much (or, for most fiction writers and poets, don't expect anything); your book is not going to sell 100,000 copies—we'll be lucky if it sells 5,000; don't look for a display ad in *The New York Times*, because there isn't going to be one; and no, you won't get on *Today* or *Oprah*; in fact, unless a major book club chooses it or some publisher makes a whopping bid for reprint rights, your book will vanish without a trace three months after publication.

Fortunately, as the ghost said to Scrooge, these are the shadows of things that will be only if you don't get busy.

To promote a magazine or newspaper piece, about all you need to do is draw up a list of influential individuals who figure to comment on it and ought to get copies, draft a covering letter to them and tell your publisher about any contacts you have with media people who might focus on your story. (If you want extra copies of your piece for your friends or your files, order them before the issue they'll appear in is printed; they're cheaper that way.) To promote a book, however, you can do a great deal more, and you'd better.

Profit and Loss and the Bigbook Bind

It's part of publishing's proverbial wisdom that each book is unique and that it therefore requires individual attention—"This isn't toothpaste we're selling" is, for reasons unknown, the standard comparison. In fact, though, publishers generally produce and distribute their wares assembly-line fashion. For this apparent contradiction, they have a ready, and thoroughly plausible, excuse: with dozens or hundreds of titles to sell and strict limits on time, money and staff, routinization is essential.

Why do publishers continue to produce so many books if they lack the resources to sell them? Why, to put it another way, does a $16-billion business accept it as a fact of life that book after book after book will fail to bring in a penny of profit? A full discussion of the reasons would make a book by itself, but three of them deserve mention here.

* Even the largest, most commercial houses sometimes publish books that don't seem likely to make any money, because editors there think those books are important to contemporary thought or literature.

* There's some truth in the toothpaste analogy, not because each book is unique (most current titles have obvious counterparts in the publishing past) but because the public will greet it as if it were until they've been educated to believe otherwise. The educational process is expensive—conventional book publishing houses, after all, have no brand-name loyalties to draw upon and no subscription systems to guarantee that money they spend initially to round up an audience will be paid off

over time—so large firms quite naturally concentrate on telling the world about those titles that have a huge potential readership and leave the rest to luck.

Since each book is a one-shot deal, publishing people must base initial commitments to a particular title on the rough guidelines their experience offers and on apparently unquenchable sparks of hope. Usually, though, the hope proves forlorn because, in the end, the routine measures that publishers have time to put into effect almost never suffice to locate and arouse a particular book's best audience; and authors, who might inject some nonroutine verve into the proceedings, don't know how to help.

*   The bigbook has the industry in a bind. On the one hand, bestsellers (not unlike toothpaste) appeal to a large general market, and that enables publishers to benefit from market research (of an admittedly informal sort) and from economies of scale. On the other hand, however, they draw funds and attention away from the majority of the books on a publisher's list, and they demand a strenuous commitment to hype.

Here's how the bigbooks grow:

1. Editors at a particular publishing house get hold of a book with bestseller potential.
2. The book gets a two-page write-up in the new catalog; editors and marketing people begin to talk it up over lunch and drinks with editors at the major book clubs and other publishing insiders, and to collect ecstatic blurbs from celebrities they work with; ads are scheduled for *PW* and major metropolitan newspapers; and a cross-country tour, complete with radio and TV appearances and local press coverage, is planned for the author.
3. Booksellers, librarians, reviewers and reprint editors, seeing the catalog, the ads and the press releases and hearing the trade gossip, get the bigbook signal loud and clear and hurry to leap on the bandwagon before anyone can accuse them of not being with-it.

4. Reviewers review, bookstores and libraries buy, and the public—responding reflexively to the hoopla—decides to get with-it too, by rushing out and grabbing that book that absolutely everybody is reading.
5. Absolutely everybody reads it.

Increasing Your Influence

The bigbook bandwagon gets a considerable part of its power from implicit comparisons (this is the cream of a very large crop, goes the unstated bigbook message); thus, it can damage your chances by defining your book as inferior (it's something other than cream, quite clearly, and perhaps no more than watery milk). And, of course, the bigbooks can also hurt you (along with any publisher's overall track record) by preempting the major portion of all sales resources (that initial advertising blitz is expensive, and so is the tour, and after sales reps push a bigbook as hard as they're often instructed to do, they won't have much energy left for selling the rest of the list).

To counter the forces that will work to keep your book just one more title on "the rest of the list," you'll have to attract an audience for it, and the most efficient way to do that is by identifying the connections that already exist between you and your work, on the one hand, and classes of readers, on the other.

Try people who know you, people who share membership with you in a formal or informal group of any sort and people who will feel a sense of kinship with your characters, your settings or your subject. Is your protagonist a liberated house-husband? Tell women's organizations and men's clubs. Does your subject involve college students? Reach the campuses. Is there a scene in Chicago, a narrative account of abortion, a proposal to abolish free public education? Across the country, people who identify in some way with these areas of interest (and with almost any others you can think of) regularly convene, and communicate through newsletters; and if you use their particular concerns to provide points of entry to selected aspects of your work, the whole of what you've done will get its fair chance to capture their attention and earn their admiration.

Once you succeed in stirring up interest, you can use evidence of your success to convince the staff at your publishing house to back you. When they see signs (even small ones) that you're a winner, they'll be more likely to make your book one of the titles they urge on booksellers, librarians, reviewers and all the other intermediaries who stand between conventionally published writers and their readers.

Persuading your publisher to get out there and sell your book is a never-ending job that demands a good deal of gall (though they don't want to be quoted, publishing people admit that demanding authors get more attention for their books). But skillful maneuvering is useful too, and for best results you'll want to devise sensible promotional plans, figure out how to fit them in with your publisher's standard operating procedures and then get up the gumption to see that they're put into effect.

The following descriptions and suggestions should tell you what you need to know to manage all three steps.

Major Departmental Development

Publicity, Promotion and Advertising

At large houses, separate departments may exist to handle each of these areas; at small firms one person is often responsible for them all, and for other things besides. In any case, though, all three are closely related and the first two are extremely important.

Probably the only request these departments will ever make of you is that you fill out a questionnaire providing them with an autobiographical sketch, a description of your book, an account of how it was conceived and written, a list of its newsworthy aspects and a roster of names and addresses of people who might provide blurb copy or otherwise help focus attention on what you've written.

In a rational world, all writers would complete these forms immediately and with care. What actually happens, however, is that publicity people have to plead for information—"We know it's a chore to fill out forms" is the way one house begins its questionnaire's covering letter, "but if you could spare a few moments to answer the attached questions, it would be a great help to us in publicizing and promoting your book"—and when they finally get writers to hand the forms in, they discover half the time that the data supplied are too sketchy to be of any use.

Bolstering this evidence of authorial sloth, there are numerous indications of authorial ignorance (writers not only have an unbounded and ungrounded faith in ads, for instance; they also seem to believe that bookstore clerks who say they've never heard of a book are saying something true and significant). Having listened to all these stories and lived through too many of them, most publicity people don't count on much help from writers. In fact, they've been badgered so often by inappropriate demands that their response to the idea of author participation tends to be horror.

Before you can make a contribution, therefore, you'll have to demonstrate that you're different, that while others may try to nag and second-guess marketing people, what you intend to do is provide extra information and elbow grease.

For starters, see what you can do about blurbs. These pre-publication comments from relevant celebrities and authorities can be the spark that ignites a publicity campaign. So make a list of important people who might say nice things about your book, and scrounge up addresses for them (see "Resources" and remember that lots of famous folk reveal their whereabouts in directories like *Who's Who* and *Contemporary Authors*). Then draft letters explaining what you need and why you think they might be happy to give it to you.

"I read what I could about each author on my list so I could personalize my approaches. For example, I learned that one author had worked in advertising so I made sure to mention that in my book the tourists on safari are advertising people," Karin

McQuillan reports. A therapist as well as a novelist, McQuillan actually enjoyed the process of asking for blurbs for her novel *Deadly Safari*, once she psyched herself up for it. "It was fun to make contact with the authors I love, tell them so, talk a bit about their books and my book. I'm always telling my clients that their needs are legitimate and that it feels good to ask for what you want even if you're told No; at least you stood up for yourself. Besides, it felt as much like sharing my enthusiasm, and joining the club, as asking for something."

Tony Hillerman, Robert B. Parker, Aaron Elkins and other giants of mystery fiction were among those who said Yes, so McQuillan's sheet of "Advance Praise" quotes became a powerful marketing tool.

To add to your marketing tool chest, look hard at your book, remembering that many of the people at your publishing house may never have read it. All too often, publicity personnel and others in charge of selling a book have to proceed knowing nothing more about it than its central subject. Thus, if your title is *A History of Fitness Fads*, they'll know enough to alert health and fitness groups and periodicals to forthcoming publication, but because they won't have read the chapter on next year's Be Fit Fair in Cleveland, they won't be able to develop potential there.

You could, though; you know every chapter, every scene, every sentence, and if you assess them as candidates for fairly standard promotional efforts, they can give you quite a lot of mileage.

Consider, for example, review copies. As a matter of course, most publicity departments send copies of the books they handle to major review media like *Publishers Weekly*, *Library Journal*, American Library Association magazines, *Kirkus*, *The New York Times*, the Washington *Post* and the Los Angeles *Times*. Columnists and magazine and newspaper editors with large, national audiences who have expressed interest in a book, or who figure to be interested in it, will also get copies.

But small periodicals can print effective reviews too, and because the publicity department may not know the ones in your field (and surely won't have time to ferret them out), it becomes your job to get up a list. Include small-town papers and neighborhood throwaways published in places you've mentioned in your book, along with pertinent special-interest journals, and mention names of contacts at these periodicals whenever possible.

As a general rule, between 100 and 500 copies of a new title go out for review. Though the press releases regularly issued by publishers vary at least as widely in number, they too constitute powerful selling tools for any sort of book. You should be able to think of good places to send them by creating appropriate conclusions for the sentence that starts, "This book will be of special interest to you because . . ."

What people or groups would be especially interested in the people or groups your book mentions? What local papers serve the places you've described? What associations care about your subject? What directories exist in the field? And how can you get your work listed? (The Bowker and Gale catalogs, which are listed in "The Self-Publishing Option Resources," will be helpful here.)

If you know about meetings of people active in your book's area, write a memo about them. If you think the book would be valuable for supplementary reading in schools, draft a letter to teachers explaining how they might use it, and pass the draft along to your editor. And if you've spotted the newsworthy side of what you've written, by all means develop your thoughts and share them as soon as you can.

Remember, too, that publicity departments frequently send announcements to notify friends, family and interested others that a particular author's book has just been published. This is a relatively inexpensive practice (much cheaper, for example, than mailing out review copies or scheduling ads), so you're not likely to meet much resistance if you press for its use.

Mailings also go out from publicity departments to radio talk shows, of which there are hundreds. Because the telephone lets authors appear on radio anywhere in the country without incurring travel expenses, you may well find that your publisher is happy to do a "phoner" mailing for you. And if they're not interested, you can do it yourself; see "Resources" for directories to use in targeting appropriate shows and their producers. Kenneth C. Davis, whose hardcover publisher had "low to modest expectations" for *Don't Know Much About History*, appeared on scores of talk shows—21 of them in the course of one "exhausting but exhilarating" July 4th weekend—to promote the paperback edition that became a bestseller. Crediting his book's success mainly to radio, Davis notes that it's a medium he's comfortable with (many writers find it far less stressful than TV) and that you get generous amounts of time to cover your subject (sometimes as much as two hours, as compared to TV time measured in minutes).

The best way of all to sell a book is face to face with a prospective buyer, which is why many publishers arrange interviews and speaking engagements for nonfiction authors (they're less good, please note, at managing to have promotional materials and bound books on hand to fill any demand the authors generate). But if no one else schedules you, you can schedule yourself.

Molly Peacock, whose books of poems include *Raw Heaven* and *Take Heart*, does a mailing every so often to people in charge of readings. Her covering letter begins, "I hope you will consider me for a place in the [Such-and-Such] poetry reading series." Then it goes on to talk about the magazines that have published her poetry and the readings she's already given. She also sends along a copy of one of her book jackets, copies of reviews, a précis of her professional accomplishments and several poems that show the quality and flavor of her work.

Readings regularly result and Peacock reports that "the psychic rewards are terrific."

The financial rewards can be pretty good too. A poet who's "completely unabashed" about selling her books when she reads, Molly Peacock has found that giving readings plus judging poetry contests plus getting grants can propel her annual income from poetry into five figures.

Readings also work well for novelists, but the best way for

nonfiction writers to meet their readers is by preparing presentations they can give before groups.

Some of the greatest success stories in contemporary publishing are traceable to talks initiated by unknown authors. Back when *I'm OK, You're OK* first came out, it had an advance sale of 7,433. During its first year, sales were roughly 20,000 copies—respectable, but by no means extraordinary. The next year, however, sales soared over 100,000, and they continued to mount each year after that until they peaked at over a million. The publisher gave the credit to the author, Thomas A. Harris, because his talks before small audiences got sales to the point where the publicity department felt justified in planning a strong promotional campaign. It's a pattern other authors have traced too.

Where speaking to groups is concerned, your knowledge of your book is again your best asset, and you should use it to select upcoming conferences and conventions that will be worth attending. Many authors have been successful in selling their own books at conventions and fairs, so you may have no trouble getting your publisher to cover your expenses at such gatherings (if you do go, try hard to get a list of names and addresses of the attendees; it could supply productive leads for mail-order sales).

Promotional devices like posters, flyers, bookmarks and order forms are useful when you speak before groups, and in theory some of your book's projected revenues will be allocated for them. In practice, though, bigbooks get much more than their share and most books get much less. If you're artistic, you may be able to compensate by designing and executing promotional materials yourself in consultation with publicity and promotion people (see the Starter Kit), and if you're realistic in your suggestions you might get the publisher to pay your out-of-pocket expenses.

As for ads, the important thing is not to plump for space in the standard book review media. Ads there are exceedingly expensive—a full page in *The New York Times Book Review* costs approximately $17,000—and their rate of return may be only a fraction of what you'd get from two tiny coupon ads in publications that focus on your area of interest. (See "A Foot in the Door Resources" for leads.)

The publicity department should be pleased if there's enough evidence of interest in your book to warrant keeping it alive. And when and if a book starts to take off, they may try to help it along by issuing periodic announcements to the trade journals about favorable new reviews or large new printings. The more developments there are, the better; so keep working to interest the local bank, the library, the schools or the stores in displaying your book; keep sending small periodicals material about it whenever a news event comes along to serve as a peg; keep looking for groups that might welcome you as a speaker; and above all, keep telling your publisher what you're doing. Each new sign of interest and enthusiasm you can report may stimulate still more attention.

Subsidiary Rights Sales

Once upon a time, there were publishers who produced books bound in cloth covers to sell in bookstores and publishers who produced books bound in paper covers to sell elsewhere. Hardcovers were used on books coming out for the first time; softcovers were for "cheap editions," and sub rights departments in hardcover houses became profit centers by selling rights to paperback reprinters.

The picture is not so simple anymore. Having realized that their profits may be greater if they're the only house issuing a book (however many formats that book may have), publishers that used to do hardcovers only and publishers that once did nothing but paperbacks now publish hardcover and softcover books; either may sell rights in one format and/or the other; and either may decide to issue reprints of material they originated.

Some authors get a measure of control over reprint deals in their contracts, but in general it's hard to affect major sub rights sales. Writers can be influential, though, with regard to serial sales (of excerpts, to magazines and newspapers, before and after publication), and, once again, your intimate knowledge of your book can make the difference between getting offers and getting ignored. If you suggest that the analysis of sitcoms on pages 85 to 90 might appeal to *TV Guide*, that chapters two and three, with some connective tissue and a new lead, would work for *Rolling Stone*, or that your section on old country inns should interest *Southern Living*, your rights director (or your agent, if that's who's handling serial sales) will be delighted—and much more effective.

Left to their own devices on serial submissions, overworked people are likely to send a complete set of galleys of your book out to a magazine that shares its general area of interest. When the galleys arrive, magazine editors will be faced with a choice: (a) to plow through three hundred pages of material in hopes of finding fifteen that might, with some work, make a piece; or (b) to ship the book back and risk missing a decent article. Quite often—and quite rightly, given time pressures and priorities—an editor will opt for the latter. If you want portions of your work to appear in the periodical press, therefore (and you will if you consider either the money or the publicity you can gain that way), you'll have to carve them out yourself and help direct them to the most appropriate openings you can find. Confer with your editor on timing, and consult "A Foot in the Door" and "Spinoffs" for leads.

Sales to Bookstores

The job of getting books into stores is performed by a sales force, which can number roughly one hundred at a very large publishing house. At least twice a year, salespeople at most large firms convene for a full-dress presentation of their house's new books. Sometimes sales conferences are held in the publisher's own home territory and editors introduce their own titles; sometimes the conferences take place at an island resort, and the editor-in-chief, along with other members of upper management, announces the entire line, describing each book and suggesting how to sell it.

It's important to get your book presented favorably at the sales conference because if the reps sense that it's a loser they'll classify it mentally as a "skip book" (one they can use to build confidence with booksellers by saying, "Between you and me, you can skip this"); and then, of course, a loser is what it will be. To avoid this fate, you should prepare a package of selling documents and pass it along to your editor in the hope that the editor, in turn, will relay copies to all the marketing people. Consider including a list of promising markets together with notes on how to reach them, an analysis of the distinctions between your book and its competition, a particularly engaging excerpt and/or a table of contents.

In addition, you might offer to talk with the assembled sales reps if they're in your area, either by addressing them at a meeting or by attending one of the parties the house may be giving for them during a sales conference.

Since more than a hundred titles may be presented at each sales meeting and since each sales rep will have approximately twenty-nine seconds to sell a book in the stores, it's a good idea to create a tag line for yours. "What I need most," noted Nancy Taylor as a sales rep for Random House, "are key words or phrases that will be sure to catch the attention of the retailer. For instance, when *Inner Tennis* came out, I jotted down 'Zen approach to tennis' and 'meditative techniques applicable to sports.' And that's what I used to sell the book. If there's no handle, it's difficult to sell a book, no matter how good it is."

When, after close to a week, sales conferences end, each sales rep goes forth—armed with catalogs, book covers, photos of authors and a quota to meet for every title—to call on accounts (a single rep may be responsible for contacting fifty or a hundred booksellers). Because most books sold to stores are fully returnable and because the sales reps' bonuses are usually based on sales minus returns, it does them no good to load retailers up with copies of a title the stores won't be able to move. Still, once the books are on the shelves the manager will try to find customers for them (or so the theory goes), and besides, quotas help publishers provide an objective correlative for impressionistic first-printing orders.

Unfortunately, despite quotas and clever sales pitches, many new books have a hard time getting into bookstores, and those that do make it onto the shelves aren't likely to stay there long. Because they know they can return most titles they stock, bookstore managers take little risk in ordering, have little incentive to sell aggressively or imaginatively and tend to go with our cultural flow toward the new, new, new and the big, big, big. Ninety days after a book's publication, booksellers who want room for other titles may simply pack it up and return it to the publisher for credit, and unless they're convinced that would be a mistake, it's just what they'll do.

Everyone agrees that present systems of distribution are unsatisfactory all around and perhaps at their worst in those moments—known to authors, publishers and booksellers alike—when it's impossible to cash in on a surge of interest in a particular book because the damn thing isn't in fact "available at your bookstore," as the ads and media coverage promised, but is, instead, stuck in the warehouse, lost in the mail or held up in its second printing by a strike at the bindery.

On the whole, the transience and unpredictability of a book's life in the stores make everybody miserable, and there's not much relief in sight. You can take a small step toward sanity, however, by reminding yourself that—just like the publicity people and the subsidiary rights people—sales reps can't be relied upon to have read your book and that they need you to tell them what's between the covers.

If you've written about patients' rights, for example, and you know that Boston, New York and San Francisco are among the cities in the vanguard of medical change, write a memo to the sales force and urge them to set high quotas for stores there. Try to isolate as many promising geographical markets as you can, whatever your subject, and prepare a list for the sales force, complete with explanations (I grew up in Newtown, Connecticut; my parents live in Boise, Idaho; chapter six is set in Helena, Montana). Selecting three cities for special attention, Joanne Leedom-Ackerman helped propel her first novel, *The Dark Path to the River*, into a second printing shortly after its publication date. With good reviews and a schedule of public appearances in hand, she arranged to autograph books and deliver posters at chain and independent bookstores in Los Angeles (where she lived), New York (where her story takes place) and Dallas (where she comes from; where her supportive publisher, Saybrook, was based; and where her novel soon made the bestseller list, which it stayed on for weeks). "Targeting a few areas and making personal contacts with the booksellers there was one of the most successful things we did," Leedom-Ackerman reports.

Special Sales

For a variety of reasons, many people never set foot in a bookstore. They do, however, go to stores that cater to their special interests: tennis players frequent sporting goods shops, knitting enthusiasts head for the yarn department, kids hang out where toys are sold, and the list goes on. In fact, all sorts of groups not only have stores that serve their needs; they have periodicals, associations, catalogs and conferences as well. Reaching readers through these and other special-interest, "nontraditional" channels is the job of the special sales department.

A good many special sales departments have developed recently, because publishers now know that special sales can bring in sizable amounts of money—more, for some books, than bookstores ever will. Suggestions from authors are usually welcome in this area, so find out who handles special sales for your publisher and then get up a memo pinpointing the nontraditional channels the house should use to get your book directly to its natural readership (see "Managing Sales" for guidance).

Sales to Libraries

In addition to selling directly to retailers, some salespeople call upon wholesalers, who get a large discount because they buy in bulk and who sell their inventory to retailers and libraries. Wholesalers (or jobbers, as they're sometimes called) sell books of all publishers and offer all the advantages typical of onestop suppliers in any industry, including simplified ordering, billing and shipment procedures.

It's their greater efficiency and their discount policies that recommend jobbers to librarians, who order from them after studying publishers' catalogs and reviews in professional journals. Since libraries are obviously a crucial market and since books lead comparatively long lives on library shelves, you'll want to establish contact with librarians in your area, and perhaps you'll decide to include an index in your book (a "no index" note at the end of a review in a library journal can mean "no reference value" to a librarian and thus no sale to you). Otherwise, you can probably rely on whoever handles library promotion to do whatever is practical for your book in this area.

Fighting the Fear of Hustling

Authors rarely lobby for their books within the houses that publish them (which means less competition for you if you follow this chapter's advice), and they're even less likely to go out by themselves in search of sales. Somehow, they seem to think, it's not dignified to hustle for anything you yourself created. Well, dignified writers do it, and for a dignified reason: believing that what they have to say is worth saying, they accept the responsibility of finding those people who will benefit from hearing it.

Even famous, well-established authors are not so smug or rich that they won't get out and give their latest book a nudge or two. A buyer for the Radius Book Store on the West Side of New York City, Susan Bergholz, reported that Joseph Heller, who was a neighbor of hers as well as the author of *Catch-22* and *God Knows*, periodically came into the store to autograph a few copies, to check the stock and positioning of his book and to see how many copies had been bought.

And other writers also roll up their sleeves to reach readers. Cases in point include Joshua Meyrowitz, whose *No Sense of Place* has won three awards and gone into multiple printings; Ann McLaughlin, whose first novel went back to press and earned her a contract for a second, and Frederic Flach, M.D., whose book *Rickie*, a dramatic account of his daughter's misdiagnosis as schizophrenic, got a second life in paperback and was optioned for TV.

Like any author with insight, these people probably realized that nothing sells a book better than personal connections. To get the most from yours, with the least psychological strain, start by talking before audiences that will think of you as a neighbor or a friend.

Arrange for a reading at a local library. Check with groups in your area that might sponsor meet-the-author get-togethers. See if a bookstore downtown will display your book and invite people to meet with you to talk about it. And whether they'll do that or not, arrange to autograph the store's copies of your book (since autographed copies are more likely to sell, it's smart also to sign copies in bookstores outside your area whenever you travel).

While you're stalking the home front, call the local papers and radio stations to volunteer for interviews or to see if they'd like to serialize your book. And by all means drop a note to the book reviewers of all local publications to tell them that a local resident has been published. In her hometown (Portland, Oregon), Rose Naftalin sold 6,000 copies of her cookbook. As that figure indicates, it's hard to overestimate the value of promotion on your own turf.

After you've used every connection your geographical and personal roots suggest, you can start to develop connections through subject matter. Consider the example of Jane Seskin— author of *Young Widow*, *Living Single* and *A Time to Love*—who prepared a brief talk about living alone and meeting people, combined those remarks with readings of her lighthearted poems about the single life and arranged to deliver the resulting presentation at a variety of singles clubs.

Having heard writer Elizabeth Janeway say that she and her economist husband, Eliot, never spoke anywhere without bringing some copies of their books to sell, Seskin carted a supply of her own books around to meetings. Because juggling money can be awkward, she often took a friend along to transact sales, but she personally autographed every copy on request. (For more information about money-making opportunities on the lecture circuit, see "Spinoffs.")

Wherever you speak and whether you bring your own personal stock or rely on your publisher to get books into the area, be sure to have a supply of flyers with order forms along for backup. Ask your editor to get the sales department to prepare some for you, and if they won't or can't, produce them yourself (see the Starter Kit for instructions). Be sure, too, to let the publicity department know at least six weeks in advance about any speaking engagements you've lined up so that they'll have time to alert the local press and bookstores and so that you'll have time to take advantage of any public-speaking services your publisher has to offer.

Some houses provide coaching for their authors before scheduled TV and personal appearances, but whether or not lessons are available, you can always make up a list of provocative questions that an interviewer might ask, and then practice answering them fast and fully. Since the average interview lasts eight minutes, there's plenty of time to establish eye contact with your audience and to mention the title of your book with fair frequency; all you need by way of preparation is a few rehearsals.

Those of you who still feel shy may be emboldened by the story of Diana Brown, told here in her own words.

As a librarian, I was well aware of the number of titles published each year, so when my first novel—*The Emerald Necklace*—appeared, my family and I put our heads together to explore what we might do to save an entertaining book from possible oblivion. We sought out all our contacts: personal, professional, educational, ethnic, and told them of the novel's release.

Attending a political convention, my husband had "campaign" buttons made up for each of us announcing "My wife [or mommy] [or I] wrote *The Emerald Necklace* by Diana Brown." These we wore to an ever increasing number of talks I presented to local groups—friends of the library, schools, service and women's clubs.

May's birthstone being the emerald, we approached a local jeweler with a chain of stores in busy shopping centers who agreed to display my book along with his emeralds, and with a sign noting it was by a local author. We also purchased a small advertisement in a local shopping guide suggesting *The Emerald Necklace* as a May birthday gift.

I wrote a press release on the novel, its progress, and my own background for distribution to local papers. When *The Emerald Necklace* was featured in *Good Housekeeping* and later by *Buenhogar* (the Spanish-language version of that magazine) we had this release translated for Spanish-language papers and radio stations in our area.

Our summer vacation was turned into a promotion trip. Armed with the press release and copies of reviews, we called on newspapers, radio and television stations along our route. Since *The Emerald Necklace* had been chosen by the Sunday supplement *Family Weekly* as suggested summer reading, we made sure to approach each newspaper that carried that magazine. The trip resulted in numerous reviews and feature stories.

Using photocopies of the book jacket, we designed our own notepaper and envelopes. We also reprinted the publisher's catalog copy, and no bill payment or letter left our home without one of these promos being inserted in the envelope. Our Christmas card was also designed from the book jacket—which happened to have been adapted from a handsome portrait by Sir Henry Raeburn.

All of these personal and family efforts resulted in *The Emerald Necklace* going into three hardcover printings. It has since been reprinted in paperback and published in England, Argentina, and Greece. Undoubtedly its success added to the publisher's enthusiasm for my later novels—including *Come Be My Love*, *The Hand of a Woman*, and *The Blue Dragon*.

The Editor Exits and Other Evils

Authors are prey to strange evil forces. When the reviewer assigned by a prestigious magazine to cover your book does a lousy job and the piece gets chucked, you get no coverage there. When delays of one sort and another mean your tap-dancing guide comes out after the craze is over, you'll have lost your audience. When two books with subjects like yours suddenly fail, you'll forgo the support of the sales force. And when your editor is feuding with the publicity director, you will suffer.

But no matter how events conspire against you, if you believe in your book you can change your luck. Here's a sampling of suggestions.

✱ When your editor leaves the house, don't panic. As soon as you hear the news, find out who might adopt your book once it's orphaned (your original editor should be able to supply some names), and then meet with all the candidates to assess their enthusiasm for your work and their ability to do well by it. Finally, after you've been assigned a new editor, make a date to explain your book's strengths in detail. (Resell your book also when a new sales manager, special sales director or other key player enters the picture.)

   If, as sometimes happens, no editor on the premises seems likely to handle your book well, then explore ways you might get the project away from its present publisher and resell it to another house (your original editor may be helpful here too, and writers with agents should seek their counsel).

✱ Authors with the money to back their convictions can hire publicists and marketing consultants (see the *Literary Market Place* listings). Some publicists won't work for a book that's already out, and no publicist or marketing consultant can promise results. Still, marketing energy and expertise have breathed new life into many a title.

✱ If you have plenty of convictions but very little money, try hiring an energetic student whom you can train to be your own personal publicity agent. With a week's study of the standard publicity guides (see "The Self-Publishing Option Resources"), even an amateur should be able to put ten good ideas into practice.

✱ To alleviate the no-books-in-the-stores problem, you can call bookstores in areas where you'll be getting publicity and explain when and why they should have your book in stock. One writer who went this route was initially afraid that bookstore managers would hang up on her, but in fact they were grateful for her calls and—more important—they did arrange to have copies of her book on sale when she was in town.

✱ Start fresh, by arranging for your book to be reissued, preferably by a publisher equipped to attract its special-interest audiences.

Books get second lives all the time. Look, for instance, at remainder dealers, who buy publishers' leftovers in bulk at below-cost prices, offer readers a bargain and sometimes sell so many copies of a particular title that they wind up reprinting it over and over again. Or consider the experiences of Feenie Ziner with her autobiographical book *A Full House*. When Norton gave up on Ziner's account of raising triplets, she resold it to The Center for the Study of Multiple Birth, which brought out a charming paperback edition.

Instead of finding a new publisher, as writers and agents often do, you may decide to become your book's new publisher. Consult a literary property lawyer and/or your agent if you have one, about severing your current publishing ties and see the next section for guidance on how to proceed after that.

The Self-Publishing
Option

*   *   *

The Case for Doing It Yourself
OR
Don't Skip This Chapter Unless You're Willing to Let Prejudice Stand Between You and What May Be Your Best Destiny

A DEMONSTRABLY FALSE series of assumptions keeps a great many writers from seriously considering self-publishing, which is a shame because a lot of people could earn more money and have more fun if they brought out their own work. Constructed with one part ignorance, one part laziness and one part unadulterated snobbery, the chain of thought might be summarized as follows: I am a writer; a writer's job is to express ideas, images and information in words; after a writer has done this job, noncreative types should pronounce it good and take it over, leaving the writer free to write some more.

At first glance, the argument seems logical enough, but closer examination reveals a fatal flaw. If expression is a writer's goal, why is a publisher necessary? Why, indeed, is anything necessary besides a desk drawer big enough to hold completed manuscripts?

The answer, of course, is that expression is really only a preliminary goal, a necessary first step toward the ultimate end of writing, which is communication.

Once you accept the fact that when you write you want to communicate, you'll realize three things: (1) you need people to communicate with; (2) you're most likely to communicate effectively with people who'll be receptive to your writing's particular style and substance; and (3) finding those people is the only way to fulfill your role as a writer.

In theory, you can get a publishing company to track your audience down for you; in practice, though, busy professionals handling masses of titles are not likely to concentrate on drawing receptive readers to yours. Thus, if you want to reach as many people as possible you'll have to plan selling campaigns on your own (and maybe execute them on your own as well) whether you're self-published or conventionally published. Those who self-publish, however, will be spared one burden: they won't have to start by putting their ideas across to a publisher with an impulse to ignore them.

Looked at in this light, do-it-yourself publishing may seem a more attractive alternative than it used to. Writers who are beginning to like the idea but who are not yet convinced that they'll be able to implement it should read the next two chapters to resolve their doubts one way or the other. And writers who are troubled by the always sticky matter of money may ease their minds with the following string of comparisons.

Self-publishers pay to have their work issued. People who use vanity presses pay to have their work issued (though they pay much more and get much less; see "Openings"). But the group that pays the highest price of all is composed of writers of bestselling books. True, they don't pay to begin with. But the advances they receive can sometimes be matched by self-publishers (see "Front-end Funding"). And besides, by the time successful books go out of print at a major house, their authors will have repaid the publisher many times over, not only for their advances but also for all expenses, through the portion of their profits that the firm keeps for itself.

Therefore? Therefore, who pays what and when and to whom is not, by itself, a useful gauge of publishing worth.

Instead of allowing yourself to be diverted by quibbles about front money or picturesque notions of the cloistered literary life, why not confront the decision to self-publish by examining self-publishing's advantages, as sketched below, to see how well they would blend with both your work and your character?

Advantages

Quality Control. Self-publishing is often the only way to produce a book or periodical that will live up to your personal standards.

Photographer Bob Adelman began putting his own books out when he found that conventional houses wouldn't or couldn't meet his specifications for design and reproduction. Working closely with designers, printers and journalists whose achievements he knew and admired, Adelman put together a book he could be proud of. Called *Street Smart: Adventures from the Lives of Children*, it's an unusually handsome volume.

Ron Jones, motivated by educational rather than aesthetic considerations, turned to self-publishing because he and several of his fellow teachers thought conventionally published textbooks inadequate. "During the six years I taught in city and country schools," Jones explained, "no one ever stole a textbook, and I think I know why. Every year textbooks pop out of the publisher's ovens with new covers and new titles, but the content is always the same. They encourage verbal skills and deductive paths of logic. They avoid the use of intuition, imagination, contemplation and direct action as problem-solving tools."

Jones and a loose confederation of parents and teachers decided to publish a "de-school primer" called *Zephyros* to stimulate thousands of students through projects like "Make Your Own Religion" or "Pretend You Are a Building." At a regulation-model textbook house, where editors must meticulously tailor their books for adoption by school boards, *Zephyros'* unorthodox learning experiences would have been either drastically modified or totally scrapped.

Freedom of Form. Despite the honored place of pamphlets in American history, publishers nowadays don't print them. They don't print narrative poems much either, or novellas or nonfiction that's longer than a normal magazine article but shorter than a normal book.

If you have something important to say that can best be expressed in 15,000 words, one of two things is apt to happen: a publishing firm will buy your manuscript, in which case you'll be asked to pad it to at least 25,000 words (so it can count as a book) or to cut it by 50% or more (so it will fit into a standard magazine format); or you'll decide to bring it out yourself, in which case you can leave it at the length that suits it.

Self-publishers are free to vary physical dimensions other than length (small commercial firms have produced books with the dimensions of cigarette packs and Frisbees, among other things). And they are free, as well, to demarcate their own literary boundaries. Laurel Speer, a poet, likes to let a manuscript "find its final form before I commit it to book form." The author of eight books published by other people as well as many poems in periodicals, Speer took a hard look at "the enormous influence-peddling, favor trading and in-groupishness" of poetry markets and "determined to seek out a fine letterpress partner and put my own books into print. I love my autonomy, my total independence of movement and choice," she reported in *Small Press Review* after several years of publishing "one of a kind poetry books."

One of a kind magazines can be produced too, and so can hybrids—magazines, say, that resemble books because they're aesthetically unified or books that resemble magazines because they're issued serially. In short, if self-publishing authors want to break old publishing molds and construct new ones, nobody can stop them.

Tangible Sources of Satisfaction. When a women's writing workshop began planning to self-publish an anthology of members' work and circulate it within the group, a lot of potential contributors got worried. With their poems and stories already in print, they thought, they'd be tempted to slack off, and then they'd never write anything worth offering an outside audience.

As things turned out, the anthology did nothing to depress creativity; on the contrary, it stimulated a surge of new composition. Having seen their words clothed in the dignity of bound and printed pages, the workshop writers found their energies fueled by pride. They'd picked the printer, after all, and checked galleys for typos and roughed out the cover and glued the binding on, and now they had a professional-looking edition to show for their efforts. In these pushbutton times, the pleasures of physical achievement are reserved mainly for children, but self-publishers, along with a handful of other adults who work with their hands building things they love, are privileged to share the I-made-it-myself elation.

Reader Response. Unlike a writer whose book circulates in the hands of a publishing company's sales force, self-publishing authors often deal face to face with wholesalers, retailers and members of the reading public, and thus create innumerable opportunities to converse about their work with people who have actually read it. When feedback from readers is favorable, it's a delight; and when it's unfavorable, it may still be instructive.

Ease of Entry. No preparatory rigmarole is required when you publish your own writing. You don't have to sell anyone on its merits until it's printed, and you don't have to know more about how to get it printed or about how to sell it when the time comes than you can learn from a book.

Furthermore, you can edge into self-publishing by degrees, without ever making a major commitment before hard evidence shows that the move will be wise. Suppose, for example, that you've written *The Complete Small-Engine Repair Manual*. With a modest cash outlay, you can get 1,000 copies printed up to offer local hardware stores, department stores and bookstores on consignment, and to retail personally at nearby vocational schools and continuing-education centers. Then, if those markets work well, you can go back to press, begin to experiment with mail orders and wholesale distribution over a wide geographical area and perhaps wind up selling hundreds of times as many copies as there were in your original print order.

Or suppose (to frame another example drawn from actual experience) that you've just moved to the Ozarks and that you want to share observations on your new homeland with friends you've left behind. If you begin by mimeographing reports to them, and if they pass your pieces on to friends and acquaintances of theirs, and if the chain continues to lengthen, you will have founded a newsletter or a magazine before long, and developed a mailing list that more scientific periodical publishers will envy.

Camaraderie. "When I decided to self-publish *Blinkies: Funny Poems to Read in a Blink*, everyone I know got into the act," reports Alma Denny, talking about her collection of light verses, most of which ran first in *The Wall Street Journal*, *Gourmet*, *English Today* and various other periodicals. "An artist offered to design a cover and do 51 cartoons for my short poems. A printer in Washington, DC (her father), set the poems up in type. (He also owns a bookstore!) She is arranging with a book packager in Ohio to do the production. A friend in Washington State wants to handle distribution and mailing. A professional PR person has asked to do the promoting. A beautiful actress wants to do readings at meetings to sell the book. And my sisters have asked for 100 copies each to sell to their Sisterhoods. What I'm saying is the idea snowballs."

Denny's notes reveal one of the nicest side effects of self-publishing. People working together toward a common goal often forge or strengthen close personal ties, and self-publishing writers can convene as big a group of collaborators as they like. Conventional houses react badly to having more than two people on the other side of a publishing contract (both profits and decision-making powers will, they fear, be spread too wide and thin). But works produced in concert do succeed when self-publishers are in charge.

The people who labor along with a self-publisher on a particular project aren't the only ones who offer aid, comfort and affection, however. Members of the country's vast small-publisher network may also be ready to help. Many small publishers are generous with advice and assistance, and coming to know them by joining their associations frequently means coming to like them as well.

Longevity. Large, established, book-publishing firms, which must make room in their catalogs for hundreds of new titles at least twice a year, can't afford to keep a book in circulation for more than a few months unless its initial rate of sale is impressive. The life span of articles in established magazines is even more severely limited; one month after the March issue comes out, it's off the stands, no matter how many copies remain unsold or how many people are just now beginning to show an interest in the piece you wrote for it.

By contrast, a self-published work can be granted the gift of time, and with time it may well attract a following. Many books that make no splash when they're released become profitable over the years as appreciative readers begin to wield the single most powerful selling tool any publishing company ever has: word of mouth. And once word of mouth begins to operate, it's relatively simple for self-publishers to capitalize on it (see "Managing Sales").

Natural Candidates

If a major publishing house with close ties to influential media people is going to give your book its bigbook treatment, then you will probably do better under its auspices than you would on your own. In other circumstances, it's not so easy to decide whether conventional publishing will be a better bet than self-publishing or vice versa.

As if to underline the availability of both self- and conventional publishing options for a wide variety of projects, dozens of writers have always moved back and forth between the two systems. Historically, the roster of self-publishers has included many names that now appear under publishing's most prestigious imprints. (William Blake, Washington Irving, Percy Bysshe Shelley, James Fenimore Cooper, Edgar Allan Poe, Walt Whitman and Mark Twain are among those cited by Bill Henderson in his classic *Publish-It-Yourself Handbook*.) And crossovers continue in present times.

Maggy Simony, for instance, began by self-publishing three volumes of *Traveler's Reading Guides*, which list and describe fiction and nonfiction about anywhere anyone might be going. Then, after getting excellent reviews in library media and write-ups in travel and consumer publications (including *The New York Times*), she sold rights to Facts on File, which brought out an 800-page, one-volume edition that also became available through the Book-of-the-Month Club and the Quality Paperback Book Club. And Vicki Lansky, who sold several of her children's books to Bantam, eventually republished some of them herself when they went out of print. Aiming at a large general audience, she now sells roughly 40,000 copies of *Birthday Parties* every year through bookstores, catalogs and other appropriate channels; with a smaller target market, she also sells about 5,000 copies a year of *KoKo Bear's Big Earache*, to pediatric ear, nose and throat specialists.

It's by no means unusual for a major house to pick up a proven self-published work; in fact, self-publishers who are tired of business aggravations and eager to devote themselves full time to new writing projects frequently go after bids from conventional houses once their books are launched—and get them. Any self-publisher who makes a deal with a big firm, though, ought to be represented by a lawyer who's thoroughly familiar with the publishing industry and who's a bit of a scrapper besides.

But if it's true that almost anything a commercial company can publish (and some things it can't) can be self-published instead, it's also true that two classes of writing are particularly well suited to the self-publishing process:

* Works that are clearly of interest to at least one well-defined, relatively large, easy-to-reach audience (because a single indi-

vidual can market them as well as an established firm, and if you do it yourself you get to keep all the profits).

✱ Works that figure to interest a very small group of readers, at least to begin with (because established firms aren't likely to take them on, and if they do, they'll probably let them die in short order without ever giving them a decent chance to live).

Whether self-publishers sell hundreds of copies or hundreds of thousands of copies will depend on their level of skill with words and with business arrangements, as well as on what it is that they've written. Diverse kinds of material offer good self-publishing potential across a wide sales spectrum, though. For instance:

Need-to-Know Pieces. The American thirst for information persists. Even on vacation, we like to improve our minds, which is why there are hundreds of educational travel programs, and why Evelyn Kaye saw a reason to create a book about them. She can make money on *Travel & Learn: The New Guide to Educational Travel* with sales of well under 1,000 copies, she estimates.

Satisfying the need for different kinds of information, Malcolm Barker published his *Book design & production for the small publisher*, winning raves from the small press community, and John Muir published his *How to Keep Your Volkswagen Alive*, which has now sold more than 2 million copies. Other writers have produced substantial profits with such items as a newsletter describing job openings in the federal government, a brochure explaining how to get rid of groundhogs and a book analyzing the management of paperwork.

Local Stories. When the locality in question is a region and the self-published work is a full-size book or periodical, sales may easily mount into the high thousands (regional books pay the rent for a good many commercial publishers). But even if both the area and the self-publishing project are defined by more modest limits, success is still possible, as witness the experience of F. Alan Shirk.

A lifelong resident of Berks County, Pennsylvania, he compiled a brief, illustrated hometown history he called *The Colonial Berks Sampler* and sold it by placing coupon ads in local newspapers and sending complimentary copies together with order blanks to local schools, libraries and civic organizations.

Scholarly Papers and Classroom Texts. Circulating ideas and information is essential in academia, but teachers who write or compile materials for distribution to their colleagues or their students can't rely on publishing houses to produce a book that only a few hundred people figure to read. Fortunately, though teachers' markets may be small, they are solid. Thus, by computing sales accurately in advance, self-publishing scholars can arrange to keep costs down to the point where they'll surely be matched by revenues.

One caveat: Now that it's easy to access and duplicate written material, it's also easy to overstep copyright boundaries. If you do decide to publish a collection of other people's work, be sure you have the permissions you need and be prepared to pay for them.

Special-Interest Literature. Clem Labine sells his *Old-House Journal* to 100,000 subscribers. Ruth Portis, who self-published *Step by Step Beadstringing—A Complete, Illustrated, Professional Approach,* sold thousands of copies partly through the Jewelers' Book Club, the Gemological Society of America and catalogs from jewelry supply companies. Glen C. Ellenbogen, author/publisher of the satirical *Journal of Polymorphous Perversity,* made a 3,300-copy bulk sale to Smith, Kline & French Laboratories, which wanted to distribute an issue featuring its pharmaceutical products (eventually, by the way, he also made a paperback sale to Ballantine, which brought out a collection of "Readings from the Journal of Polymorphous Perversity" called *Oral Sadism and the Vegetarian Personality*).

Like Labine, Portis and Ellenbogen, hundreds of other self-publishers have tapped into specialized markets with gratifying consequences.

If what you've written will serve a special-interest audience, you may find it relatively easy to get financial help when you put on your publisher's hat. But even if you bear all initial expenses yourself, you shouldn't be out of pocket for long, and you should reap major rewards in the form of response quite quickly when you serve a public that's hungry for word of its avocational enthusiasms.

Novels, Short Fiction and Poems. Because more fiction and poetry seems to be written each year than existing companies of any size can handle, some novelists and poets see no alternative but to self-publish. Whether last resort or first choice, self-publishing in this area can have thoroughly agreeable results.

Harriet Herman started out with a 1,000-copy print order when she published the first edition of *The Forest Princess*, her fairy tale about a heroine instead of a hero. Within two months she'd sold every book she had. A second printing of 2,000 copies sold out within a year, and a third (3,000 copies) followed suit. Herman then reported in the magazine *The Self-Publishing Writer* that she was planning a fourth edition of *The Forest Princess* (which she also produced and showed on television as a film-strip); she's self-published a sequel; and she sold United Kingdom rights to both books to a British publishing firm.

Robert Lane ended up with even more overseas sales. His novel about a schizophrenic child is called *A Solitary Dance* and was published originally by Serrell & Simons (i.e., Bob and his wife, Mary). They then sold rights to Reader's Digest Condensed Books, New American Library's Signet paperback line, several foreign publishers and a couple of book clubs. At last count, more than two million copies of *A Solitary Dance* were in print in sixteen countries and nine languages.

Activist Arguments. In nonmilitary battles, the call to arms is often sounded by words on paper, which makes newsletters, pamphlets and magazines perennially popular formats for rallying supporters around a multiplicity of causes.

Not long ago, a small North Carolina collective of women who called themselves Lollipop and who shared Harriet Herman's concern with nonsexist children's literature successfully self-published a book called *Exactly Like Me*. At about the same time, the Corporate Action Program—a Washington, DC, group with "an abiding faith in the power of people to shape their own destinies, and the belief that institutions should be servants, not masters, of our social needs and goals"—offered the public its *Corporate Action Guide*. And more recently, John Javna and Julie Bennett self-published *50 Simple Things You Can Do to Save the Earth*. Because its message is urgent, it made sense to get it out fast through their Earthworks Press rather than wait for an established publisher to take it and process it.

Through advertising, subsidies from interested organizations or sales revenues, activist self-publishers may manage to cover expenses and perhaps to produce profits as well. But most writers who aim to change the world with their words are prepared to look elsewhere for economic sustenance. What they want from publishing is the chance to deliver a message of importance to an audience of responsive individuals, wherever they are and whatever their numbers.

If self-publishing did not already exist, such motives might suffice to create it. As matters stand, though, the option is open to all and clearly to be preferred by a good many writers for a variety of kinds of writing. Moreover, as the chapters that follow will show, it's becoming easier to exercise with every passing day.

A Complete Starter Kit of
Self-Publishing Skills

WITH
Applications for Anybody's Promotional Materials

TAKE A SIMPLE task like tying shoelaces, write out step-by-step instructions for a person who's never done it before, and the response you'll get will be, Thanks just the same but it sounds awfully complicated and I think I'll stick to moccasins.

Something similar happens when beginners read up on self-publishing. As with tying shoelaces, though, the steps involved in producing what you've written are much simpler than they sound and it's easy to get the hang of them if you just leap fearlessly into action; any mistakes you make will probably be both correctable and instructive, and they will certainly not be fatal.

Skeptics may protest that self-publishing requires mastery not of one new activity, but of a whole series of unfamiliar processes. And that's quite true. It's equally true, however, that you don't have to handle any or all of these processes completely alone. Free guidance is available (read on); help is not hard to buy (see this section's "Resources"); and, as you progress through production, you can effect any number of trade-offs between expenditures of your time and energy, on one side of the equation, and of money to procure professionals' services, on the other.

So rest assured that with judicious use of manuals and specialists, with a minor investment in equipment and with a modicum of background information, any amateur can mastermind the creation of a bound book, a pamphlet, a periodical or—please note— an effective piece of promotional material for whatever's being published, no matter who's publishing it.

Editing

Most writers get so heartily sick of reworking their words that they can barely get their eyes and minds to focus on the pages when the time comes to edit their manuscripts. In such a situation, it makes sense to look around for someone else who could do the job, but many self-publishing writers don't bother. Instead, they sometimes simply skip the editing stage, sometimes (1) because they believe it's of little value, sometimes (2) because they're afraid of having their work distorted, and sometimes (3) because they don't know how to find a good editor.

Points one and two are debatable, although every piece of writing can benefit from sensible editing (many will be significantly improved) and good editors don't distort (on the contrary, they clarify and strengthen). If you agree and decide to look for an editor who'd be right for your work, you might start by finding out who edited books you admire and asking them if they'd do yours (call or write the publisher's publicity departments to get names if the books don't supply internal evidence). In the event that the editors can't afford the time or you can't afford their fee, perhaps they'll suggest colleagues you might contact.

Alternatively, you can choose a freelance editor from those who are listed in *Literary Market Place* or enrolled as members of the Editorial Freelancers Association (see this section's "Resources"). It's important, of course, to get references and samples before you make a commitment. If you created your work on a computer, you should try to get an editor who can work on copies of your diskettes. And in any case you should arrange to have the editor proceed in well-defined stages. That way, if serious disagreements arise over the edited version of Chapter 1, you and the editor can either devise ways to avoid such snags later or you can call it quits.

Copy-editing

The same approaches should suffice to find a good copy editor, but because copy-editing demands an entirely different mental set than writing, some authors can handle this step themselves.

To copy-edit a manuscript (as the second chapter of "The Sale and Its Sequels" shows), you must make sure that it is correct and consistent fact by fact, word by word and even letter by letter; and the best way to do that is by following a copy-editing style manual (you should find at least one that's to your taste listed in "Resources"). On its simplest level, copy-editing style is what determines whether you use "blond" rather than "blonde," and no matter how complicated its prescriptions get, style's function is simply to ensure consistency in the interest of clarity.

Descriptions as well as spelling ought to be consistent throughout a manuscript (don't drive your readers to distraction by presenting them with a character who's dainty and petite on page 16 and a strapping Amazon on page 92), and what you choose to stick to matters less than choosing to stick to something.

If you imagine, all the while you're copy-editing, that your manuscript is the work of a slipshod and possibly feeble-minded soul, you'll find it easy to adopt the most effective copy-editing attitude: suspicion. Go slowly and question everything: is Wales correctly described as a peninsula; could anyone really fly to Rome in daylight all the way; does that say "dilemmma"; is "accurrate" spelled right; doesn't that plural verb refer back to a singular subject; and wouldn't the thought be clearer if it were presented in two sentences rather than one?

Though a careful copy editor will check all proper nouns, all facts (even fiction has them) and all words that look the slightest bit odd, the most important statements to verify are those that might lead to legal difficulties. If you are writing anything that is derogatory and/or untrue about living people or functioning businesses, you may face a libel suit or a suit for invasion of privacy. Additional legal pitfalls open up when writers quote too extensively from other people's material, or when they print matter that might be adjudged obscene. Moreover, a new legal danger zone has arisen as a result of our culture's increasing emphasis on self-help; a reader with vertigo who falls off a branch and is seriously hurt while following the advice in your "Blueprints for a Treehouse" may think there are grounds to sue you.

This last trouble spot is the hardest to deal with, but common sense may be of some help (don't assume that your readers will realize they should unplug the toaster before they start fiddling with its innards, for example; or that they'll think to consult their doctors before embarking on a strenuous diet or exercise program).

Otherwise, your best course is to get hold of one or more of the legal guides mentioned in "Resources"; after you've read them you'll know better whether you need to call in a lawyer or take any other measures to protect yourself from legal action. Just remember that even those people who win lawsuits find litigation expensive and aggravating. Consequently, it's sound policy to recast all potentially dangerous material in your manuscript unless doing so involves violating your principles.

It's smart to copyedit with pencil on paper even if you've composed on a screen, and to mark all changes, no matter what their purpose, with standard proofreading symbols (see the relevant "Tools" in "Resources" or use the list you'll find in your dictionary). Then, when your work is as correct, consistent and clear as you can make it, be sure to claim your own legal rights and the status your work deserves in the eyes of librarians, booksellers and reviewers by registering your copyright, applying for an ISBN or ISSN (a.k.a. International Standard Book Number and International Standard Serial Number) and getting a bar code. See "Resources" for information on how to proceed—and start early.

Design and Production

Thanks to computers and laser printers, self-publishers can now get books, magazines, newsletters and promotional pieces ready to be printed without going through several costly production steps that used to be mandatory.

But there's a catch. The ability to use a page layout program doesn't make you a designer any more than the ability to use a word-processing program makes you a writer. Then too, you may not be interested in graphic arts or you may not have time to learn them.

So consider three basic options when you're planning to produce your own work: doing it all, hiring a graphic artist to create design specifications for you to follow, and hiring a desktop publishing company not only to create a design but also to get your material in shape for printing.

Doing It All

If what you're publishing is a book that consists of straight text, consult one or more of the design and production guides listed in "Resources" and absorb the elementary advice that follows. When you've formulated a tentative design/production plan, talk briefly with a few promising printers (see below) and make sure it's a good plan from the printers' point of view. Then proceed to create camera-ready copy (i.e., pages ready to be printed) using a powerful word-processing program and a laser printer.

As you work, keep two principles firmly in mind: (a) What written material looks like will have a good deal to do with how it's received. If it's sloppy or jumbled, if the body type is too small to read easily or the headings are so big and black that—no matter what they say—they always seem to be threats, then the power of your carefully assembled words will be vitiated, and (b) Beginners do best by keeping things standard and simple.

One standard to adhere to is that of page size. You'll save money by choosing the dimensions that both paper companies and printers are accustomed to. For books and pamphlets, this generally means a page that's roughly 5½ by 8½ inches or 6 by 9 inches; and for magazines, journals and newsletters, one that's 7 by 10 inches or 8½ by 11 inches. Check with printers you're considering to see exactly what sizes their equipment handles most economically.

Having chosen a size for your page, you then must decide on margins (use your own books or magazines as models, and remember that unless the bottom margin is larger than the top your page will look droopy) and on how to arrange text, heads, artwork and white space effectively within them. A smattering of technical terms should enable you to move comfortably through these decision-making points and those that will arise later:

Body type: type that's used for text rather than for headings. (i.e., titles). Body type is measured in points (which are defined below) from the top of a letter like *h* to the bottom of a letter like *p*—that is, from the highest to the lowest extremities of the alphabet in a particular typeface.

Display type: type that's used for headings (or "heads") rather than for text; also measured in points.

Justification: the spacing of a line of type so that it will extend fully to both right- and left-hand margins. When lines of type do not extend to meet the right-hand margin, the copy is *ragged right.*

Layout: a blueprint of sorts, showing how text, titles, artwork and all the other elements of a work to be printed should be arranged.

Leading: the space between lines of type (the term was coined in the days when printers worked with lead type and had to insert strips of lead above and below lines of text to create space between them).

Letter space: logically enough, the space between the letters of a word. Adjusting these spaces is useful for justification, but letter-spaced words sometimes look funny, so scrutinize your own print-outs or ask to see sample copy before you agree to have a designer letter-space your work.

Pica: the printer's unit of measurement. A pica equals

approximately one-sixth of an inch and is used for expressing column widths and other important dimensions of a page.

Points: divisions of the pica (12 points = 1 pica), used to express such things as body-type sizes and amounts of leading. Points are symbolized by what looks like a straight, single quotation mark.

Running heads: the titles that are repeated at the top or bottom of book and periodical pages.

Typeface: a particular design of type. Each face has a name (like Helvetica or Bodoni Book) and consists of all capital and lower-case letters and a full range of numbers and punctuation marks in a variety of point sizes. Italic and boldface variations on any given face are generally available and are called Helvetica (or whatever) itals or bold for short.

Word space: just what it says, and adjustable within narrow limits to justify columns of text or to squeeze or extend headlines.

Text

Given a variety of typefaces to choose from, it's possible, within certain limits, to select one that will make a particular manuscript fit into a particular number of pages. Copy-fitting techniques depend on simple arithmetic and are not hard to learn, but using them to good purpose requires a thorough knowledge of typography.

For a first self-publishing venture, therefore, you might as well not worry about making your manuscript into a printed work of a preordained size. Just find a book or periodical you'd like your work to resemble and call the publisher's art director to ask for its basic text specs. Most likely, a standard point size—10-point is usual for books, and 9-point will work nicely for newsletters and magazines—in a standard face like Baskerville or Century with a standard 1 or 2 points of leading will serve you well. The rule of thumb is, Choose a point size that's roughly half the pica width of a line of printed text. If it turns out in the end that you need a few extra pages to satisfy the requirements of the printing press you can always add editorial and/or promotional material and/or blank sheets front and back.

Heads

"If you can't make it good, make it red. And if you can't make it red, make it big." This maxim about headlines, uttered with tongue only slightly in cheek, translates as, Don't be afraid to be splashy, and you should take that exhortation to heart, especially when you plan your cover. The largest display type you'll ever use will probably appear there; it's by designing the front of your book as if it were a billboard that you get your best chance of doing justice to what's inside.

Specs for heads between the covers are somewhat harder to arrive at than specs for body copy, but one easy solution is to use a headline face with the same name your body typeface has. On more difficult choices, consult the guides in "Resources" or your printer. Again, a printed work that you admire will make a fine model and you can't go far wrong by sticking with a conventional face and simply varying its size to indicate relative importance (36- or 30-point might, for instance, be perfect for part titles, with 30- or 24-point chapter heads and 18- or 14-point for the subheads within chapters).

Artwork

For some self-publishers, artwork is an integral part of the project; others want pictures to illustrate or to decorate, and sometimes they have trouble finding good ones. If you're in this second category, try the public relations departments of large organizations involved with work that's relevant to your subject (what they supply will be free); various sources of noncopyrighted drawings (see "Tools" in "Resources"); appropriate governmental agencies (through their PR departments); and the picture sources listed in *LMP*. Be sure to get permission in writing to use their pictures from people you or other individuals photograph. Perhaps you can copy the release form your local newspaper uses.

Layout

Three observations will stand amateur designers in good stead as they begin their first layouts: (1) The simpler the better; symmetrical and centered arrangements pose the fewest problems. (2) The fundamental unit of design is the spread—or pair of facing pages that the reader's eyes take in with a single glance. (3) White space (i.e., blank space) is important; if you don't leave enough of it or you don't arrange it well, you'll end up with dense, uninviting pages.

By drawing on published books or magazines for models and using some of the guides listed in "Resources," beginners can construct layouts that range from serviceable to handsome. Working with straight text, you'll have only a few questions to answer. How much space should chapter heads get (for instance), or should each article start on a new page, and what should the running heads look like? After you've solved such problems, all you'll have to do is fill each succeeding page with text until it's time to repeat the opening-page format once again.

While you're developing your layout you may be confronted with text that's too long or too short and pictures that are too big or too little. Almost any text can be cut (developing the knack of cutting copy so that no scars show is itself a rewarding activity) and pictures are easy to adjust. If they're the wrong size for the space you want them to occupy, they can usually be cropped and/ or inexpensively enlarged or reduced.

For scaling pictures, there's a beautifully simple method: draw a rectangle exactly the same size as the picture you have; then draw a diagonal line across it from bottom left to top right and mark off the dimension you must satisfy on one side (i.e., if your column width is 3¼ inches and you want the picture to fit into one column, put your mark 3¼ inches from the left on the bottom of your rectangle); finally, draw a line from this mark to the point where it meets the diagonal and measure it. The figure you get is the height your picture will be when its width is 3¼ inches.

Black-and-white line drawings will reproduce as is. So will computer generated decorative borders and rules of assorted sizes (which can be used to create boxed copy, underlined heads and the like). Photographs, however, must be processed for the press, and you should send yours out to be turned into prints called PMTs or Veloxes that offset presses can handle. Your printer can advise you on specifications, and you can ask the printer (or a friendly local typesetter, designer or publisher) for advice on what photo processor to patronize.

Get every piece of artwork properly sized, copied and placed on a printout of your pages. Then recall your copy-editing personality and view each spread with a jaundiced eye. Are the section heads all the right sizes? Are the running heads in place? Did you remember to provide page numbers? Also known as folios, page numbers can be centered below the text or placed in outside corners; they are always odd on right-hand pages and even on the left (page 1 is the right-hand page facing the inside front cover in a periodical and the first page of chapter one or the first part-title page in a book; pages that precede a book's page 1 should get Roman rather than Arabic numerals or not be numbered at all.).

Examine current books to see the proper deployment of front and back matter, and be sure—for both books and periodicals— to insert your correct copyright notice in the place prescribed by the Copyright Office.

After everything is just as it should be, take a few minutes to consider whether using colored paper or ink would be desirable. Sepia stock might give a family chronicle just the right nostalgic look; dollar-bill green chapter headings might enhance the message of a personal finance manual; a screen of color might set off a sidebar to best advantage.

Because color gives you a relatively cheap way to add life and interest to your book or periodical—and because it makes promotional materials far more noticeable—it's worth exploring the options and incurring some extra expense. Ask your printer about incremental costs and check to see that any colors you choose for a cover will reproduce well together in black-and-white since that's how most promotional materials will appear.

Design/Production Duets

If you're publishing something more complicated than an all-text book, or if you have no feel for graphics, the least expensive option is hiring a designer to create a set of specs that you can follow with your own equipment—i.e., with a computer and a word-processing program for simple designs and with a computer and a program such as PageMaker, Ventura or Quark for more complicated layouts. The designer you hire can be a desktop publishing specialist (see leads in "Resources"), but designers who don't work with computers will be fine too, provided they understand what your program can do.

So look again at what's in the library and the bookstore, select several books or magazines with the personality you want for yours, and call the publishers to find out who designed them. Or see if the art director of a publication you admire can moonlight to work for you or an art student will do your job at bargain rates (many art directors and graphic artists teach part-time and can identify talented students who are hungry, and ready, for outside assignments).

Felix Kramer, president of Kramer Communications, favors a "safety net" system for self-publishers who buy design as a set of specs. After a client gets his design specifications, a three-stage learning process ensues: "The first time they watch me; the second time I watch them and the third time they call with questions." Design costs, Kramer notes, often run between $500 and $1,000 for a book. Bids you get may vary from these figures, though, depending on how complicated your job is, whether you want the designer to create a cover and whether the designer will also have to create or acquire artwork such as drawings or photographs.

Of course, you may want your designer to do all production tasks once you realize how much page layout programs cost in time and aggravation as well as in money. To find desktop publishing specialists, use the leads in "Resources" and check your local Yellow Pages. Then hire carefully. You should be saving money (traditional typesetting and layout often run $15–$25 per simple camera-ready page) but costs are not negligible (don't be surprised by quotes of $10 and up per page).

A good way to start, once you've identified prospects, is by looking over their portfolios and asking several different designers for estimates. As Judith Grossman suggests, it's wise to see if samples show projects like yours and to make sure you feel comfortable with the personality and style of the person you hire. Grossman, who runs the Inprint Graphic Design studio, also notes that you should get an estimate before work begins and that it's important to spell out what services you're buying.

What will the specs pertain to? Just the text? Covers, jackets, front and back matter? Will the design studio provide sample pages and in what form? Do you see sketches first? One version or more? What about revises? How many sets of page proofs will the studio provide, and how many do you need? Are you paying by page or by time? Is artwork (photographs, illustrations, graphs, tables) included or will you pay for that separately, piece by piece? How much will the studio charge you for changes you may want to make? Will the person you interviewed actually do the work or will someone else be responsible, and if so who is that person?

Grossman, Kramer and virtually every other desktop publishing pro who has worked with amateurs have a warning to issue: don't do too much. By all means, find out what codes to insert as you create your manuscript since that will save time (and therefore money) later on. Otherwise, though, stick to straight typing or expect to incur extra charges for unscrambling and undoing your well-intentioned but addlepated specs.

Printing

Printers star often in publishing horror stories. Poor quality, late delivery, short shipments, mixups too peculiar to predict—even large firms run up against such snags. To avoid as many headaches as possible, study the sections on printing in the design and self-publishing manuals listed in "Resources" and profit by other people's current experiences.

If you're working with a designer, ask for recommendations. Pinpoint several good but not expensive-looking books or periodicals and call their art directors or their production managers to find out which printers they use and whether they'd advise you to use them too. Check "Resources" for guidance on buying printing. And then send a Request for Quotation to at least six firms. Don't hesitate to approach giants like R.R. Donnelley as well as smaller printers and local copy shops. Modern technology enables even huge printers to do short runs (i.e., print relatively few copies) economically and well, and several small houses swear that some of the biggest are best.

In hopes of having a solid basis for comparison, you should send the same Request for Quotation form to each printer you contact (sample forms are available from books listed in "Resources"). Be prepared, though; some will respond with their own forms, and variations in price may be enormous. The cost of 500 copies of a 100-page $5\frac{1}{2}$- by $8\frac{1}{2}$-inch book that's delivered camera-ready to be printed on 50-pound white paper may range, for example, from something like $1,400 up to twice that or even more. Unit costs will decline, of course, as print orders rise and if you're ordering thousands of copies rather than hundreds you should be able to get as good a deal as an established publisher would.

Because factors other than price are important, the lowest bid may not be the one to accept. Before you hire anybody, examine samples and references; look for evidence of pride in the work that the printer does; ask how their equipment meshes with yours; establish clearly what changes will cost at various points; think about whether you want a printer who's nearby so you can oversee operations, and arrange to get the particulars of your agreement in writing.

Most printers gladly offer suggestions about paper and ink and produce samples on request. Moreover, plenty of leads to information on these subjects appear in "Resources." You won't go wrong, though, if you pick 30-pound newsprint for a newspaper, 50- or 60-pound stock for a book and 80- to 100-pound paper for soft covers, and you're safe in letting your printer choose ink for you.

Soft covers? you say; don't I want to produce a real (i.e., hardcover) book? Until recently, the answer would have been a qualified yes; binding some copies (though not all) in hardcover was mandatory, because reviewers wouldn't write about paperbacks and libraries wouldn't buy them. Today, however, the cover composition of a book is increasingly, and often totally, irrelevant in the minds of both librarians and reviewers. Your markup on the hardcover may be better but softcovers are favored in most stores and often preferred by readers who've been conditioned to think of them as bargains. And besides, because they're lighter they're cheaper to mail, which will mean a lot when you start sending out the promotional copies and filling the orders that the next chapter tells you how to generate.

Hard covers or soft, you can rely on a carefully selected printer to handle binding for you. Just remember that when printers talk about "perfect" binding they're not promising flawless work; instead, they're referring to the popular method of gluing pages together inside a square-backed cover.

Material that's ready for final printing should be submitted simply as pages from a laser printer or as sharper versions of those pages in Linotronic output produced by "imagesetters" whom either you or your printer can hire. If you've only found printers who insist on typesetting from hard copy or diskettes or reproducing from old-fashioned "mechanicals," keep looking.

Print Runs and Pricing

Even economic simpletons know that what you'll net on sales of your work will be the difference between what you get for it and what you spend for it. What you get, however, will be largely determined by what you spend (on production, promotion and distribution) and by what you charge (too high a price will have just as negative an effect on your balance sheet as one that's too low); while what you spend and what you charge may be largely determined by what you think you can get.

Leading publishing firms, which have been thrashing around inside this vicious circle for centuries, have developed a system for determining the major getting and spending variables: cover price and print order. They carefully assess unit costs for assorted quantities (which they estimate fairly accurately) in the light of projected sales (which they estimate with wildly varying degrees of success) and of current dogma about cover-price ranges. Then, when the book in question is one editors really want to do, they crunch the numbers until the bottom line looks appealing.

A more rational way to proceed is by focusing first on your market. Identify the people who are most likely to want your work and then try to figure out how many of them there are, how you might reach them, how important your book could be in their lives and how much they'd pay for it (how much do they pay now for comparable sources of information and/or entertainment? what do they tell you they'd pay for your material?).

"My principal advice is: Do not be afraid to charge top dollar," says James J. Brodell. When Brodell self-published *How to Purchase a Newspaper and Succeed* in 1983, he thought about pricing in terms of "what I would charge someone for a consultancy involving a newspaper property they sought to purchase." Then he decided on $22.50, "not bad," as he points out, "for a slim paperback." Using two trade publications that "reach everyone who is thinking about purchasing a newspaper," Brodell sold 900 copies and got feedback that the book was well worth what it cost.

Whatever price you set on your published work, it must, of course, be high enough to let you (1) recoup your production and marketing expenses, remembering that booksellers and some other intermediaries will get a big cut of the take; (2) cover your other expenses, like rent and labor; and (3) produce at least a modest profit. If readers won't pay that high a price, however, you'd better know it early on; and if they'll pay more, that's surely a useful bit of knowledge.

Many self-publishers hedge their bets to some extent by starting with small printings and asking printers to keep plates and film of their work, or by binding only part of the first edition, for instance. But essentially what's required of you at this stage is a small but sprightly leap of faith.

Self-publishing writers who take care to cushion that leap of faith with a sensible program of action will soon find enough solid information through experience to arrive at later decisions much more rationally.

Managing Sales

IF THE BIG, established publishers—with all their money, personnel and media connections—have a tough time getting most of their books and periodicals off the ground, what chance do self-publishers have? Though you may be surprised to hear it, they have a good one, and it's getting better every day.

Self-publishing writers have three important advantages over writers who are conventionally published when it comes to selling their work.

* Self-publishers get closer to their readers. Conventionally published authors are separated from their audiences by two sets of people: the publishing-company staff members, whom the author relies on; and the wholesalers, retailers, librarians and media personnel, whom the staff members rely on.

    Working through double ranks of intermediaries is seldom the most efficient way to accomplish anything, and it's especially inefficient when the goal in view is person-to-person communication, as it is for writer and reader. It is a definite plus, therefore, to eliminate intermediaries, particularly if you have the option of getting them to work for you when you want them—which self-publishers now do. (In fact, if their budgets permit, self-publishers can hire someone to assist with or execute almost every selling task they'll confront; see "Resources.")

181

✻ Self-publishing writers don't have to sell thousands of copies in order to have their work survive in print; editions numbering in the low hundreds make splendid economic sense so long as expenses can be kept down. Often, you can select a size for your first printing that will virtually ensure that you break even on it. And because a small first edition can serve as a trial run, later, and perhaps larger, print orders will be less risky.

✻ A self-publisher has only one person's work to promote—his or her own. Thus, the energy and time self-publishers can devote to selling a single product far exceed what big publishers could offer. And unlike conventionally published big-book authors (who'll be sent on grueling promotional tours to face interviewers who haven't read their books and booksellers who don't have copies in stock), self-publishers can go where they know they're wanted and arrange to create and to satisfy demand for their writing as they travel.

Instead of being exhausted and frustrated by promotional activities, self-publishers are generally stimulated. Selling makes a nice change of pace from writing (which you can do for only a part of the day anyway), and it's financially and psychologically rewarding besides. When he visited bookstores all across the country to spur sales of his novel *The Grassman* and a selection of books from his own press, Len Fulton found ample confirmation of the view that a book's best sales rep is its author, the person "who shares all the continuity."

Fulton conceived of his trip as part of the logical publishing sequence, in which "the artist was the biceps, the publisher the forearm, the bookstore the fingers which touch out to what will be touched." His work, he felt, deserved "a full blood-run to the ends of the fingers." Doubtless yours deserves no less.

Because self-published writers and conventionally published writers should use essentially the same techniques in reaching out to readers, everyone who's interested in selling self-published work should read "Why and How to Be Your Own Best Sales Force" (in "The Sale and Its Sequels") and adopt its stress on identifying connections to potential readers as a first principle. A mental blend of the information from that chapter with the self-publishing framework outlined below should then yield a fine base for self-publishing sales operations.

Publicizing and Promoting

Some of the first people a self-publisher should become acquainted with are the editors and publishers at small publishing companies (they're reachable through their associations and various "Foot in the Door Resources," and in many cases they're eager to share their experience). And one of the first things a self-publisher will discover in conversations and correspondence with established independents is that they're often self-publishers too (though they may publish other writers' work as well as their own). Which leads to marketing tip No. 1: imitate them by choosing a name for your publishing venture. Issuing your book from the Marble Avenue Press (instead of under your own name) will give it a certain cachet and signal its legitimacy for those people—and there still are some—who insist on equating self-publishing with vanity publishing.

Be sure to include your address, phone and fax numbers along with the name of your press in the very front of your book or periodical, to make ordering easy. Putting a coupon order form and an 800 number on a back page may also stimulate orders. (See "Resources" for information on the telephone as a sales tool.)

Like a conventional publisher's staff, a self-publisher's first priority is to get momentum going in advance of publication. Everything conventionally published writers can do for their work, self-published writers can do too, but the former won't be primarily responsible for securing blurbs, reviews and listings, and the latter will.

Blurbs

Try the famous-name blurb tactic if (a) you have access to any well-known personalities whose praise might help attract reviewers' attention, or (b) you think that if particular celebrities read your work they'd find it valuable, perhaps even exciting, and agree to be quoted to that effect. For names and addresses of potential blurb writers, consult *Who's Who in America*, *Contemporary Authors* and relevant specialized directories. And if you send your work out for advance comments, accompany it with a covering letter that explains why you think it will interest the particular person you're addressing.

Whether or not you succeed in getting quotable comments from superstars, you should request advance quotes from leading lights in your book's field whose credentials will give weight to what they say. "The most compelling account of life under the sea I have ever read" may do almost as much for sales if it's signed by Prof. John Doe, School of Oceanography, Underwater U., as it would if it had come from Jacques Cousteau.

Reviews

Once you have copies and comments to distribute, be careful not to mail them out too early or too late. Check lead times for the review organs you hope will cover your work, and arrange to deliver it a month or two before the editors finalize the issue whose publication date coincides with yours. (Be sure to include a slip announcing your pub date, price and ordering information, and to use the special book rate for mailing; it's cheaper.)

As to where to send review copies, you needn't be reluctant to approach prestigious national publications, which will be hospitable to any book if it's professionally produced and submitted and if it suits their readers' needs. Remember, though, to send galleys— not bound books—to *Publishers Weekly*, *Kirkus Reviews*, *The New York Times Book Review* and powerful monthlies that pride themselves on running reviews either before a book comes out or right around its publication date. If what editors there get from you is a finished book, they're likely to ignore it because they'll assume (a) that pub date is imminent or past and (b) that they therefore don't have the three to four months they need to get a review into print.

Self-publishers can select other standard reviewing outlets from the lists in the latest *Literary Market Place* and the latest *Book Publishing Resource Guide* and they can draw up their own lists of potential reviewers at special-interest journals and local magazines and newspapers. On clearly outside bets, it's fine to send only a descriptive announcement—the small firm's version of the big publisher's catalog—instead of your book itself, with a note saying that review copies are available on request.

While self-publishers shouldn't count on getting reviewed in major magazines (any more than authors with established publishers should), they can anticipate a warm reception from numerous special-interest journals. Use "Resources" to find names and addresses and then, because new review possibilities are springing up all the time, join COSMEP, the International Association of Independent Publishers, and PMA, the Publishers Marketing Association, so you can get useful leads through their newsletters and enter promising sales channels through their programs. Since libraries can be a strong and supportive market for independently published books and periodicals, *Library Journal*, *School Library Journal* (if that's appropriate) and *Booklist* should also get galleys at least three months before publication date, and *Choice* should get a copy of your finished product. It's helpful to send a covering letter that explains why you think library patrons will want your work, and it's wise to follow up with polite reminder letters as necessary.

The best time to make a library sale is after reviews run in these magazines because librarians trust them and heed their recommendations in ordering. And today you won't have to work as hard as self-publishers once had to, since library periodicals are more and more unwilling to let review copies from little publishers get lost in the avalanche of big publishers' materials.

Listings

A number of standard reference works are used regularly by booksellers, librarians and members of the reading public, and it's to the advantage of all published authors to be mentioned in as many as the nature of their work allows. Make sure to apply for inclusion in the Bowker directories (especially the *Books in Print* volumes and/or *Ulrich's International Periodicals Directory*), the *Cumulative Book Index* and the Dustbooks skein of small-press information; go through the Bowker, Dustbooks, Gale Research and H. W. Wilson catalogs to identify all publications from these houses that should mention what you're publishing (addresses appear in "The Self-Publishing Option Resources"); and study the "Foot in the Door Resources" listings as well as this section's "Resources" to find additional relevant directories.

Nonfiction on your subject can also serve to publicize your work. As you come across books with appropriate bibliographies, write to acquaint their authors with the work you're doing in the field, and ask them to mention it when they lecture and when they do revised editions.

Sales Channels

Once word is out that your work exists and is available, the next step is enabling readers to get hold of it. Several kinds of inter-mediaries are in business to help publishers do just that.

Bookstores

Many of these intermediaries focus on bookstore distribution, servicing accounts either by sending sales reps to visit with cata-logs and book covers in hand (in the style of large houses) or simply by mailing new catalogs several times a year. Some outfits have built up good reputations among booksellers, so that books may sell many more copies if presented through their catalogs than if introduced to store managers by the publishers themselves.

But the main advantage a good distributor offers is this: booksellers are more inclined to buy from distributors than from individuals because they trust them more to fulfill obligations and simplify procedures; and booksellers are more inclined to pay distributors than individuals because business with them is ongoing.

Not long ago, a self-publisher's chief problem with respect to reaching bookstores was the dearth of distributors; in the near future, the basic quandary may be how to choose among them. All will take a cut of your profits, of course, but some want to make a killing with a hot commercial property while others focus on helping the cause of serious literature, and some are financially sound while others may be teetering on the edge of insolvency. Your best bet, if you want to have a distributor, is to judge each one you consider according to its strengths and what it can do for you.

To narrow the field, ask congenial publishers to tell you what distributors they've found reliable and effective, look to fellow members of COSMEP and PMA for recommendations, talk with local booksellers about which distributors they prefer to deal with and consult "Resources." After you have a list of names and addresses, write to each distributor you're interested in and ask for a catalog and for information about services, fees and timetables.

Every catalog you read should give you a good feel for the kind of book that distributor represents best. Some handle ongoing presses but not one-shot self publishers, so you may have to cross those off your list; and others will strike you as clearly inappropriate (if yours is a how-to title, a catalog in which page after page describes experimental literature is not for you).

Once you have a final roster of likely candidates, you should answer the following questions to your own satisfaction before you sign on with any of them. (If you can't find the information you want in the literature you've received, write and ask for more data.)

❋ Does this distributor have its own sales force, hire independent sales reps or rely exclusively on a catalog?

❋ What size cut does the distributor take? California-based Bookpeople, for instance, buys on consignment at 52 percent off the retail price, and in turn sells to stores at a 40 percent discount. You'll have to figure out what discount is reasonable for you.

❋ What territory does the distributor cover and how many accounts does it service? How does it deal with bookstore chains and wholesalers? Can it handle sales to nonbook outlets and/or sales to consumers via direct mail; and, if so, which markets do you want the distributor to represent you in and which would you rather keep for yourself?

Since many distributors service only a part of the country, you may need to contract with more than one for a book that has national appeal, or to pick just the right one if your book is designed for a particular geographic or special-interest audience. The point is to get the coverage you need.

Self-publishers who decide to approach booksellers on their own should begin by settling down in the library to study the *American Book Trade Directory*. A Bowker publication, it lists thousands of bookstores and hundreds of wholesalers in North America by state (or Canadian province) and then by city and specialty, and it has a list of bookstore chain headquarters too.

Step two is compiling your own list of booksellers and wholesalers in your area and/or in the locations or with the specialties appropriate for your book (specialized bookstores exist for mysteries, science fiction, sports books, travel books and books on a surprisingly large range of other subjects). And step three is getting in touch with the buyers at every place on that list (the manager or owner, whose name you'll usually find in the directory, can steer you to the proper person in a large and departmentalized operation).

Try to schedule a talk with each buyer—over the phone or, if possible, face-to-face—when things aren't too busy, and be prepared to explain why your book will sell once it's on the shelves.

Booksellers, it's important to remember, generally rely on publishers to promote books, so you'll make more headway if you can talk about the publicity you'll be getting locally, the public speaking you'll be doing in the region and perhaps the in-store events you could run.

Often it makes sense to suggest a program or display that will highlight several books; for example, you might select a dozen crafts titles (including yours), arrange them in the bookstore window with samples of your handiwork and demonstrate techniques at the store one day from 4 to 6 P.M.; or you might make common cause with another author who disagrees with your book's position on mandatory retirement, create a window display featuring both books and placards revealing the crux of the argument and invite the public to an open debate on the issue inside the store.

Since one order from a large chain or wholesaler can make your book widely available throughout the country, you'll want to contact the giants (like Ingram and Baker & Taylor, among wholesalers, and Waldenbooks, B. Dalton and Crown among the chains) as well as selected independent booksellers, smaller chains and appropriate local, regional or specialized wholesalers.

When you sell to stores on your own, get payment in advance or resign yourself to giving away a lot of copies for nothing. And try as hard as you can to sell on a nonreturnable basis. This will mean offering a bigger discount than normal—perhaps over 50 percent—but it's sound practice, because unless store managers have paid for your book, they'll have little, if any, incentive to sell it. Most sales forces are still stuck to fully returnable policies on the dubious—and incorrect—grounds that the industry has to do business this way. But that doesn't necessarily mean you have to get hamstrung by the full-right-of-return rule too.

Better Stores and Other Nontraditional Outlets

Most book distributors will insist on holding the exclusive rights to sell your book to bookstores, but self-publishers of both books and periodicals can do plenty of selling themselves to nonbook stores of all kinds. In fact, in imaginative marketing to nonbook outlets, small and self-publishers have taken a definite lead over big firms. What began as a necessity (because there was no effective way for little houses to get what they published into bookstores) has thus become an asset (because bookstores are such bad places to launch anything but bestsellers). Today, health food stores, craft shops, hardware stores, warehouse clubs and variety stores are all accustomed to selling written work along with their other wares.

Some books succeed handsomely in outlets like these without ever penetrating the bookstore market, and some succeed first in such "nontraditional" or "special sales" channels and then, once word of mouth has begun to build, they find favor with booksellers. Whatever the pattern, unconventional approaches to marketing are likely to serve self-publishers well.

Take the first step in exploring special sales opportunities for your work by listing the kinds of nonbookstore retail outlets your readers are likely to frequent. Next, prepare a selling speech, explaining how your book will help a retailer move basic nonbook stock and try the speech out on the managers of appropriate stores nearby. If one or more of them will take some books on consignment and customers buy those books, you can set your sights on national distribution.

Let's say, for example, that the local sporting goods store proves a fine outlet for your *Backpacking with Kids* guide. They're making money on each copy they sell and they're making more money on backpacks, whose sales are up 30%. Ask the manager which wholesalers service the store, contact those wholesalers, explain your experience with the Acme Sports Center in Hometown, Kansas, and declare that other sporting goods stores would profit by stocking your book too. Then offer to sell them as many copies as they want at a large discount—you may have to go well over 50 percent—nonreturnable.

Next, make a list of mail-order catalogs that might offer your book in their pages ("Resources" will lead you to likely candidates), and send for copies of the ones that sound promising to see if they carry books like yours and/or other products that would obviously appeal to your readership. Mail-order catalogs of all kinds are increasingly apt to include books; so far, how-to and novelty titles have been particularly successful.

Third, look into premium sale possibilities. The hardest kind of special sale to make, a premium sale is also often the most lucrative kind. Premiums—in the form of toaster ovens, calculators and a wide variety of other goods besides books—are items business offer to attract new customers and prompt current buyers to buy more. Since a premium sale may involve tens or even hundreds of thousands of copies—and dollars—it's worth trying for if you can make a connection between your book and a product or service. One self-publisher persuaded a company that makes fondue pots to package a copy of her fondue cookbook with each order. Perhaps you can arrange for a moving company to buy your moving manual in bulk for its clients, or work a deal with a magazine whose subscribers might renew more readily if they got your book free when they signed on for another year.

Because the list of good nontraditional sales channels for your work can be very long indeed, it pays to exercise your imagination. *Cheap Chic*, a guide for dressing well on a shoestring budget, was marketed effectively in clothing and secondhand stores; *How to Make Furniture Without Tools* sold well in lumber-yards; one industrious soul got beauty salons to stock books for women that they could read under the drier, and with a little ingenuity, maybe you can top that. To spot companies that favor premium ploys, examine your junk mail and keep your eyes peeled when you shop. And when you have a prospect list, see the *Thomas Register of American Manufacturers* (listed in "Money Resources"); you'll find company names and addresses there.

Direct Routes to Readers

Although conventional publishing houses often classify mail-order campaigns and other direct approaches to readers as "special sales," they shouldn't be special for you. Instead, they should form the core of your sales campaign.

Selling to readers is, after all, the purpose and the promise of all publishing. Every writer's efforts are directed, in the final analysis, to reaching them.

Self-publishers have three primary ways to get directly in touch with the people they want as readers—via the mail, advertising and personal appearances. In planning each approach, be sure to include provisions for feedback—in the form of orders, with payment, as well as in the form of verbal give and take—and when you begin to get results, keep a record of the names and addresses of everyone who places an order from any source. In the event that you publish another book or periodical or issue a revised edition, you'll have a successful, free mailing list at your fingertips.

Direct Mail

A popular means of distribution among small publishers, direct mail offers the best way to appeal—one-to-one—to groups of people around the country who are likely to want your work and who might not ordinarily hear about it or be able to get hold of it.

Getting a direct-mail package together can be an elaborate and expensive proposition (and it is in the hands of most sizable houses), but self-publishers can keep costs down if they simply prepare a description of the benefits their books or magazines provide, a collection of enthusiastic (and preferably prestigious) comments and a tear-off order blank. When a table of contents says best what the work is like, it might accompany the description, and when the author's experience or credentials are relevant, they should be mentioned too. Whatever its specific content, however, mail-order copy must always answer the question potential readers will be asking themselves: What's in it for me?

You may want to use slightly different approaches to reach slightly different segments of your public, but whether you mail one letter or a variety, choosing wisely where to send them is essential. As you'll discover when you explore mailing lists, every imaginable interest is represented. You can rent a list of people who've bought inflatable chairs as easily as you can rent one of Ph.D. holders. Prices start at about $50 for 1,000 names, and the more narrowly you can define your market the better your chances will be of getting your money's worth.

If your work focuses on a very precise subject—like directing a summer camp, say—and you know there's an association of camp directors, you can go straight to that group and ask for the use of their membership roll (you may even get the list free if you're on it yourself).

In the event that neither your background nor your subject matter leads you directly to ideal lists, you should consult "Tools" in "Resources"; see especially *LMP, Book Publishing Resource Guide* and Standard Rate and Data Service.

After you've come up with a few lists that seem to match the audiences you want to reach, ask the broker for each list what response rate other people have gotten with it (2 percent is considered pretty good), and solicit the broker's advice on your project. Then, using common sense mixed with courage, you'll have to decide for yourself whether a mailing will be cost-effective. Remember, expenses will include preparation of copy and purchase of paper, envelopes and postage (unless you can persuade a group whose list you're using to stuff your piece in with its regular mailing, in which case they'll foot the postage bill). In addition, you may need to budget money for return envelopes (possibly also with postage). And of course there are those list rental fees.

Using the self-publishing Starter Kit will let you keep some of these costs down, and so will starting with a small test mailing to just part of a list. Even the pros test before they "roll out" with a major direct mail campaign because it's all but impossible to tell in advance what the response will be. If your test pulls well, great; mail to more of that list and test others. If it doesn't, keep testing or refocus on alternative marketing channels.

Direct-Response Advertising

Nobody in the industry has any hard knowledge as to whether ads without ordering information sell books. Given the inadequacy of most publishers' distribution efforts, however, it seems unlikely that they do, so use ads *with* order information—a coupon for sales by mail and a toll-free number for telephone sales. That way, it'll be easy for readers to buy and for you to measure the success of your advertising. Self-publishers who don't have toll-free numbers of their own should see if a local bookseller would like to fill telephone orders via an 800 number. Consult "Resources" for other possibilities.

There's no better place to run a direct response ad than in a periodical that's printing a review or an excerpt of your work. Logical advertising outlets also include magazines, newsletters and newspapers that share your area of interest. *National Wildlife*, for example, might provide a good environment for an ad about a children's book on a prairie-dog town; while the *Vassar Quarterly* could pull orders for a history of higher education for women.

Ask the advertising departments of local newspapers, magazines and radio stations where you want to run your ad for advice on how to prepare copy (it's in their interest that your ad succeed, so don't be shy). Or hire an agency. And if you plan to advertise in more than one place, key each order form (on the coupon in the *Hometown Gazette*, for instance, instruct people to address their orders to Dept. HG, and use Dept. DN as part of the address cited on the coupon in the *Doglover's Newsletter*); that way, when only 3 orders come in on the HG blank but you get 150 marked DN, you can arrange to keep running Doglovers' ads until the response tapers off, and to pull out of your local paper.

Classified ads, which are cheap, may work for some books and periodicals. Per inquiry ads are relatively inexpensive too; since you pay for space for a PI ad by splitting your revenues from it with the periodical that runs it, your only up-front costs are for production. And exchange ads are free. Magazines often swap advertising, so if you're putting one out you ought to see what kind of a deal you can arrange with kindred publishing spirits. How much room you'll be accorded in someone else's periodical will depend upon relative circulation figures and/or upon good will.

Personal Appearances

Each group you can reach by mail and through advertising you can probably also reach in person, with far more exciting results. Refer back to "Why and How to Be Your Own Best Sales Force," and please remember that almost every one of this country's thousands of organizations has scheduled meetings. Check the *Encyclopedia of Associations* to see what conventions are held in your area or might be worth traveling to.

But neither scheduled events nor the examples in this book exhaust the avenues for selling a book in person, so strive for impromptu, innovative strategies. "Sometimes, when I don't have anything pressing to do," says Russell M. Genet, a self-publisher who's an authority on astronomy, "I'll go through the journals in my field and write individual authors short notes on their papers (probably the only responses they ever get) and also pop in flyers for my books. I get about a 90 percent order rate from this."

For additional inspiration—and evidence that the strangest schemes sometimes work magnificently—note the experience of Charleen Whisnant Swansea, editor and publisher of Red Clay Books.

When Swansea's first book came off the press, she took stock of who among her friends, acquaintances and colleagues could help her sell it. Capitalizing on one of her previous jobs—she'd been a traveling sales rep for a company that made false teeth—she decided to retrace her old route and convince dentists that those dog-eared magazines in their waiting rooms were not lively enough reading for their clients.

You should spruce up the reading racks by buying my book, she told them. And they did.

Libraries

Have you sent review copies to the magazines librarians trust? Have you visited the libraries in your area to acquaint the staff with what you've published and with your availability as a reader or a lecturer? If you got a good review in one of the library journals, have you reprinted it on a postcard and sent it to librarians around the country? Have you considered getting Quality Books to handle distribution to libraries for you (see "Resources" for the address and phone number)?

If so, you've done what should be done to generate sales to the library market, although you will need to take one additional step. When orders come in, either directly from librarians or via a wholesaler like Baker & Taylor, fill them promptly and make your paperwork exemplary. Many small publishers already have excellent relationships with libraries and you'll benefit by joining their ranks.

Sub Rights Buyers

With every passing year, self-publishers win new respect from the publishing establishment, partly because by now several self-published books have snagged the prize the establishment values most—space on the national bestseller lists (*The One Minute Manager* was originally issued by its authors, for instance), and partly because many self-published books have sold in numbers that make some conventional bestsellers look sick.

Nowadays, self-publishers who want to sell rights in their books to full-fledged publishing houses have precedents to point to—trailblazers like Richard Bolles' *What Color Is Your Parachute?* (sold to Ten Speed, it made—and stayed on—the charts), *The Book of Questions* by Gregory Stock (which has now sold more than a million copies in its Workman edition), Ernest Callenbach's *Ecotopia* (a Bantam release with sales well into six figures) and Zig Ziglar's *See You at the Top* (with hardcover copies in print from Pelican edging up on 1.5 million).

Like well-established publishers, well-established book clubs are receptive to submissions from self-publishers. Be bold, therefore, and try your book on any clubs listed in *Literary Market Place* and *Book Publishing Resource Guide* that seem right for it.

And if you think you have a book that a bigger publisher, a book club, a foreign publisher, an audiotape producer or anybody else ought to buy rights to, but you find that potential buyers are psychologically unprepared to deal with an author, try getting an agent to represent you. See *LMP* for leads, ask friendly small publishers for recommendations and turn to the "Money" chapter called "Spinoffs" for more guidance on generating sub rights sales.

Money

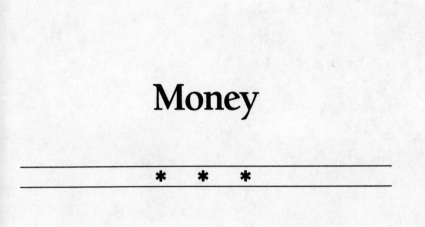

* * *

Front-end Funding

BEFORE YOU CAN begin a major piece of writing you'll need to know how you're to support yourself while you work on it. If you're otherwise employed and writing part-time, you may not have a problem. If you're rich, there's no problem, of course. And if your publisher has provided an enormous advance, you have nothing to worry about, at least until you launch your next project. But if you're among the vast majority of writers, you'll have to scramble to make ends meet.

To supplement whatever income you derive directly from writing, tap any or all of the money sources outlined below.

Grants

Browsing through the directories that list grants available to struggling writers should prove heartening, both because you'll see how many people and groups are trying to help, and because you'll find at least one program, and probably more, for which you're eligible. Even unknown authors have grants earmarked especially for them; for instance, Delacorte Press (a part of the Bantam Doubleday Dell empire) gives a prize to a first young adult novel and PEN's Ernest Hemingway Foundation Award goes to writers having first books of fiction published.

You can find out who's giving what by sending for *Grants and*

Awards Available to American Writers, which is put out by PEN, the international writers' group, and by checking books listed in "Resources." In addition, read *Poets & Writers Magazine* for announcements of new awards (and reminders about deadline dates for old ones); look at prefaces and acknowledgments sections of books in your field to see whether one foundation or another is especially receptive to your kind of project; and write your state council for the arts and the National Endowment for the Arts to ask for information about financial aid.

As a rule, grants are designed either to support a writer's work in general—to advance the writer's "career" is the usual language—or to fund a particular project. Those who apply for career-advancement money are generally judged on the basis of samples of their strongest work. Barry Targan, whose fiction was selected for Martha Foley's prestigious anthology *Best American Short Stories* for three years running, says of a National Endowment for the Arts grant that he won: "The application form itself is quite simple and straightforward, and even though it asks what you will use the grant for (you can only honestly answer—to continue to write, for support while you do write), still I think what matters most is the feeling the judges have for the samples of writing that you submit. In my own case, the fact that I'd won the Iowa School of Letters Award for Short Fiction may have helped, but many other people who received grants have published very little."

Those who want grants for particular projects have to satisfy more complicated requirements. In addition to filling out application forms, they will probably be asked to write project descriptions, estimate the budgets necessary for their execution and solicit letters of recommendation.

All this takes a good deal of time, but it's worth doing right since you're shooting for thousands of dollars. And a good way to discover what the right approach is for any specific grant is to talk with the people who've won it. The roster of previous winners that generally comes along with each application form may seem intimidatingly star-studded at first, but because many of the famous names on it got their grants while they were still unknown, they should be willing to empathize with your needs now. So explore the winners list for clues about what level of achievement is expected and what types of projects have been funded in the past, and then muster the courage to call a couple of successful grant-getters and ask for advice. Tell them about your proposal and admit it if this is your first foray into the grants game.

Susan Jacoby—who got several grants, including an Alicia Patterson Foundation fellowship, to help finance her book about new immigrants—endorses this route, as do other writers who've tried it. "Talking with someone who's recently won a grant from the foundation you're applying to gives you an insider's edge," Jacoby explains. "Each foundation has its own style: some like polysyllabic, academic presentations; others prefer it straight and simple. What's desirable and what's not changes as the composition of the selection board changes, so it's important that you talk with someone who won recently."

To go with whatever firsthand advice you can get, here are some general rules of grant-seeking:

* Incorporate selected elements of the effective book proposal (as described in "Procedures") in your project description. Emphasize the credentials and expertise you bring to your work. Explain why your project is worth undertaking and what its significance is in relation to other work in the field. If you've received an advance from a publisher, mention it, and say why you need additional funding.

* Once you've drafted a proposal you're satisfied with, circulate it among friends for suggestions; include at least one writer who has already won a grant, if you can.

* Make up a professional-looking budget. This means estimating your living expenses as accurately as possible, and in general using hard figures whenever you can, instead of guessing.

* Contact the leading authorities in your field for letters of recommendation, and try to set up meetings with them

individually. If you can't arrange meetings, write and describe your project; explain what you've accomplished thus far; and ask each authority if they'd be willing to recommend you for the grants you need. When you make it clear that your work will constitute a real contribution to their field, they'll probably agree to support your application.

In follow-up correspondence with sponsors who seem truly interested in your work, you might ask whether they can suggest any other foundations you ought to try. And you should be sure, of course, to thank every sponsor and to apprise them of the outcome of your efforts. Whatever grants you win—or fail to win—this time around, you may need their help again.

* Don't assume that you're limited to holding one grant at a time. Having money from X rarely precludes a writer from applying for more from Y and Z.

* If there's anything on the application form that you don't understand, call and ask for clarifications and explanations.

Writers' Colonies

There's scarcely a writer alive who hasn't felt at one point or another that a little peace and quiet was the key to getting some real work done. At a dozen or so writers' colonies scattered throughout the United States, peace and quiet are abundantly available, along with free room and board in most cases (at some colonies writers are asked to contribute by buying their own groceries and preparing their own meals).

Colonies come in a wide variety of styles, from Yaddo, outside Saratoga Springs, New York (with its mansion, formal rose garden, statuary, tennis courts, swimming pool and box-lunch delivery) to Cummington Community of the Arts in Massachusetts (the only retreat that has a children's program and invites everyone to pitch in with the day-to-day chores) to the Writers Room "an urban writers' colony" in Greenwich Village that rents offices and desk space but not living quarters).

Some colonies actively encourage beginners to apply (the Fine Arts Work Center in Provincetown, Massachusetts, exists for emerging writers alone), but all say that writers with talent—published or not—will be welcomed, and most accept both fiction and nonfiction writers on the basis of samples of their work. See this section's "Resources" for help in figuring out where you might best apply.

No matter how like utopia they may sound, writers' colonies are not useful for everyone. Having your own cabin in the woods will free you from the distractions of kids at home, phones in the office and other assorted turmoil, but it won't necessarily activate your muse. As one writer who has stayed at a number of colonies put it: "You don't get inspiration by looking at the trees." Nor is the problem of self-discipline any easier to handle at a colony than it is at home, although some writers do find that living in a community composed exclusively of artists shames and/or encourages them to buckle down. Those who get the most from colony life usually arrive with a specific goal in mind: five poems; the first three chapters; a rough draft. The goals you set for yourself will naturally depend in part on how long you plan to stay (some colonies ask that you spend no less than a month on the premises, while others have flexible residence requirements), but even if you don't have time to get a great deal of writing done, you may find colony conditions just right for making valuable discoveries, as Anne Grant, a documentary writer and director, did when she stayed at the Millay Colony for the Arts in Austerlitz, New York, for ten days to work on her study *Elizabeth Cady Stanton's Quarrel with God*.

"I had imagined I could finish my book," she said, looking back on the experience, "but I completed only twenty pages and a lengthy outline. I accomplished something else, though. For the first time in my adult life, I discovered my natural rhythms of waking, eating and sleeping, my flow of energy and thought when I am not interrupted. At home, whenever I failed to accomplish as much as I had planned, I would reproach myself and resent my family. At the Millay Colony, I found that even under the best conditions it takes time to develop an idea and even more time to create art."

With colonies as with grants, don't be dismayed if at first you don't succeed. Understandably, the waiting lists at most retreats are long, so you may very well have to try and try again.

Economic Ingenuity

Let's say you desperately need to get away right now in order to pull your manuscript into shape, and there's no room to be had at any of the colonies you applied to. What do you do? Well, you could decide that the world's an unfair place, shelve the manuscript, and sulk; or you could choose to abandon dependence on other people's largesse and substitute reliance on your own wits. One good way to keep yourself in funds, after all, is to devise clever ways to avoid giving up those you've got.

Do some friends of yours have second homes that they're not using and that they might allow you to live in for a couple of weeks if you volunteered to paint the kitchen during your stay? Can you afford to have a neighborhood teenager sit for your preschoolers between three and six o'clock while you work in the empty apartment of a friend who's at her office?

Most writers become experts at cash-conserving improvisations of this sort out of sheer necessity. But devising money-saving moves can be pleasurable as well as practical if you enjoy the idea of outwitting such capitalist evils as inflation and planned obsolescence by reviving secondhand clothing and furniture, for instance, or by using a barter system (maybe the electrician will fix your stove for nothing if you teach his kid grammar).

Unlike local tradespeople, the IRS never accepts payment in services, but though you can't avoid paying cash to the government, you can keep your tax bills down. Get hold of the IRS pamphlets for self-employed workers (your local office will have a list), and remember that you're personally responsible for making Social Security payments.

One other thing all writers can do to put themselves in a favorable position at tax time is keep an expenses diary. Simply carry a pocket calendar with you and jot down records of any money you spend on work-related matters (including transportation to and from editors' offices, postage and supplies, copying costs, phone calls, magazine subscriptions necessary for your project, professional membership dues and the like). Keep all receipts; mark clearly what each one is for, unless it's self-evident; and in dealing with businesses that don't normally issue them, bring your own form (you can buy a pack at any stationery store) and get it signed. Faithfully recording your expenses should help you take full advantage of applicable tax deductions and keep the costs of tax preparation down.

Some writers' organizations help their members save money by offering informational seminars, charter flights, group insurance plans and the like. And they may also provide an incidental financial benefit: membership in a major writers' group indicates to the IRS that you are indeed a professional writer and therefore entitled to all the tax breaks attendant on that occupation.

Wages

For many men and women, writing is a sometime thing, an avocation they pursue to further their goals in business or the professions. But even people whose main ambition is to write can hold down full-time nonwriting jobs that give them economic security along with other benefits.

Look at Dana Gioia, for example. Gioia, a poet who has been profiled in *Esquire* and published in *The New Yorker* and *The Hudson Review*, found that managing new business development for General Foods didn't just let him put bread on the table and a roof over his head; it also opened up new perspectives by immersing him in workaday concerns and large-scale business decisions, and it boosted his confidence besides. "Nothing, I assume, not even the Nobel Prize, would keep a real writer from feeling some anxiety about his work, but making some visible progress in a career does help give a writer, especially a beginning writer, a base of security to work from," he told Daryln Brewer of *Poets & Writers Magazine*.

Writers who work for software manufacturers, life insurance companies, stockbrokers and law firms report similar benefits.

Subsidy Publishing

Riffle through the pages of the women's magazines and you'll notice before long that the clothes and cosmetics featured in the editorial departments tend to come from the very same companies that fill the advertising columns. Almost all magazines depend on advertising revenues for economic viability, but some are more fussy than others about the nature of the links between ads and editorial attention, and a few manage to run plenty of ads that relate to articles without relinquishing control over content in any way.

A similar system exists to fund books and pamphlets. Subsidy publishing, as the practice is called, involves interesting a business, a charitable organization or any other institution that has money to spend in financing a written work prior to publication, and sometimes giving the sponsor a say about its contents. What the company gets out of the deal is a marketing tool, frequently a premium; what the writer gets is a sponsor, except that instead of the Medicis or the Ford Foundation, this time it's Amalgamated Widgets.

Established book publishers often make subsidy deals, but subsidy publishing is not well known among writers, most of whom discover it by accident, if at all, the way Ann Reed and Marilyn Pfaltz did as they were making the rounds of New York houses with their cookbook, *Your Secret Servant*.

When a friendly editor who didn't want the book for her list suggested that it might make a good premium, Reed and Pfaltz asked her what she meant by that, and then switched targets. Instead of offering their manuscript to publishing houses, they began offering it to advertising agencies, and fairly soon they found one that wanted to use it as an incentive to draw new accounts to a banking client's offices. The bank paid enough for its copies of *Your Secret Servant* so that the authors could print and bind 5,000 extra books for their own purposes. With the finished work in hand, selling publishers was simpler. Scribner's bought the 5,000 copies and kept the book in print for a number of years.

To find the organizations that might subsidize you, figure out what institutional aims your work might serve (maybe a company that manufactures luggage would like to fund your anthology of expeditions and distribute it as its Christmas gift this year, for instance; or maybe the Lions would underwrite your history of fraternal organizations). Then call or write potential sponsors themselves, or match companies with appropriate books by using the leads you'll find in "Money Resources."

Like all forms of patronage, subsidy publishing may raise moral issues. But if you're honest with yourself, your sponsor and your public, there's nothing to stop you from having clean hands, a pure heart and a healthy bank balance all at the same time.

Spinoffs

THE SINGLE BEST key to financial success in writing is recycling. Both the materials and the skills that go into creating a piece of written work can be reused in a great variety of profitable ways, and while those who've written books have the widest range of recycling options, everyone who's written anything should be able to make it do at least double duty for pay. Or triple. Or more.

Check your contract before you start the recycling processes, though, to see which rights you control and which you'll need to clear through your publisher.

Transforming the Whole

To switch from worrying about how to keep the wolf from the door to worrying about whether to be bullish or bearish with your surplus funds, get your story made into a successful movie or television program. TV and movie people prefer to buy bestsellers, of course, because they want presold audiences for their products, but little-known books, too, have been transformed for large and small screens.

Mostly, it's a matter of luck. An aggressive and talented agent who specializes in dramatic properties can be a great asset (you might start a data bank, like the one outlined for editors and literary agents in "Openings," in order to figure out which Hollywood agents would be good for, and receptive to, what you've written). The affection approach (see "Openings" again) may be worth trying with a producer, a director or an actor whose work strikes you as similar in significant ways to your own. And who you know can be crucial, as the saga of *Dances with Wolves* demonstrates. Its author, Michael Blake, described the story to Jim Wilson and Kevin Costner, his friends in the film business, back in the mid-'80s. Costner urged him to get it published as a book first. Endorsing that strategy, Wilson persuaded a literary agent to represent it. After a string of turndowns and a period of severe poverty, Blake got a buyer. Fawcett issued his book as a paperback original in 1988. That deal didn't solve Blake's poverty problem— the advance was $6,500—but then, sure enough, Costner and Wilson made the story into a phenomenally successful movie, with Blake's screenplay. The film then spawned a tie-in title (from Newmarket Press) that became the all-time bestselling illustrated movie book.

Now of course you probably don't know Kevin Costner personally. But you don't have to. The lesson here is that you should look for personal connections in the film world and work them hard. Is your cousin's sister-in-law an editor at Paramount? Ask him to ask her to call your book to the attention of a producer or two. It probably won't lead to big bucks and glitzy awards. But it might.

Outside the glamorous world of Hollywood, luck plays a smaller part in transforming written work for profit, and you can depend upon energy and intelligence instead to help you toward your goals. Among the many possibilities worth exploring, several stand out. For example:

✱ *Audiocassettes*. Audio is a growth area in publishing today. Driving, walking, riding the subway, or just sitting on a park bench, thousands of Americans now regularly listen to books on tape that are produced by companies founded expressly for the purpose and by booksellers, publishers and special-interest concerns that make cassettes as a sideline. Check your contractual rights and your publisher's capabilities and intentions in this area and see the cassettes in stock at nearby bookstores for leads to companies you might approach.

Audio books come in abridged and unabridged versions but because abridgements are the norm you should prepare yourself to sit still for cuts and find out whether you can make them or approve them. Then think about your speaking voice and style. If you can read your work better than, or as well as, a professional actor, perhaps you can do the narration and get a bigger share of the gate. Sales of 10,000–15,000 copies of an audio book aren't unusual so there's noticeable money to be made here.

✻ *Export.* Some books travel well and, if you think hard about what sorts of people in which foreign countries would respond to what you've written, perhaps yours will be one of them. To get a sense of what's currently selling abroad, read *Publishers Weekly*'s articles on publishing overseas. And then consult your publisher or your agent (if you have one) or some of the exporters and export representatives listed in *LMP* about how to effect foreign sales.

Great Britain, of course, provides a promising market for many American titles because language is no barrier, but scientific and even semiscientific writing may draw English-speaking audiences around the world, and so might essentially visual works for both children and adults.

Foreign publishers may buy copies of the American book, or buy rights to publish an edition of their own.

✻ *Translation.* Whether or not there's an English-speaking foreign market for an American writer's work, there may be a market—or several markets—for it in translation. Again, you ought to come up with a list of logical candidates and then discuss the possibilities with your publisher and/or your literary agent and/or appropriate agents listed in *LMP*.

Share whatever grounds for optimism you have (are books about the same subject regularly featured on French bestseller lists; has the leading English-Spanish translator in the United

States agreed to do your novel if you get a buyer for it in Latin America?). No exporter can afford to take lightly the obvious hazards that come with translation rights, so they'll all be hungry for evidence that supports projections of success.

✻ *Videocassettes*. Translating words on paper into visual images with sounds attached is a tricky task but it can pay off handsomely—as witness the durable video versions of Jane Fonda's exercise books—so it's worth investigating for certain kinds of nonfiction. Suppose, for example, that you've written a book about living with a handicapped child; the techniques and attitudes it explains would probably be clearest if they were visually depicted as well as verbally described. Visual presentations could obviously be at least as useful with instruction manuals of various sorts—how to refinish your antique furniture, care for your houseplants, understand body language.

To find likely prospects for sales of video rights to your material, canvass companies that already reach appropriate audiences. Organizations that serve nurses might adapt a book on touch therapy, for instance, and large corporations might adapt one that explains how to get the most out of meetings.

✻ *Cable TV*. Paralleling the growth of small, special-interest operations in book and periodical publishing, small, special-interest television channels have been multiplying lately. Local cable programs differ widely from one another—and from the local and network programs that used to monopolize TV—but they have some things in common. In general, their need for new material is insatiable, their budgets are small, and their reliance on print materials for program ideas is marked.

Check out cable shows in your area and/or study the periodicals that cover cable to identify possible buyers of rights in your work; and when you find a likely prospect, try to come up with a proposal that meets the demands of television by remembering that people want lots of action and entertainment when they click on a TV set.

✱ *Awards*. Numerous cash prizes are given each year to outstanding works in a staggering variety of categories (best first novel; best book about Ohio history; best article on dental disease), and applying for them is relatively easy. Use the directories listed in "Money Resources" to see what prizes your work might win, decide how much (if anything) you're willing to pay for entry fees, and then start filling out forms. Applications for some awards will have to come from your publisher, who will probably be glad to do the necessary paperwork. Just tell your editor what you're after and what kind of help you need.

Re-producing the Parts

Sometimes a section of a book can be lifted, virtually intact, out of the rest of a manuscript and stood firmly on its own feet. In such cases, the author needs only to figure out which periodicals might like to run it and arrange to give them their chance.

More often, however, books refuse to disassemble neatly, and carving articles or stories from their pages takes careful craftsmanship.

Once you've decided which parts of your story merit publication on their own (perhaps you'll have to supply a new lead or a few passages of transition or a local news peg before any of them does), you can approach magazines, newspapers and syndicates with your selections (see "Resources" and, if you feel the need of a refresher course, "A Foot in the Door"). You should offer to sell either first serial rights (that is, the rights to the first appearance in print of this work) or second serial rights (i.e., the rights to republish, perhaps in a slightly different form). For obvious reasons, first serial rights go for more money.

Send as many different adaptations of your material as you can prepare to as many appropriate outlets as you can find, and use the biographical note that runs with them to identify yourself as the author of their parent work. You'll want readers who are enthusiastic about an excerpt to realize that they can buy a copy of its source. Ideally, you'll be able to make that easy to do; try hard to get periodicals to print full ordering information—including a toll-free number—along with your pieces.

Don't stop, though, when you've gotten a bunch of excerpts into print and a bit of action going. Fan the flames by developing reprint possibilities. Should the *Reader's Digest* see the chapter of your book that appeared in *Essence*? Would airline magazines or trade journals or special-interest newsletters or local papers pick up your piece from *Inc.*?

The effort involved in sending tearsheets out to periodicals that might reprint from them is minimal, and likely to be fully repaid even if all you get is additional exposure. There'll be big money in the offing, though, for anyone who does win the vote at the *Digest*.

Deploying Writing Skills

If you decide to use your writing skills in order to earn enough money to use your writing skills the way you really want to use them, you have several interesting options.

One thing you can do is write other people's books. Celebrities and executives and experts of various sorts with good stories to tell often lack the time and talent to tell them well. As a result, they and their agents and editors frequently go looking for ghost-writers and collaborators.

When you're tapped to write for or with somebody else, you may get a flat fee or a percentage of the royalties or both. Try for a nonreturnable fixed payment up front in addition to, or as an advance against, the percentage, and expect to work hard for your money however it's paid. There's no such thing as "an easy book," according to William Novak, who's done autobiographies with celebrities such as Lee Iacocca, the "Mayflower Madam" and Magic Johnson as well as books, including *The Big Book of Jewish Humor*, on his own.

Novak reports that he enjoys writing as part of a team. If you think you'd like that too, ask your acquaintances in publishing about assignments, and then, once you're hired, arrange to be billed as a co-author if you can, and be absolutely certain you get credit somewhere in it. (Drawing up a written agreement at the outset about the terms of a collaboration is a good way to ensure that these and other focuses for dissension don't cause trouble later.)

Expending less effort (and no doubt earning less in the way of psychic rewards), you can take up writing fillers, short features and greeting-card verse. Successful practitioners of these and comparable minor arts have, predictably, written books that tell how you too can cash in on them, and although you can sneer if you want to, this may be a good way to pay the grocery bills.

Other opportunities to write for money exist in organizations that need newsletters, companies that need house organs, government bodies that need speech-writing staffs and myriad other concerns. Let your own ingenuity be a guide to the ones that will work well for you.

Book packagers also hire writers. Sometimes known as book producers or book developers, packagers come up with ideas for books, find people to write them and sell the finished products—in the form of fully edited manuscripts, sets of camera-ready pages or thousands of bound volumes—to publishing houses. Authors who work for packagers can negotiate a variety of deals involving flat fees and/or shares of earnings.

To get packagers to think about hiring you, write to tell them about your special expertise and your writing credits, and enclose brief samples of your best work. See "Resources" for leads to particular book producers and send for descriptive literature from those you find appealing.

Purveying Publishing Know-How

Instead of working for a packager, you may want to consider becoming one, as hundreds of people have done during the past few years.

Packagers often, but not always, have editorial experience and contacts. And packaged books are usually nonfiction, with titles like *Dial an Expert: A Consumer's Guide to Free Expertise Available by Phone* (Stonesong Press) or *The Audubon Society Nature Guides* (Chanticleer Press) or *Alternatives to Drugs* (Sarah Lazin Books) or *Theme Gardens* (Regina Ryan Publishing Enterprises, Inc.). But writers with a fund of ideas, a flair for selling and the ability to stay calm and efficient under pressure can also succeed as packagers. And novels get packaged too, especially genre fiction like historical sagas, mystery series, action/adventure stories and romantic tales for women.

Those of you who like the idea of turning your ideas for fiction and nonfiction into proposals and then getting other people to write, produce and distribute the books you've dreamed up might seek advice from book producers in your area. Review "The Self-Publishing Option" if you decide to be the kind of packager who sells finished books, not just finished manuscripts.

Arguably, of course, if you're going to produce finished books, you might as well handle distribution too and create your own publishing company.

Your safest move in that case is to specialize. By concentrating on one subject area or one kind of writing that appeals to a particular group of people, a publisher can build a following and eventually instill a strong brand-name loyalty that will help draw readers to new books from the house.

Some firms specialize successfully in books about a geographical region; *50 Hikes in New Hampshire's White Mountains* went through two editions and four printings in its first six years and spawned a series of related books at New Hampshire Publishing Company, for instance.

Other companies focus on a topic or two. Examples run the gamut from advertising and assertiveness training to yeast infections and Zen masterpieces, and any subject can work as long as you know your way around it, identify its devotees and devise reliable, cost-effective ways to reach them.

Whatever you publish, you'd be wise to search for out-of-print books on your topic that you can simply reissue and for related books other publishers may be glad to license to you because they can't penetrate the markets you get to and/or because their sales are minimal. Add titles like these to your list and you're likely to find that it reaches critical mass much faster than it would with new releases only.

But you needn't stop there. Out-of-print and underappreciated books can themselves constitute a publishing program. A number of publishers specialize in such hidden treasures. Consider Phil Zuckerman's Applewood Books Americana Reprints, for example. That line's many titles include work by Benjamin Franklin, George Washington and Walt Whitman, early versions of selected volumes in the Nancy Drew and Hardy Boys series and the original version of *Rudolph the Red-Nosed Reindeer*. When you can reissue a book in a facsimile edition, you incur no costs for typesetting and layout, and when you can publish one whose copyright has lapsed, you won't have to pay royalties. Even works still copyrighted can usually be had for modest fees, though, when no one has been paying much attention to them for a while.

Experienced authors can also sell certain publishing skills and services. If you've become adept at using a page layout program, for example, by all means make your expertise generate extra income (see "Resources" for specific guidance). If you've developed editing, copy-editing or proofreading skills, you ought to tap the ready market for them as well; try publishing houses, newspapers, ad agencies and almost any other business that involves the preparation of materials to be printed (which almost any business does). And if you've developed as much marketing knowhow as self-publishers Dan Poynter of Para Publishing, Tom and Marilyn Ross of Communication Creativity and John Kremer of Open Horizons, you might follow their lead by creating books, newsletters, workshops and all manner of other goods and services that show small publishers how to connect with readers. See "The Self-Publishing Option Resources" for a better idea of their various approaches.

You can get advice on selling publishing expertise from independent publishers around the country (who may advise you, too, on marketing valuable artifacts—like your mailing list).

Lecturing

Lecturing is lucrative; in fact, it's what supports a good many well-known writers. For months every year, these prominent authors crisscross the country to speak before civic and corporate groups and on college campuses, and many of them earn well over a thousand dollars per speech. (The take for beginners is lower, of course.)

The lecture bureaus that schedule celebrities' talks (*LMP* has a list) are prepared to welcome new clients, but, as in any other business, a recommendation from a respected source and a strong presentation will increase the odds for acceptance.

Both in approaching lecture agents and in fulfilling the engagements they'll get you if they take you on, you should be aware that what works when you write won't necessarily work when you talk. For a piece of writing, as Bill Leigh of the Leigh Bureau has explained, is directed to a class of individuals, but a speech is directed to a group; and what people in groups want to hear is the voice of authority. You should concentrate, therefore, not on your writing but on its subject; stress your theme, your points and your credentials. And use the intimate, first-person approach that's so powerful in print sparingly, if at all, on the platform.

Teaching

Though it doesn't pay as well as lecturing, teaching makes a good sideline for writers too, and draws on many of the same skills. Enrollments in writing and journalism classes are strong today, and almost every area of the country has continuing-education programs that might be hospitable to new courses. If you're interested in teaching, explore opportunities at prisons and rehabilitation centers as well as at schools and universities in your region;

and send for catalogs. Maybe one of the instructors listed will agree to advise you about drafting and submitting a course proposal.

Teaching has several attractions. Serious writers report that helping others learn writing techniques gives them new insights into their own creative processes, and that contact with both students and fellow instructors is often stimulating. Furthermore, the pay is steady, at least as long as the semester lasts, and much longer than that in most cases.

Endnote

* * *

Righting the Scales of Success

DOWN DEEP WHERE it matters—on some subrational level—it's natural for authors to suspect that pub date constitutes the publishing industry's equivalent of the theater's opening night. And it would be nice if it did. After the long and lonely work of writing and the petty aggravations of production, there ought to come a time when the audience cheers and the critics dole out stars and a person knows for sure whether to pop open the champagne at a party or slink off to suffer alone.

In the normal course of events, however, a writer's audience is apt to remain silent (people almost never volunteer comments on what they've read unless it made them mad); potential critics will probably pay no attention (reviewers ignore magazine pieces and the vast majority of new books); and any responses that do come an author's way are liable to be hell on the impulse that wants certainty because they'll straggle in over such a long period of time and be so liberally sprinkled with waffle words ("Despite its flaws . . ."; "Despite its promise . . ."; "Despite its very real merits . . .").

But if random reactions are imperfect indicators of accomplishment, the supposedly scientific polls known as bestseller surveys are even worse. Credited by the public with mirroring its response to what's published, all the bestseller lists actually aim to reveal is which trade books are selling well in bookstores, and they rank even that small fraction of what people read more in terms of rate of sale than in terms of sales per se. As a result, a book that sells

223

2,000 copies a week for ten weeks in a particular set of stores may make the list, while another book that sells hundreds of thousands of copies over a five-year period will never get near it.

Worse still, and more important, bestseller lists don't generally rank anything right. The bookstore managers who supply data to compilers have learned over the years that the bestseller label stimulates demand, and they're not above reporting inflated sales figures for a specific book simply because—having been persuaded to order large quantities of it—they want it hyped.

On at least one memorable occasion, booksellers cited a book that hadn't been written yet, let alone published and sold, as a current bestseller, and although their motivations may have been a bit obscure in that instance, it is clear enough on the whole that bookstore managers (and publishers too) can and do regularly skew bestseller standings, so that nobody knows just what they may mean.

Given this set of circumstances, most writers find that publication day comes and goes and leaves in its wake nothing but a gnawing sense of anticlimax that can lead eventually to a debilitating conviction of failure. In fact, only two kinds of authors are likely to get a fair share of pleasure from getting published: (1) those whose books the major houses, book clubs and TV and movie studios catapult to commercial success (no matter what your personal hierarchy of values is, almost everybody in our culture gets a warm feeling at some level from winning fame and money); and (2) those who've learned from this book, or from any other source, how to go where readers they respect will appreciate them and how to appreciate themselves.

Techniques for reaching appropriate and appreciative audiences have already been outlined—in "Why and How to Be Your Own Best Sales Force" and in "Managing Sales"—but techniques for arranging to appreciate yourself are harder to explain, partly because the subject is fraught with tension. In the light of our Puritan heritage, it's hard not to believe that to appreciate yourself is to be proud, and to be proud is to be vain, and to be vain is to be threatened by comeuppance.

Forget that. If you got your work published and read, you have plenty to be proud about, and the more parts of the publishing process you completed successfully, the more plaudits you've earned. Furthermore, nobody's in a better position than you are to evaluate the extent and nature of your accomplishments.

The Achievement Awards list that follows is designed as a playful first step to help people who write learn to sing their own praises. At the outset, you may feel uncomfortable claiming credit for anything on it but the items that you can recite with a faintly self-mocking air. In the end, however, perhaps you'll abandon all pretense of sophistication, add freely to the list in your mind, and accept all legitimate commendations—whatever their cultural authority—with unself-conscious joy.

Start by assuming that you're fully entitled to applause if you have:

* Had a manuscript accepted (over 90 percent of the material submitted to publishing houses is regularly turned down).
* Discovered a way to issue a book or periodical on your own.
* Produced an aesthetically pleasing piece of work.
* Elicited congratulatory letters and phone calls from family and friends (who may or may not have read whatever it was you wrote).
* Elicited congratulatory letters and phone calls from total strangers who've not only read your work but liked it enough to comment on it.
* Gotten enthusiastic and insightful reviews.
* Gotten bad reviews with good lines in them.
* Created a tangible literary object with your name on it that snuggles on the shelf between James and Kafka.
* Built friendships—with your editor, agent, art director, readers, small-press publishers, distant colleagues.
* Mastered a new skill (page layout, proofreading, public speaking).
* Become eligible for membership in the Authors Guild and for all the grants and prizes only published writers can win.

* Found and informed the audience that will benefit by your work, even though it numbers only 2,000 readers and they're scattered all over the country.
* Furthered a cause.
* Generated interest in whatever you do next.
* Managed to escape the 9-to-5 rat race without descending to a subsistence standard of living.
* Learned a new language ("I want the picture flopped and a 9-point caption; that's the wrong font").
* Established a track record (getting published is always easier when you have a past to parade as well as a future to promise).
* Completed what you started. Now, instead of a wistful interior monologue—"Someday I've got to write that up"—you can be party to a spirited public dialogue—"Your piece [magazine, book] made me think [laugh, weep, see more clearly, want to tell you that . . .]."

And if ever you lose sight, for a moment, of the mysterious force that prompted you to sit down and write to begin with, listen to R. V. Cassill: "Writing is a way of coming to terms with the world and with oneself. The whole spirit of writing is to overcome narrowness and fear by giving order, measure, and significance to the flux of experience constantly dinning into our lives." And that's no small achievement.

Resources

* * *

How to Use Resources

This next section is designed to function as a giant Swiss Army knife. Implements in it will serve almost any purpose you dream up, so long as you use them creatively and with care.

If you keep it somewhere handy, you'll benefit by browsing back and forth among the listings in your spare moments, picking out different ones to use at different times in somewhat different ways and allowing your mind to play with the possibilities.

Before you make a sizable commitment to anyone or anything mentioned here, please investigate with your own aims in view. Obviously, you'll have to determine not only what you need but also whether, when you need it, and if it still fits the description it merited when its writeup went to press.

Because prices are unstable, they're not listed, but every book and periodical recommended here was available in libraries and/or for sale at a reasonable cost when it was selected as a Resource.

When the asterisk appears, it indicates goods or services that are exceptionally valuable to authors.

Getting the Words Right Resources

THE LISTINGS BELOW will help you uncover fresh material and find the time, the temerity and the talent to write it up successfully.

Advice, Analysis and Reportage

Alberti, Robert E. *Your Perfect Write: The Manual for Self-Help Writers.* **Impact Publishers, P.O. Box 1094, San Luis Obispo, CA 93406. 1985.**

Alberti knows what he's talking about; he heads Impact Publishers, which specializes in self-help books.

American Poetry Review. **1721 Walnut Street, Philadelphia, PA 19103. Published bimonthly.**

Essays about poetry, reviews of poetry and interviews with poets appear here along with work by new and established poets.

American Society of Journalists and Authors. *Tools of the Writer's Trade: Writers Tell All About the Equipment and Services They Find the Best.* **Edited by Dodi Schultz. HarperCollins, 10 East 53 Street, New York, NY 10022. 1990.**

ASJA members share discoveries and opinions about computers, reference materials, professional connections and a host of other nitty-gritty topics.

Atkins, Gary, and William Rivers. *Reporting with Understanding*. Iowa State University Press, 2121 South State Avenue, Ames, IA 50010. 1987.

Examples, exercises, analysis and advice on how to get and present information, with emphasis in later chapters on special interests, including political, environmental and minority affairs.

Barzun, Jacques. *On Writing, Editing, and Publishing: Essays Explicative and Hortatory*. University of Chicago Press, 5801 South Ellis Avenue, Chicago, IL 60637. Second edition, 1986.

Writer's block, jargon and style are among the topics Barzun's classy lectures address.

Blue, Martha. *See* "The Self-Publishing Option Resources."

Bly, Carol. *The Passionate, Accurate Story: Making Your Heart's Truth into Literature*. Milkweed Editions, P.O. Box 3226, Minneapolis, MN 55403. 1990.

It's rare and refreshing to find a writer who not only believes in fiction with moral force but can illuminate the process of creating it.

Boston, Bruce O. *Language on a Leash*. Editorial Experts, Inc., 85 S. Bragg Street, Suite 400, Alexandria, VA 22312. 1988.

A stylish collection of essays for people who care about the English language, by a writer who stakes out an attractive middle ground between the purists and the overly permissive.

✱ Brande, Dorothea. *Becoming a Writer*. Jeremy P. Tarcher, Inc., 5858 Wilshire Boulevard, Suite 22, Los Angeles, CA 90036. 1981.

This book aims to "teach the beginner not how to write, but how to be a writer." Focusing mainly on fiction, Dorothea Brande asserts that there really is a magic about writing and that it can be taught. What she has to say is as eye-opening today as it was when it first appeared in 1934.

Brown, Rita Mae. *Starting from Scratch: A Different Kind of Writers' Manual*. Bantam Books, 666 Fifth Avenue, New York, NY 10103. 1988.

The author of *Rubyfruit Jungle* and *High Hearts* (among other novels) has definite ideas about how writers should live and learn. Her ebullient, bossy book includes imaginative exercises.

Burnett, Hallie. *On Writing the Short Story.* **HarperCollins, 10 East 53 Street, New York, NY 10022. 1983.**

Teacher, editor and writer Hallie Burnett presents essays about plot, character, style and the other elements of good short fiction along with six stories that illustrate her points.

* **Burroway, Janet.** *Writing Fiction: A Guide to Narrative Craft.* **Scott Foresman, 1900 E. Lake Avenue, Glenview, IL 60025; 800-782-2665. Second edition, 1987.**

A creative writing textbook that's a joy to read. Janet Burroway, whose own prose is a delight, focuses on stories by twenty-one leading modern writers—including Jamaica Kincaid, Bobbie Ann Mason, Peter Taylor and Raymond Carver—to explore form and structure, the writing process, methods of character presentation and other essential aspects of fiction.

Calderazzo, John. *Writing from Scratch: Freelancing.* **Littlefield Adams Quality Paperbacks, 8705 Bollman Place, Savage, MD 20763. 1990.**

Friendly first-person prose about creating and placing periodical pieces.

Carroll, David L. *A Manual of Writer's Tricks.* **Paragon House, 90 Fifth Avenue, New York, NY 10011. 1990.**

Taken as suggestions rather than directives, Carroll's "tricks" will be helpful, particularly the procedural ones like "Don't attempt serious rewriting when you're tired or in a bad mood."

* **Cassill, R. V.** *Writing Fiction.* **Prentice-Hall, 15 Columbus Circle. New York, NY 10023. Second edition, 1975.**

Cassill, who's written some highly acclaimed fiction himself, advocates learning to write by reading the best writing available and by comparing your writing with that by more experienced hands. He includes readings along with his text and explains how to analyze the ways writers produce their effects. A fine book that covers all the stages necessary in writing fiction, including getting started.

* **Chasen, Jerry Simon, and Kenneth P. Norwick.** *The Rights of Authors, Artists, and Other Creative People.* **Southern Illinois University Press, Box 3697, Carbondale, IL 62901. 1992.**

A remarkable thing happens when you read what Jerry Chasen and

Ken Norwick have to say here. You actually begin to understand how the law works and how it might apply to your particular situation. This is an excellent guide for all writers, and especially useful for anyone who's been deluded into thinking that legal rules are hard, fast, mysterious and totally unpredictable.

Dickey, James. *Self-Interviews*. Recorded and edited by Barbara and James Reiss. Louisiana State University Press, Baton Rouge, LA 70893. 1970.

A fascinating tour of the mind of a poet. In an appealing conversational voice, Dickey interweaves observations about writing poems with reportage about his life. For material about Dickey's fiction, *see Sorties* (also published by LSU Press), which presents journal entries along with a handful of essays.

✳ Dillard, Annie. *The Writing Life*. Harper Perennial, 10 East 53 Street, New York, NY 10022. 1989.

Annie Dillard writes magnificently about writing (and every other topic she's tackled, as witness her Pulitzer Prize winner, *Pilgrim at Tinker Creek*). Give yourself a treat; read this, soon and often.

Edelstein, Scott. *The No-Experience-Necessary Writer's Course*. Scarborough House, Chelsea, MI 48118. 1990.

Familiar but generally intelligent prescriptions and exercises for beginners.

***First Person Singular: Writers on Their Craft*. Compiled by Joyce Carol Oates. Ontario Review Press/George Braziller, George Braziller, Inc., 60 Madison Avenue, New York, NY 10010. 1983.**

An illuminating collection of essays by and interviews with more than two dozen leading writers, including Gail Godwin, Anne Tyler, Mary Gordon and E.L. Doctorow.

Fontaine, André, and William A. Glavin, Jr. *The Art of Writing Nonfiction*. Syracuse University Press, 1600 Jamesville Avenue, Syracuse, NY 13244-5160. Second edition, 1987.

A more accurate title for this helpful handbook would have been *The Art of Writing the Interpretive Story*, "interpretive journalism" being the authors' term for the "new journalism" pioneered by Tom Wolfe and others.

Gaudet, Marcia, and Carl Wooten. *Porch Talk with Ernest Gaines: Conversations on the Writer's Craft.* Louisiana State University Press, Baton Rouge, LA 70893. 1990.

The author of *The Autobiography of Miss Jane Pitman* and other fine fiction shares his ideas and experiences in an engaging series of interviews.

Goldberg, Natalie. *Writing Down the Bones: Freeing the Writer Within.* Shambhala Publications, Inc., Horticultural Hall, 300 Massachusetts Avenue, Boston, MA 02115. 1986.

Natalie Goldberg, a teacher of writing and a student of Zen Buddhism, offers practical advice about writing and "about using writing as . . . a way to help you penetrate your life and become sane."

Goldfarb, Ronald L., and Gail E. Ross. *The Writer's Lawyer: Essential Legal Advice for Writers and Editors in All Media.* Times Books, 201 East 50 Street, New York, NY 10022. 1989.

Use this knowledgeable discussion to heighten your awareness of legal issues that often crop up in connection with writing. *See also,* Chasen and Norwick, above, and Pinkerton and *Writer's Guide to Copyright,* below.

Higgins, George V. *On Writing: Advice for Those Who Write to Publish (or Would Like To).* Henry Holt and Company, 115 West 18 Street, New York, NY 10011. 1990.

Professor and prolific novelist, Higgins has written a lengthy lecture that's both entertaining and educational, although the Olympian tone may put some readers off.

* Horowitz, Lois. *Knowing Where to Look: The Ultimate Guide to Research.* Writer's Digest Books, 1507 Dana Avenue, Cincinnati, OH 45207. 1984.

Don't dismiss the subtitle as hyperbole. This is a meaty, comprehensive and thoroughly readable guide. Sections on indexes and on looking for addresses, statistics and other particular kinds of information are especially valuable.

How to Write an Uncommonly Good Novel. Edited by Carol Hoover. Ariadne Press, 4817 Tallahassee Avenue, Rockville, MD. 20853. 1990.

Members of the Washington, DC, based Writers Mentors Group

cover a range of topics, including point of view, humor, foreshadowing, rhythm and revising.

Hughes, Elaine Farris. *Writing from the Inner Self.* **HarperCollins, 10 East 53 Street, New York, NY 10022. 1991.**

Delightful as well as practical, this guide to stimulating creativity and overcoming writer's block is an ingenious blend of writing and meditation exercises.

* **Jerome, Judson.** *The Poet's Handbook.* **Writer's Digest Books, 1507 Dana Avenue, Cincinnati, OH 45207. 1980.**

A remarkably deft tutorial, based partly on Jerome's column in *Writer's Digest* magazine, for everyone who wants to write "effective comprehensible poetry."

Killien, Christi, and Sheila Bender. *Writing in a Convertible with the Top Down: A Unique Guide for Writers.* **Warner Books, 1271 Sixth Avenue, New York, NY 10020. 1992.**

In letters back and forth, Killien and Bender comment wisely and constructively on writing as a process. You may want to follow their lead by creating your own intimate, long-distance writers group with someone you admire and trust, and in any event you'll enjoy sitting in on theirs.

Kilpatrick, James J. *The Writer's Art.* **Andrews & McMeel, 4900 Main Street, Kansas City, MO 64112; 800-826-4216. 1984.**

What to do and what not to do to become a better writer. Kilpatrick is an opinionated and engaging instructor who provides wonderful examples to prove his points.

Kirby, David. *Writing Poetry: Where Poems Come From and How to Write Them.* **The Writer, Inc., 120 Boylston Street, Boston, MA 02116-4615. 1989.**

An energizing discussion by English professor and poet David Kirby, who believes in poetry as a route to fresh, original thinking, a path to the "back door of knowledge."

Klauser, Henriette Anne. *Writing on Both Sides of the Brain: Breakthrough Techniques for People Who Write.* **HarperCollins, 10 East 53 Street, New York, NY 10022. 1987.**

First you use the right side of your brain to create; then you use the left side to edit. According to Henriette Anne Klauser, who runs Writing

Resource Workshops, it's when we try to write and edit simultaneously that we run into problems. Her incisive, manual explains just how you can separate the two functions and why you'll be glad you did.

Leader, Zachary. *Writer's Block.* **Johns Hopkins University Press, 701 West 40 Street, Suite 275, Baltimore, MD 21211. 1991.**

Leader's "theoretical and historical enquiry" is stimulating scholarly reading.

Loring, Ann, and Evelyn Kaye. *Write and Sell Your TV Drama.* **Alek Publishing Company, 147 Sylvan Avenue, Leonia, NJ 07605. 1984.**

Clear, step-by-step instructions derived from a course Loring taught at the New School in New York.

Maggio, Rosalie. *The Dictionary of Bias-Free Usage: A Guide to Non-discriminatory Language.* **Oryx Press, 4041 North Central at Indian School Road, Phoenix, AZ 85012-3397. 1991.**

Use this admirably comprehensive dictionary to check on sexist overtones and undertones in your language, and to get rid of them. *See also* Miller and Swift, below.

McCormack, Thomas. *The Fiction Editor.* **St. Martin's Press, 175 Fifth Avenue, New York, NY 10010. 1988.**

The head of St. Martin's Press offers conceptual tools that both writers and editors can use to diagnose and solve problems with fiction manuscripts. Pungent, persuasive, engaging and edifying.

Meyer, Herbert E., and Jill M. Meyer. *How to Write.* **Storm King Press/Random House, P.O. Box 2089, Friday Harbor, WA 98250. 1986.**

The authors analyze and illustrate the decisions, steps, skills and techniques that go into writing any kind of prose, and they come up with a tidy prescription. Brisk, clear, sound advice that's most easily applicable to nonfiction.

Meyrowitz, Joshua. *No Sense of Place: The Impact of Electronic Media on Social Behavior.* **Oxford University Press, 200 Madison Avenue, New York, NY 10016. 1985.**

Professor Meyrowitz's masterly analysis includes a fascinating discussion of the powers (and limitations) of print.

* Miller, Casey, and Kate Swift. *The Handbook of Nonsexist Writing*. HarperCollins, 10 East 53 Street, New York, NY 10022. Second edition, 1988.

   It is possible—even easy, after a bit of practice—to use nonsexist language without awkwardness or ostentation. This book shows how. Highly recommended.

Moffat, Mary Jane. *The Times of Our Lives: A Guide to Writing Autobiography and Memoir*. John Daniel and Company, P.O. Box 21922, Santa Barbara, CA 93121. Second edition, 1989.

   A slim volume full of practical wisdom by the author of her own memoir, *City of Roses*, which Tillie Olsen called "a magical evocation of a girlhood."

Murray, Donald. *Writing for Your Readers: Notes on the Writer's Craft from* The Boston Globe. Globe Pequot Press, P.O. Box 2, Chester, CT 06412. 1983.

   Although Murray has journalists in mind, the tips he offers will prove valuable for all sorts of writers. See especially his suggestions about crafting good strong leads.

Noble, William. *Make That Scene: A Writer's Guide to Setting, Mood and Atmosphere*. Paul S. Eriksson, Publisher, 208 Battell Building, Middlebury, VT 05753. 1988.

   Noble, the author of other books for writers on such subjects as dialogue, structure and plagiarism, offers advice generously sprinkled with examples.

On Being a Writer. Edited by Bill Strickland. Writer's Digest Books, 1507 Dana Avenue, Cincinnati, OH 45207. 1989.

   Interviews that originally appeared in *Writer's Digest* with William Faulkner, Tom Robbins, Ellen Goodman, and more than two dozen other disparate authors.

Patterson, Benton Rain. *Write to Be Read: A Practical Guide to Feature Writing*. Iowa State University Press, 2121 South State Avenue, Ames, IA 50010. 1986.

   Good solid guidance from a pro. Pointers on finding an angle and organizing a piece are especially helpful.

Pinkerton, Linda F. *The Writer's Law Primer*. **Lyons & Burford, 31 West 21 Street, New York, NY 10010. 1990.**

A broad, quick introduction that's easy to read except for the sexist pronouns.

Poets & Writers Magazine.

See "Advice, Analysis and Reportage" in "A Foot in the Door Resources."

***Poets at Work: The* Paris Review *Interviews*. Edited by George Plimpton. Viking Penguin, 375 Hudson St., New York, NY 10014. 1989.**

Sixteen poets, including Robert Frost, Allen Ginsburg, Anne Sexton and John Ashbery, talk here about their writing and their lives. Another focused Plimpton collection, *Women Writers at Work*, is also available from Viking Penguin.

***The Poet's Craft: Interviews from* The New York Quarterly. Edited by William Packard. Paragon House Publishers, 90 Fifth Avenue, New York, NY 10011. 1987.**

Richard Wilbur, Diane Wakoski, Erica Jong and Gary Snyder are among the twenty-five poets who share views and experiences in Packard's collection.

Poynter, Dan, and Mindy Bingham. *Is There a Book Inside You? A Step-By-Step Plan for Writing Your Book*. **Para Publishing, P.O. Box 4232, Santa Barbara, CA 93140-4232. Third edition, 1991.**

If you're intrigued by the question the title poses and not sure what the answer is in your case, use the exercises here to find out.

Rico, Gabriele Lusser. *Writing the Natural Way: Using Right-Brain Techniques to Release Your Expressive Powers*. **Jeremy P. Tarcher, Inc., 5858 Wilshire Boulevard, Suite 200, Los Angeles, CA 90036. 1983.**

Gabriele Lusser Rico offers undergraduates and others a system designed to foster self-expression.

Rivers, William L. *Finding Facts: Interviewing, Observing, Using Reference Sources*. **Prentice-Hall, One Gulf + Western Plaza, New York, NY 10023. 1975.**

A brilliant discussion—with persuasive examples—of the elusiveness of truth and the power of perception to distort, this makes an excellent complement to Alden Todd's *Finding Facts Fast* (see below).

Rivers, William L. *Writing Opinion: Reviews*. Iowa State University Press, 2121 South State Avenue, Ames, Iowa 50010. 1988.

You can count on Rivers for good advice and examples. See especially his chapter on book reviews if you like the idea of compiling credits by writing them.

* Roberts, Ellen E. M. *The Children's Picture Book: How to Write It, How to Sell It*. Writer's Digest Books, 1507 Dana Avenue, Cincinnati, OH 45207. 1981.

You don't just get detailed, practical guidance from Ellen Roberts's handsome, illustrated book; you also get the heartwarming feeling that this canny, experienced children's book editor wants to see you create a picture book that's as good—and as successful—as you can possibly make it. Highly recommended. (*See also* Litowinsky in "A Foot in the Door Resources.")

Seuling, Barbara. *How to Write a Children's Book and Get It Published*. Scribners, 866 Third Avenue, New York, NY 10022. Revised edition, 1991.

Knowledgeable, encouraging, step-by-step guidance for beginners.

Shelnutt, Eve. *The Writing Room: Keys to the Craft of Fiction and Poetry*. Longstreet Press, 2150 Newmarket Parkway, Suite 102, Marietta, GA 30067. 1989.

An accomplished writer and teacher interweaves essays, stories and poems by "writers in the process of development and change" to illuminate useful ways of thinking about writing.

* Strunk, William, Jr., and E. B. White. *The Elements of Style*. Macmillan, 866 Third Avenue, New York, NY 10022. Third edition, 1979.

By now this collection of clearly and amusingly written "rules" of style is considered virtually sacrosanct. A valuable and thoroughly enjoyable classic.

* Todd, Alden. *Finding Facts Fast: How to Find Out What You Want and Need to Know*. Ten Speed Press, P.O. Box 7123, Berkeley, CA 94707. Second edition, 1979.

As this entire "Resources" section demonstrates, there's no dearth of places, people and publications to consult when you're in need of information. In fact, your major problem may be selecting wisely from among the available sources of data, and it's advice on this question that Todd gives in his remarkably thorough and readable manual. Highly recommended for anyone whose writing projects include research.

Ueland, Brenda. *If You Want to Write.* **Graywolf Press, P.O. Box 75006, St. Paul, MN 55175. Second edition, 1987.**

"Everybody is talented, original and has something important to say." That's Brenda Ueland's position, based on her experiences as a writer and a writing teacher. First published in 1938, *If You Want to Write* dispenses courage as well as advice. Most useful for fiction.

Ullmann, John, and Jan Colbert. *The Reporter's Handbook: An Investigator's Guide to Documents and Techniques.* **St. Martin's Press, 175 Fifth Avenue, New York, NY 10010. Second edition, 1991.**

Investigative reporters share hard-won know-how. This authoritative, admirably organized volume is packed with information.

Vargas Llosa, Mario. *A Writer's Reality.* **Syracuse University Press, 1600 Jamesville Avenue, Syracuse, NY 13244-5160. 1991.**

Eight incisive lectures by the author of *Aunt Julia and the Scriptwriter* and other acclaimed novels.

Venolia, Jan. *Write Right! A Desktop Digest of Punctuation, Grammar, and Style.* **Ten Speed Press/Periwinkle Press, P.O. Box 7123, Berkeley, CA 94707. Revised edition, 1988.**

A chatty, well-organized handbook.

Wallace, Robert. *Writing Poems.* **Scott, Foresman, 1900 E. Lake Avenue, Glenview, IL 60025. Second edition, 1987.**

This rich, inventive and encouraging book is designed to "provide the circumstances" that foster learning for poets. Focusing on form, content and process, Wallace writes with grace and sophistication about work by many contemporary poets, including himself and some of his students. And he provides excellent exercises in his "Questions and Suggestions" sections.

Weiss, Jason. *Writing at Risk: Interviews in Paris with Uncommon Writers.* **University of Iowa Press, 119 West Park Road, Iowa City, IA 52242. 1991.**

Julio Cortazar, Eugene Ionesco, Milan Kundera and Nathalie Sarraute are among Weiss's subjects, and they have something important in common, he believes: "public approval placed a distant second for these artists compared to the stages of understanding achieved."

Welty, Eudora. *One Writer's Beginnings*. **Warner Books, 1271 Sixth Avenue, New York, NY 10020. 1984.**

Eudora Welty's charming memoirs illuminate a fiction writer's mind-set.

Wooley, Catherine. *Writing for Children*. **NAL Books. 375 Hudson Street, New York, NY 10014. 1989.**

Lessons from a lifetime of writing children's books. Wooley has had dozens published, some under her own name and some as Jane Thayer.

The Writer. **The Writer, Inc., 120 Boylston Street, Boston, MA 02116-4615. Published monthly.**

This venerable magazine features instructive essays by published writers along with news tidbits and lists of special-interest markets. The Writer also publishes books for beginning writers. Send for information.

The Writer's Chapbook. **Edited by George Plimpton. Viking, 40 West 23 Street, New York, NY 10010. 1989.**

Plimpton has organized material from 120 *Paris Review* interviews under several dozen subjects—"On Work Habits," "On Symbols," "On Potboilers" . . . Writers quoted include Hersey, Heller and Huxley.

Writer's Digest.

See "Advice, Analysis and Reportage" in "A Foot in the Door Resources."

* *A Writer's Guide to Copyright*. **Poets & Writers, Inc., 72 Spring Street, New York, NY 10012. Second edition, 1989.**

A clear, concise, inexpensive guide, complete with a copyright checklist, and sample forms, including a Random House contract.

The Writer's Quotation Book: A Literary Companion. **Edited by James Charlton. The Pushcart Press, P.O. Box 380, Wainscott, NY 11975. Third Edition, 1991.**

Stylish insights into writing from leading writers of yesterday and today. The editor's juxtapositions add to the appeal. Consider, for instance: "Anything that is written to please the author is worthless" (Blaise Pascal) followed immediately by "Any writer overwhelmingly honest about pleasing himself is almost sure to please others" (Marianne Moore).

◆ Zinsser, William. *On Writing Well: An Informal Guide to Writing Nonfiction.* HarperCollins, 10 East 53 Street, New York, NY 10022. Fourth edition, 1990.

Zinsser is not only a good teacher; he's wonderful company as he explains and exemplifies style, audience, interviews, business writing and other aspects of the writer's craft.

Zinsser, William. *Writing with a Word Processor.* HarperCollins, 10 East 53 Street, New York, NY 10022. 1983.

If you're opposed to writing on a computer, let William Zinsser give you the whole story of why and how even a "mechanical boob" learned to love word processing.

Tools

AWP Official Guide to Writing Programs. Associated Writing Programs/Dustbooks, P.O. Box 100, Paradise, CA 95967. Updated periodically.

Writing programs throughout the U.S. and Canada are described here.

Chase's Annual Events. Contemporary Books, 180 North Michigan Avenue, Chicago, IL 60601. Updated annually.

Fun to read and useful for finding news pegs on which to hang light pieces for hometown papers or small magazines, the calendar created by William and Helen Chase will also alert you to upcoming fairs, conventions and exhibits that might be worth covering or simply attending. Over 10,000 entries in all.

"Directory of Accredited Home Study Schools." National Home Study Council, 1601 18th Street, NW, Washington, DC 20009. Updated periodically.

Before you sign up for a home study program, write for this free list.

A Directory of American Poets and Fiction Writers. Poets & Writers, Inc., 72 Spring Street, New York, NY 10012. Updated periodically.

Unlike most directories of contemporary writers, this one is inexpensive enough so that you can own it yourself. More than 6,000 entries (Saul Bellow, Anne Tyler and John Irving . . .) include addresses and phone numbers. A good tool for contacting professional writers.

Directory of Special Libraries and Information Centers. **Edited by Janice A. DeMaggio. Gale Research Inc., P.O. Box 33477. Detroit, MI 48232-5477. Updated periodically.**

Check the index for troves of information on the subject you're researching.

"Editorial Services," *Literary Market Place* **(see below).**

Plenty of professional writers are ready to give you a hand in expressing what you have to say, and this list will lead you to a number of them. In approaching a potential collaborator, be sure to ask for an estimate and to check references. *See also* Editorial Freelancers Association, below.

Encyclopedia of Associations. **Edited by Deborah M. Burek. Gale Research Inc., P.O. Box 33477. Detroit, MI 48232-5477. Updated periodically.**

The roughly 20,000 organizations and reference centers listed here can supply information and leads on almost any topic. Indexed in terms of geography as well as area of interest, entries are extremely informative.

Gale Research Inc. Catalog. **Gale Research Inc., P.O. Box 33477. Detroit, MI 48232-5477.**

This free catalog will familiarize you with a wide variety of reference books that will help you in all kinds of research.

Guide to Reference Books. **Edited by Eugene P. Sheehy. American Library Association, 50 East Huron Street, Chicago, IL 60611. Updated periodically.**

The ultimate reference book: 14,000 titles are categorized and clearly described. Available at your library.

The Guide to Writers Conferences. **Shaw Associates, 625 Biltmore Way, Suite 1406, Coral Gables, FL 33134. Updated periodically.**

Workshops, retreats, residencies and writers organizations are covered too, and the lengthy list of conferences is indexed in several useful ways. *See also* Writers Conferences, below.

The Independent Study Catalog: NUCEA's Guide to Independent Study Through Correspondence Instruction. **Edited by John H. Wells and Barbara C. Ready. Peterson's Guides, Box 2123, Princeton, NJ 08543-2123; 800-EDU-DATA. Updated periodically.**

Information about 10,000 high-school, college and graduate courses from The National University Continuing Education Association.

Lesko, Matthew. *Information U.S.A.* **Viking Penguin, 375 Hudson Street, New York, NY 10014. Updated periodically.**

Lesko's theory is that someone somewhere in the government can tell you anything you need to know. Use this hefty directory to get to the right sources for your work as efficiently as possible.

Literary Market Place. **R. R. Bowker, 121 Chanlon Road, New Providence, NJ 07974. Updated annually.**

As subsequent "Resources" entries will show, *LMP* has many virtues. In connection with writing, its most useful sections are "Courses for the Book Trade" (which lists programs that teach publishing skills along with programs that teach writing) and "Writers' Conferences & Workshops" (which provides a small list of the perennials that you should supplement; *see The Guide to Writers Conferences*, above, and *Writers Conferences*, below).

Oryx Press Catalog, **4041 North Central, Phoenix, AZ 85012-3397; 800-279-ORYX; fax: 800-279-4663.**

Oryx Press publishes a number of useful books for people who write on science and technology, and when you buy them by mail you get a money-back guarantee.

Readers' Guide to Periodical Literature. **H. W. Wilson Company, 950 University Avenue, Bronx, NY 10452. Updated periodically.**

The leading bibliography of articles from mass-circulation and other fairly general magazines, the *Readers' Guide* is useful for tracking down a piece you read some time ago that's relevant now to your work; for finding out what's appeared in the periodical press about a subject you're investigating; and for introducing yourself to varied angles on the same topic (*see* "Basics"). To get the most mileage from this guide, be sure to look under every subject heading that might possibly pertain to your needs.

Research Centers Directory. **Edited by Karen Hill. Gale Research Inc., P.O. Box 33477. Detroit, MI 48232-5477. Updated periodically.**

A guide to university-related and other nonprofit research organizations, this directory supplies excellent leads to experts and expertise. Use the subject index.

Statistics Sources. Edited by Jacqueline Wasserman O'Brien and Steven R. Wasserman. Gale Research Inc., P.O. Box 33477. Detroit, MI 48232-5477. Updated periodically.

Arranged by subject, *Statistics Sources* will tell you where to find organizations and publications that can supply data you need.

Subject Guide to Books in Print. R. R. Bowker, 121 Chanlon Road, New Providence, NJ 07974. Updated annually.

To get a good idea of what's already been written about your subject, consult this compilation. Useful for a style survey as well as for research leads, the *Subject Guide* is on hand at most libraries.

* Swidan, Eleanor A. *Reference Sources: A Brief Guide*. Enoch Pratt Free Library, Publications Office, 400 Cathedral Street, Baltimore, MD 21201-4484. Updated periodically.

A superb introduction to the best reference sources, divided into general and special subject categories. The annotated listings should give reference-room users confidence that they'll be able to ferret out whatever facts they're after.

The Writer's Advisor. Compiled by Leland G. Alkire, Jr. Gale Research Inc., P.O. Box 33477. Detroit, MI 48232-5477. 1985.

Annotated listings of approximately 800 books and 3,000 articles on varied aspects of writing, from "Characterization, Voice, and Viewpoint" to "Tax Considerations."

Writers Conferences. Poets & Writers, 72 Spring Street, New York, NY 10012. Updated annually; issued in March.

Look here for information on approximately 200 writers conferences in the U.S. and overseas.

The Writers Directory. St. James Press, 233 East Ontario Street, Chicago, IL 60611. Updated periodically.

Brief biographies, with addresses, of more than 15,000 writers who have had at least one full-length work published in English. Get hold of this directory at the library to track down professional writers you'd like to contact, and check its subject index to add to your list.

People, Places and Programs

Associated Writing Programs, Old Dominion University, Norfolk, VA 23529-0079.
A clearinghouse for information, AWP puts out a newsletter and a catalog of writing programs, presents awards and publishes work by outstanding student writers. *See* "Money Resources" for information on their placement service.

Dial-a-Writer Referral Service, American Society of Journalists and Authors, 1501 Broadway, Suite 302, New York, NY 10036; 212-997-0947; fax: 212-768-7414.
Ask for help in locating potential co-authors in your area if you feel sure that your own efforts at composition are bound to be inadequate for one reason or another. When writers surface whom you might like to work with, study what they've already published, ask for and check their references and draw up a written agreement specifying the terms of the deal with you.

Editorial Freelancers Association, Inc., P.O. Box 2050, Madison Square Station, New York, NY 10159; 212-677-3357.
You may find just the right editor, collaborator or ghostwriter by using the EFA's Job Phone. As above, remember to ask for writing samples, to get and check references and to be clear about the deal you're making.

International Women's Writing Guild, Box 810, Gracie Station, New York, NY 10028.
"An alliance open to all women connected to the written word," the Guild aims to encourage and support both published and aspiring writers through (among other things) its newsletter, its annual conference at Skidmore College and its programs elsewhere in the U.S. and abroad.

The Poetry Project, St. Mark's Church, 131 East 10 Street, New York, NY 10003; 212-674-0910.
Members get invited to readings and workshops featuring writers such as Kenneth Koch, Elmore Leonard and John Ashbery.

✱ **Poets & Writers, Inc., 72 Spring Street, New York, NY 10012; 212-226-3586.**

The people at Poets & Writers have figured out lots of ways to improve the quality of a writer's life. The group's publications are designed especially for writers of fiction and poetry but they're helpful to writers of all sorts. Among them are *Poets & Writers Magazine* and the *Directory of American Poets and Fiction Writers*. Send for the informational brochure, and if you write fiction or poetry ask to be listed in the next edition of the directory.

Tools of the Trade: Books for Communicators, P.O. Box 12093, Seminary Post Office, Alexandria, VA 22304; 703-683-4186; fax: 703-683-5837.

One-stop shopping from home for many or most of the books you'll find listed below. Miriam Ross keeps more than 1,000 titles in stock and will be glad to order others that you want. Write for details.

U.S. government.

A prime source of information on countless subjects. Write to the public relations staff of appropriate departments to request help in getting the data you want and *see* Lesko's *Information U.S.A.*, above.

The Writers Room, Inc., 153 Waverly Place, New York, NY 10014; 212-807-9519.

Dozens of writers rent space at modest rates in New York City's Writers Room, which functions as a support system and a grapevine as well as an office. Interested writers in the New York area are invited to send for applications. If you live elsewhere, check around for a comparable facility, and if you can't find one, think about asking the New York room's board of directors for guidance on setting one up.

A Foot in the Door Resources

S INCE MAKING SALES to publishers depends on who you know, what you know and how you present each project, many of the resources mentioned here are designed to serve as introductions not only to markets but to people and procedures you'll find helpful as you approach publishing firms.

Advice, Analysis and Reportage

Adams, Jane. *How to Sell What You Write.* **Putnam/Perigee, 200 Madison Avenue, New York, NY 10016. 1984.**

Adams advises writers to think of their work as Product created for two different markets—the publishers or producers, whom she calls Buyers, and the readers, or Customers. It's a sound schematic, well worth keeping in mind. *See also* her pointers on reaching many markets with variants of the same material.

Allen, Linda Buchanan. *Write and Sell Your Free-Lance Article.* **The Writer, Inc., 120 Boylston Street, Boston, MA 02116. 1991.**

A friendly primer by a freelancer who specializes in writing about the environment and outdoor activity.

Book Publishing Career Directory. **Edited by Ronald W. Fry. Gale Research, Inc., P.O. Box 33477, Detroit, MI 48232-5477. Updated periodically.**

Reports by insiders about what kind of work they do and about breaking in to their special areas. Informative and generally encouraging.

Burgett, Gordon. *How to Sell More Than 75% of Your Freelance Writing*. Prima Publishing and Communications, P.O. Box 1260B1, Rocklin, CA 95677. 1990.

By using queries, concentrating on nonfiction and submitting to several editors simultaneously, that's how. Burgett, who has lots of publication credits himself, has done several books on selling written work and offers seminars on the subject.

The Business of Book Publishing: Papers by Practitioners. Edited by Elizabeth A. Geiser and Arnold Dolin, with Gladys S. Topkis. Westview Press, 5500 Central Avenue, Boulder, CO 80301-2847. 1985.

This anthology stems from the solid, stimulating Publishing Institute held each summer at the University of Denver (see below).

Coser, Lewis A., Charles Kadushin and Walter W. Powell. *Books: The Culture and Commerce of Publishing*. University of Chicago Press, 5801 South Ellis Avenue, Chicago IL 60637. 1982.

Based in large part on interviews with eighty-five editors from fifty-six houses (most of them in the New York metropolitan area), this sociological analysis of book publishing has some interesting observations to offer—among them, the finding that only 25 percent of the new authors at trade houses in the sample made their initial contacts with their publishers through agents.

Curtis, Richard. *How to Be Your Own Literary Agent: The Business of Getting Your Book Published*. Houghton Mifflin, One Beacon Street, Boston, MA 02108. 1984.

Curtis, who's both an agent and an author, is spunky and candid about dealing with large mainstream book publishers. *How to Be a Savvy, Helpful Client of a Literary Agent or a Literary Property Lawyer* would be a better title for his book, though, since it isn't smart for writers to represent themselves in negotiations with big firms.

Day, Robert A. *How to Write & Publish a Scientific Paper*. Oryx Press, 4041 North Central at Indian School Road, Phoenix, AZ 85012. Third edition, 1988.

Knowledgeable and readable.

Freelance Writer's Report. Cassell Communications, P.O. Box 9844, Fort Lauderdale, FL 33310; 305-485-0795. Published monthly.

Dana Cassell's lively, durable newsletter is packed with short, informative items. *The Fiction Writer*, a new quarterly magazine from the same publisher, premiered in 1991.

Hinckley, Karen, and Barbara Hinckley. *American Best Sellers: A Reader's Guide to Popular Fiction.* **Indiana University Press, Tenth and Morton Streets, Bloomington, IN 47405. 1989.**

A mother and daughter team not only list and describe bestsellers from the '60s to the '80s; they analyze the books in terms of authors, categories, characters and themes. A fascinating compilation.

Litowinsky, Olga. *Writing and Publishing Books for Children in the 1990s: The Inside Story from the Editor's Desk.* **Walker and Company, 720 Fifth Avenue, New York, NY 10019. 1992.**

This particular editor's desk was situated variously at Delacorte, Scribners, Viking Penguin and Macmillan. Her advice covers books for young people at all age levels and she offers interesting observations about trends.

Luey, Beth. *Handbook for Academic Authors.* **Cambridge University Press, 40 West 20 Street, New York, NY 10011. Second edition, 1990.**

A comprehensive, comprehensible guide for anyone working on articles for scholarly journals or textbooks and other books for the academic market. Luey, a writer, scholar and sometime publisher herself, is the editor of *Publishing Research Quarterly.*

Magazines Career Directory. **Edited by Ronald W. Fry. Gale Research, Inc., P.O. Box 33477, Detroit MI 48232-5477. Updated periodically.**

Tips from people who work at magazines big and small about what kinds of jobs exist and how to get them.

Newspapers Career Directory. **Edited by Ronald W. Fry. Gale Research, Inc., P.O. Box 33477, Detroit MI 48232-5477. Updated periodically.**

Like the other volumes (on books and magazines) in the Career Directory series, this one offers advice from practitioners on a wide range of job opportunities.

Parsons, Paul. *Getting Published: The Acquisition Process at University Presses.* **University of Tennessee Press, Knoxville, TN 37996-0325. 1989.**
Skillful reportage, using insiders' testimony, about how university presses of various sorts decide what to publish.

Poet. P.O. Box 54947, Oklahoma City, OK 73154. Published four times a year.
Peggy Cooper's lively magazine includes how-to and reportorial pieces, lists of grants and awards and book reviews, plus, of course, poetry.

* *Poets & Writers Magazine.* **Poets & Writers, Inc., 72 Spring Street, New York, NY 10012. Published bimonthly.**
Along with timely, solid information (when and how to apply for grants and awards, what various writers' colonies offer, where to find fellow writers in your area), *Poets & Writers Magazine* has feature stories that shed light both on creating prose and poetry and on attracting readers to written work.

Powell, Walter W. *Getting into Print: The Decision-Making Process in Scholarly Publishing.* **University of Chicago Press, 5801 South Ellis Avenue, Chicago, IL 60637. 1985.**
Focusing on two scholarly presses that he observed closely, Powell punctures publishing myths and reveals realities. His trenchant observations conclude with a skippable chapter on organizational theory.

Sautter, Carl. *How to Sell Your Screenplay: The Real Rules of Film and Television.* **New Chapter Press, Inc., Old Pound Road, Pound Ridge, NY 10576. Second edition, 1992.**
Sautter, who co-authored the much-praised "black-and-white" episode of "Moonlighting," offers detailed advice on how to become a screenwriter. Consistently entertaining as well as admirably instructive.

Scribner, Charles, Jr. *In the Company of Writers: A Life in Publishing.* **Scribners, 866 Third Avenue, New York, NY 10022. 1990.**
Derived from an oral history by Joel R. Gardner, this modest autobiography by a scion of the Scribner family provides glimpses of editors and writers in action.

Tebbel, John. *Between Covers: The Rise and Transformation of Book Publishing in America*. Oxford University Press, 200 Madison Avenue, New York, NY 10016. 1987.

The one-volume edition of Tebbel's classic four-volume *History of Book Publishing* starts with the seventeenth century, goes through the 1970s and focuses mainly on large trade publishing houses. A brief final chapter sketches the publishing landscape in the mid-'80s.

Tebbel, John, and Mary Ellen Zuckerman. *The Magazine in America: 1741–1990*. Oxford University Press, 200 Madison Avenue, New York, NY 10016. 1991.

Readable and remarkably thorough, *The Magazine in America* concentrates on 20th-century periodicals—the people and purposes behind them and the trends they mirrored and fueled.

West, Michelle. *The No-Bull Guide to Getting Published and Making It as a Writer*. Winslow Publishing, Box 38012, 550 Eglinton Avenue W., Toronto, Ontario M5N 3 A8, Canada. 1986.

Advice full of energy on writing for magazines.

The Writer.
See "Getting the Words Right Resources."

Writer's Digest, 1507 Dana Avenue, Cincinnati, OH 45207. Published monthly.

Geared primarily to beginners, the articles in *Writer's Digest* sometimes promise more than they can deliver. On the other hand, there's savvy guidance in here too. Read skeptically and you'll be able to separate the practical advice from the puffery.

The Writer's Handbook. Edited by Sylvia K. Burack. The Writer, Inc., 120 Boylston Street, Boston, MA 02116. Updated periodically.

A raft of well-known writers, editors and agents have contributed tips to this compilation, and a list of more than 2,000 markets is in it too.

Writer's Yearbook. Writer's Digest, 1507 Dana Avenue, Cincinnati, OH 45207. Published annually.

The *Yearbook* is essentially a fatter-than-normal issue of the monthly *Writer's Digest*.

Tools

The Bloomsbury Review: A Book Magazine, Owaissa Communications Co., Inc., 1028 Bannock Street, Denver, CO 80204. Published bi-monthly.

A lively periodical that provides a wider window on the world of books than more renowned review media.

Booklist. American Library Association, 50 East Huron Street, Chicago, IL 60611. Published twice monthly September–June, monthly July–August.

Together with *Choice* and *Library Journal* (both of which are listed below), *Booklist* exerts a great deal of influence on librarians as they ponder what books to buy. Skimming its reviews, you can begin to sense the patterns of public taste that libraries both reflect and help to create.

Book Review Digest. The H. W. Wilson Company, 950 University Avenue, Bronx, NY 10452-9978. Published periodically.

Tidbits from reviews of some 6,000 books a year appear here. Check to see (1) how critics reacted to recent books like yours and (2) which of them might be especially receptive to your work.

Bowker Catalog. R. R. Bowker, 121 Chanlon Road, New Providence, NJ 07974. Free on request.

Bowker codifies and disseminates information about publishing. Simply looking at the products in the catalog should give you fresh ideas about placement, and perhaps you'll also want to get hold of some of the reference works.

Chase's Annual Events.

See "Getting the Words Right Resources."

Choice. Association of College and Research Libraries, American Library Association, 100 Riverview Center, Middletown, CT 06457. Published monthly except combined in July and August.

See *Booklist*, above, and get hold of a copy.

Clardy, Andrea Fleck. *Words to the Wise: A Writer's Guide to Feminist and Lesbian Periodicals & Publishers.* Firebrand Books, 141 The Commons, Ithaca, NY 14850. Updated periodically.

If you've written anything for a feminist and/or lesbian audience, use this informative annotated guide. It covers more than 150 book and periodical publishers.

COSMEP Newsletter. **COSMEP, The International Association of Independent Publishers, P.O. Box 420703, San Francisco, CA 94142-0703. Published monthly.**

COSMEP's newsletter provides views of the tastes and needs of hundreds of small publishers. If your library doesn't subscribe, write for information on how you can.

DeFrancis, Beth. *The Writer's Guide to Metropolitan Washington: Where to Sell What You Write.* **Woodbine House, 5615 Fishers Lane, Rockville, MD 20852; 800-843-7323. 1991.**

You don't have to be in Washington to benefit from this book. Published with Washington Independent Writers, it describes associations, packagers, businesses and government bodies as well as publishers per se in and around the nation's capital who might buy what you have to sell.

Directory of Literary Magazines. **Moyer Bell Ltd., Colonial Hill/ RFD 1, Mt. Kisco, NY 10549. Updated periodically.**

Prepared in cooperation with the Council of Literary Magazines and Presses, this new directory covers roughly 500 periodicals around the country that publish fiction, nonfiction and poetry.

Directory of Poetry Publishers. **Dustbooks, P.O. Box 100, Paradise, CA 95967; 800-477-6110. Updated periodically.**

Detailed listings describe more than 2,000 magazines and publishing houses that welcome poetry, and there's a useful subject index.

Editor & Publisher International Year Book. **Editor & Publisher, 11 West 19th Street, New York, NY 10011-4234. Updated annually.**

This directory of newspapers names department heads and gives circulation figures and other valuable data for each entry. Useful for selling stories with a local slant.

✳ *Gale Directory of Publications and Broadcast Media.* **Edited by Karen E. Koek and Julie Winklepleck. Gale Research Inc, P.O. Box 33477, Detroit, MI 48232-5477. Updated periodically.**

Annotated listings of thousands of newspapers, magazines, trade publications, radio and TV stations and cable companies, arranged by geographic location and indexed by key words. One or more of these entries may make good targets for material with a special-interest focus or a pronounced local slant.

Gentz, William H. *Religious Writers Marketplace*. Running Press, 125 South Twenty-second Street, Philadelphia, PA 19103. Third edition, 1989.

An exemplary directory, this covers radio, TV and movies along with periodicals and book publishers of all sorts serving varied denominations. Short intelligent essays complement the well-organized, well annotated listings.

***The Guide to Writers Conferences*. Shaw Associates, 625 Biltmore Way, Coral Gables, FL 33134. Updated periodically.**

Retreats, residencies and organizations are listed along with conferences, and there are several useful appendixes, including a conference calendar, geographic and subject indexes, and a list of conferences that give scholarships. Thorough and easy to use. *See also Writers Conferences*, below.

Herman, Jeff. *Insider's Guide to Book Editors, Publishers, and Literary Agents, 1992–1993*. Prima Publishing and Communications, P.O. Box 126OJHB, Rocklin, CA 95677. 1992.

Virtually the only place you'll find descriptive material about editor after editor, Herman's book also offers essays, sample agreements and generously annotated listings of selected agents. (Remember to check that any editor you target hasn't moved since the book came out.)

***The Horn Book,* 14 Beacon Street, Boston, MA 02108. Published bimonthly.**

Like *School Library Journal*, below, this is a major review periodical for children's books.

***Hudson's Subscription Newsletter Directory*. Hudson's Media Directories, 44 West Market Street, P.O. Box 311, Rhinebeck, NY 12572. Updated periodically.**

Browse through your library's copy to see if you can find markets for your work among the thousands of newsletters listed here and indexed by subject.

International Directory of Little Magazines and Small Presses. Edited by Len Fulton. Dustbooks, P.O. Box 100, Paradise, CA 95967; 800-477-6110. Updated periodically.

Descriptions of 5,000 markets appear in this affordable paperback, and its geographic and subject indexes make appropriate people easy to target.

Journalism Career and Scholarship Guide. Dow Jones Newspaper Fund, P.O. Box 300, Princeton, NJ 08543-0300. Updated periodically.

A fund of information for people interested in becoming journalists.

Library Journal, P.O. Box 1977, Marion, OH 43305. Published twice monthly with certain double issues.

See Booklist, above.

Literary Agents of North America: The Complete Guide to U.S. and Canadian Literary Agencies. Author Aid/Research Associates International, 340 East 52nd Street, New York, NY 10022. Updated periodically.

More than 1,000 agents are listed, some with richly detailed write-ups; some with simple bare-bones facts. This directory's five indexes—subject, policy, size, geographical location and people—make it an unusually useful volume, provided you remember that an agent isn't essential.

❋ *Literary Market Place.* R. R. Bowker, 121 Chanlon Road, New Providence, NJ 07974. Updated annually.

As noted in "Getting the Words Right Resources," *LMP* is an indispensable reference work. When you're working on getting your foot in the door, study the following sections:"U.S. Book Publishers" (note especially the subject listing, which, although general, is handy, and the geographical location listing, which is a gold mine of good leads, particularly for regional books); "Reference Books for the Trade" (here you'll find specialized titles that may be relevant to your current work, along with leads to books about the publishing industry); "Literary Awards, Contests & Grants" (if you win, you'll have acquired credentials that editors will respect); "Writers' Conferences & Workshops" (a partial but useful listing); "Literary Agents" (with names, addresses, phone numbers and some annotations); "Courses for the Book Trade" and "Employment Agencies" (specializing in publishing positions).

News Inc., **49 East 21 Street, New York, NY 10010. Published monthly except during the summer.**

A magazine about newspapers that focuses mainly on business issues. Creative browsing may give you some insights into editorial needs and personnel, however.

Newsletters in Print. **Edited by Brigitte T. Darnay. Gale Research, Inc. P.O. Box 33477, Detroit, MI 48232-5477.**

Ten thousand places to look for information—and for buyers of your information.

PMA Newsletter. **Publishers Marketing Association, 2401 Pacific Coast Highway, Suite 102, Hermosa Beach, CA 90254; 213-372-2732; fax: 213-374-3342. Published monthly.**

Like the *COSMEP Newsletter* (see above), PMA's periodical will introduce you to many interesting publishers and publishing possibilities.

Poet's Market: Where & How to Publish Your Poetry. **Edited by Judson Jerome et al. Writer's Digest Books, 1507 Dana Avenue, Cincinnati, OH 45207. Updated annually.**

Unusually informative listings cover 1,700 publications. To make this directory even more enlightening, the editors include short, chatty "close-ups" of a dozen poetry publishers and information about poets' resources—contests, grants, conferences, colonies, organizations and the like.

Publishers Directory. **Edited by Thomas M. Bachmann. Gale Research Inc., P.O. Box 33477, Detroit, MI 48232-5477. Updated periodically.**

Roughly 20,000 small and specialized publishers are listed. Try your library for a copy.

Publishers' Trade List Annual. **R. R. Bowker, 121 Chanlon Road, New Providence, NJ 07974. Updated annually.**

Browsing through these volumes—which offer a huge collection of current book catalogs—can lead to worthwhile discoveries about the strengths, weaknesses and idiosyncrasies of individual houses. Probably the most comprehensive introduction anywhere to the personalities of individual houses and imprints.

✳ *Publishers Weekly,* **249 West 17th Street, New York, NY 10011.**

PW, as it's familiarly known, has no equal as a source of up-to-date information about book publishing facts, figures, ideas and individuals. You can arrange to join the insiders who read it regularly by using your library's subscription copies or by subscribing yourself.Although it's aimed primarily at people who work with books, it frequently announces new periodicals, which provide promising markets (*see Samir Husni's Guide to New Magazines,* below).

The Pushcart Prize: Best of the Small Presses. Edited by Bill Henderson. Pushcart Press, P.O. Box 380, Wainscott, NY 11975. Published annually.

Look to the latest volumes of Bill Henderson's anthology not only for fine poetry and prose but also for insight into what literary publishers are currently enthusiastic about.

Rotten Rejections: A Literary Companion. Edited by André Bernard. Pushcart Press, P.O. Box 380, Wainscott, NY 11975. 1990.

A great pick-me-up for those times when turndowns get you down. *Rotten Rejections* shows you what editors said as they spurned *The Clan of the Cave Bear, The Spy Who Came in from the Cold* and a host of other titles they must have gone on to kick themselves about.

Readers' Guide to Periodical Literature. The H. W. Wilson Company, 950 University Avenue, Bronx, NY 10452-9978. Updated periodically.

Available in libraries, this standard and invaluable reference tool covers a variety of popular magazines. Use the subject headings to identify those that are likely to want your work and then tap the library's resources again to read a few issues and familiarize yourself with their style and their slant.

Samir Husni's Guide to New Magazines. Dept. of Journalism, The University of Mississippi, University, MS 38677. Published annually.

Organized by subject category, Husni's 1991 edition covered 536 periodicals born in 1990. It's well worth checking out the latest version because magazines are usually hungrier for material when they're new than they are after they've become known.

School Library Journal, P.O. Box 1978, Marion, OH 43305. **Published monthly.**

An excellent way to get an overview of current children's books and what librarians think of them.

Small Press: The Magazine of Independent Publishing. **Small Press, Inc., Colonial Hill/RFD 1, Mt. Kisco, NY 10549-9871. Published bimonthly.**

Lively reading with good leads to smaller publishing companies that may be right for your work and able to do a good job with it. Read author bios with as much care as the articles themselves.

Standard Periodical Directory. **Edited by Matthew Manning. Gale Research, Inc. P.O. Box 33477, Detroit, MI 48232-5477. Updated periodically.**

Listings arranged by subject cover 65,000 periodicals in the U.S. and Canada.

Story, **P.O. Box 396, Mt. Morris, IL 61054. Published quarterly.**

Richard and Lois Rosenthal have revived *Story* magazine to publish short fiction and nothing but short fiction.

✻ *Subject Guide to Books in Print.* **R. R. Bowker, 121 Chanlon Road, New Providence, NJ 07974. Updated annually.**

Try your local bookstore or library for copies of these volumes. They're excellent tools both for trend spotting and for manuscript marketing.

✻ *Subject Guide to Children's Books in Print.* **R. R. Bowker, 121 Chanlon Road, New Providence, NJ 07974. Updated periodically.**

Thousands of titles—fiction and nonfiction—are indexed here. A good way to identify kindred spirits at publishing houses if you write for kids.

Tarila, Sophia, *New Marketing Opportunities.* **First Editions, P.O. Box 2578, Sedona, AZ 86336. 1990.**

Are the readers you seek part of the "New Age" market? If so, consult this two-volume directory of conduits to them.

Utne Reader. **P.O. Box 1974, Marion, OH 43306-4074. Published bimonthly.**

Composed of material from the "alternative press," the *Utne Reader* can introduce you to ideas that differ from, and perhaps foreshadow, what you'll find in mainstream periodicals.

Wrenn, Jenny. *Guide to Women Book Publishers in the United States for 1990*. Clothespin Fever Press, 5529 N. Figeruoa, Los Angeles, CA 90042. 1990.

Women book publishers—feminist and otherwise—are listed here and indexed by subject specialty, location, ethnicity and contact person.

Writers Conferences. Poets & Writers, Inc., 72 Spring Street, New York, NY 10012. Published annually in March.

A guide to roughly 200 gatherings with terse, extremely informative listings. Once you've studied the descriptions, you can send for literature about the conferences that interest you most, and then—taking account of the topics, the speakers, the chances for getting criticism and the condition of your pocketbook—choose those that will serve your current needs best.

Writer's Digest Catalog. Writer's Digest Books, 1507 Dana Avenue, Cincinnati, OH 45207.

Get hold of this catalog to find specialized guides not reviewed here that are relevant to your work.

Writer's Market: Where & How to Sell What You Write. Writer's Digest Books, 1507 Dana Avenue, Cincinnati, OH 45207. Updated annually.

Writer's Market flags thousands of publishing opportunities. If you do a bit of extra investigating to learn more about the ones that seem relevant before you approach an editor, these leads should serve you well.

Writers Northwest Handbook. Media Weavers, Blue Heron Publishing, Inc., Route 3, Box 376, Hillsboro, OR 97124. Updated periodically.

Essays and tips accompany a lengthy list of markets—almost 2,800 publishers are active in the region.

Writer's Profit Catalog. 174 Holland Avenue, New Milford, NJ 07646.

Guidance for writers from Robert W. Bly, who focuses on marketing and moneymaking and produces books, short reports, cassettes and seminars. Send for his catalog to see which products might serve your needs.

People, Places and Programs

Association of Authors' Representatives, Inc., 10 Astor Place, Third Floor, New York, NY 10003; 212 353 3709.

Formed in 1991 when the SAR (Society of Authors Representatives) merged with ILAA (the Independent Literary Agents Association), the AAR is an organization of conscientious professionals. If you send them a stamped, self-addressed envelope, they'll send you a list of their members.

The Children's Book Council, 568 Broadway, Suite 404, New York, NY 10012; 212-966-1990.

Write to the CBC if you'd like a list of its members (publishers, editors and art directors) and/or brief descriptions of members' publishing programs. You'll need to enclose a self-addressed envelope with an ounce's worth of postage on it for the former and 2 ounces' worth for the latter.

Howard University Press Book Publishing Institute, 2900 Van Ness Street, NW, Washington, DC 20008; 202-806-8465; fax: 202-806-8474.

This intensive introduction to book publishing runs for five weeks during the summer. Send for a free descriptive brochure.

Mystery Writers of America, 17 East 47 Street, 6th Floor, New York, NY 10017; 212-888-8171.

Meetings and a newsletter are among the benefits MWA offers. If you write crime/mystery/suspense, you're eligible for membership. Send for the group's brochure.

Poets & Writers, Inc.
See "Getting the Words Right Resources."

Poets House, 72 Spring Street, Second Floor, New York, NY 10012; 212-431-7920.

A place to make contact with poets (*see* "The Sale and Its Sequels Resources"), and to become acquainted with the publishers who buy poetry. There's a sizable collection of books, periodicals and tapes too.

Publishing Institute, 2075 South University Blvd., D-114, Denver, CO 80210.

Run with zest and acumen by Elizabeth Geiser, this four-week summer program at the University of Denver offers much-praised workshops and lectures about varied aspects of book publishing, with a helpful dose of career counseling. Write for details and application forms.

Radcliffe Publishing Course, 77 Brattle Street, Cambridge, MA 02138; 617-495-8678; fax: 617-495-8422.

Another well-regarded program for people interested in training for publishing jobs, this summertime course takes six weeks and covers both book and magazine publishing.

Tools of the Trade.

One-stop shopping for the books listed here that you'd like to own. *See* "Getting the Words Right Resources."

Sensible Solutions, Inc., 275 Madison Avenue, Suite 1518, New York, NY 10016; 212-687-1761; fax: 212-986-3218.

A consulting firm headed by Judith Appelbaum and Florence Janovic, Sensible Solutions grew out of *How to Get Happily Published*. Its marketing plans are designed to help writers approach book publishers and—once books have been placed—to round up readers.

Society of Children's Book Writers, P.O. Box 66296, Mar Vista Station, Los Angeles, CA 90066.

Through its publications and gatherings, the SCBW serves editors, agents, librarians, teachers and producers who are involved with children's books, as well as people—published and unpublished—who write and illustrate them. The group also offers insurance and grants to members.

University of Chicago Publishing Program, University of Chicago Office of Continuing Education, Business and Professional Programs, 5835 S. Kimbark Avenue, Chicago, IL 60637.

Several courses focus on marketing manuscripts. Send for a catalog to see the specifics of what's offered.

The Sale and Its Sequels Resources

T O HELP YOUR work reach its best audience, it's wise to proceed as though you were responsible for getting it out to readers. Those of you who are ambitious, therefore, will want to study and use "The Self-Publishing Option Resources" along with books, periodicals, programs and people described below that meet your needs.

Advice, Analysis and Reportage

* Balkin, Richard. *A Writer's Guide to Contract Negotiations*. Writer's Digest Books, 1507 Dana Avenue, Cincinnati, OH 45207. 1985.

Candid, substantive guidance from a literary agent. *See also* Chasen and Norwick, Levine and the other legal guides listed in "Resources."

Barzun, Jacques. *On Writing, Editing, and Publishing: Essays Explicative and Hortatory*. University of Chicago Press, 5801 South Ellis Avenue, Chicago, IL 60637. Second edition, 1986.

Barzun's targets in these stylish pieces include over-reaching copy editors and talk-show hosts. The essays on writing and writer's block are especially interesting.

Bloch, Douglas (with Robert Brock). *Phone Power: How to Successfully Telemarket Your Product or Service*. Pallas Communications, 4226 NE 23rd Avenue, Portland, OR 97211. 1988.

Lots of sample scripts that you may be able to adapt.

Brent, Stuart. *The Seven Stairs.* **Simon & Schuster/Touchstone, 1230 Avenue of the Americas, New York, NY 10020. 1982.**

A charming memoir by the legendary, literary Chicago bookseller. It's fun to get to know him and enlightening to see the bookselling business through his eyes.

Bunnin, Brad, and Peter Beren. *The Writer's Legal Companion.* **Addison-Wesley, Route 128, Reading, MA 01867. 1988.**

Called *Author Law and Strategies* in its first incarnation, this self-help guide will alert you to legal issues and help you figure out what action, if any, to take about them.

Callenbach, Ernest. *Publisher's Lunch.* **Ten Speed Press. P.O. Box 7123. Berkeley, CA 94707. 1989.**

The form is fiction—about a man/woman, editor/author relationship developed through lunch-hour conversation—but you can learn a lot here about the facts of publishing life.

✱ **Chasen, Jerry Simon, and Kenneth P. Norwick.** *The Rights of Authors, Artists, and Other Creative People.* **Southern Illinois University Press, Box 3697, Carbondale, IL 62901. 1992.**

The best way to avoid legal problems and safeguard legal rights is to understand how the law actually works, and you will when you've read this book. Highly recommended. (*See also* Balkin, and Bunnin and Beren, above; Crawford and Levine, below, and legal guides listed in other "Resources" sections).

Crawford, Tad. *The Writer's Legal Guide.* **Allworth Press, 10 East 23 Street, Suite 400, New York, NY 10010. 1978.**

Comprehensive and readable, Crawford's book covers copyright, contracts, libel, obscenity and taxes, among other things. New developments have dated a couple of chapters, but this remains a useful introduction to the laws that affect writers.

Cuddihy, Michael. *Try Ironwood: An Editor Remembers.* **Rowan Tree Press, 124 Chestnut Street, Boston, MA 02108. 1990.**

Memoirs by the poet who became founder and editor of *Ironwood*, the literary magazine.

✱ **Dessauer, John P.** *Book Publishing: A Basic Introduction.* **Continuum Publishing Co., 370 Lexington Avenue, New York, NY 10017. 1989.**

This updated version of John P. Dessauer's classic work covers all facets of publishing and analyzes the way they relate to the wide world of readers.

Direct Mail and Mail Order Handbook. **Edited by Richard S. Hodgson. Dartnell Corporation, 4660 Ravenswood Avenue, Chicago, IL 60640. Third edition, 1980.**

A huge book that should tell you everything you'll ever need to know about reaching your readers—and enabling them to do business with you—by mail. Direct-mail pros swear by it.

Editor to Author: The Letters of Maxwell E. Perkins. **Edited by John Hall Wheelock. Cherokee Publishing Co., Box 1730, Marietta, GA 30061; 800-548-8778. 1950.**

What an exemplary editor does, as reflected in letters from the legendary Max Perkins to both well-known and little-known writers.

Feldman, Elane. *The Writer's Guide to Self-Promotion & Publicity.* **Writer's Digest Books, 1507 Dana Avenue, Cincinnati, OH 45207. 1990.**

A generous array of pointers and examples from an experienced publicist.

Fletcher, Tana, and Julia Rockler. *Getting Publicity: A Do-It-Yourself Guide for Small Business and Non-Profit Groups.* **Self-Counsel Press, 1704 N. State Street, Bellingham, WA 98225. 1990.**

The text is full of practical tips and the tone is upbeat and energizing.

Glenn, Peggy. *Publicity for Books and Authors: A Do-It-Yourself Handbook for Small Publishing Firms and Enterprising Authors.* **Aames-Allen Publishing Co., 1106 Main Street, Huntington Beach, CA 92648. 1985.**

Glenn, who began publishing her own books in 1980, is a smart and engaging tutor. Her thoroughly practical handbook shows how books of all sorts can capture time on the air and space in the press.

Hubbard, J.T.W. *Magazine Editing for Professionals.* **Syracuse University Press, 1600 Jamesville Avenue, Syracuse, NY 13244-5160. Second edition, 1989.**

Use this to get insights into your editor's actions. (It's a good place to get some ideas about writing too; *see* especially the sections on "Story Organization.")

Jerome, John. *The Writing Trade: A Year in the Life*. Viking Penguin, 375 Hudson Street, New York, NY 10014. 1992.

Jerome, who earns his living as "a competent but essentially invisible writer," shares his experiences in this frank and winning, month-by-month account.

* Kremer, John. *1001 Ways to Market Your Books—For Publishers and Authors*. Open Horizons, 51 N. Fifth Street, Fairfield, IA 52556. Updated periodically.

With the inspiration and information offered here, any writer will be better able to attract readers. An essential resource that's even better when coupled with Kremer's bimontly newsletter, *Book Marketing Update*.

* Levine, Mark L. *Negotiating A Book Contract: A Guide for Authors, Agents and Lawyers*. Moyer Bell Limited, Colonial Hill/RFD 1, Mt. Kisco, NY 10549. 1988.

Mark Levine leads you step-by-step through the clauses common in book contracts, explaining what you should try to delete, add or otherwise alter. Intelligent, intelligible advice.

Levinson, Jay Conrad. *Guerrilla Marketing Weapons: 100 Affordable Marketing Methods of Maximizing Profits from Your Small Business*. Penguin/Plume, 375 Hudson Street, New York, NY 10014. 1990.

Ideas in here will work for writing as well as widgets, and there are plenty of them.

Luxenberg, Stan. *Books in Chains: Chain Bookstores and Marketplace Censorship*. National Writers Union, 13 Astor Place, New York, NY 10003. 1991.

Despite the tabloid-style title, this is a well-researched, well-reported study of the way large bookstore chains operate. Bear in mind though, that the Pantheon story is misstated, that the chains' reliance on best-sellers is overemphasized, and that books are accessible to readers in vast numbers through many channels besides bookstores, chain or otherwise.

McCormack, Thomas. *The Fiction Editor*. St. Martin's Press, 175 Fifth Avenue, New York, NY 10010. 1988.

What to hope for from your editor if you write fiction. And if you get less than you hoped for, tools you can use to make your book better.

Moyer, Page Emory. *The ABC's of a Really Good Speech.* **Circle Press, 38 The Circle, East Hampton, NY 11937. 1990.**

Effective, easy-to-access advice. Writers who'd like to connect with readers through talks can use this to learn basic technique and build confidence.

* Parker, Roger C. *Looking Good in Print: A Guide to Basic Design for Desktop Publishing.* **Ventana Press, P.O. Box 2468, Chapel Hill, NC 27515. Second edition, 1990.**

The illustrations, which are wonderful, will help you understand and appreciate design options for any kind of print production, not just desktop publishing. And together with the lively text, they'll also enable you to create effective promotional materials.

Playle, Ron. *Selling to Catalog Houses.* **Playle Publications, Inc., P.O. Box 775, Des Moines, IA 50303. 1989.**

Use the nuts-and-bolts advice on pricing and presentation as you devise strategies for this major mail order market.

Poets & Writers Magazine.

See "A Foot in the Door Resources."

Publishing Research Quarterly. **Transaction Periodicals Consortium, Rutgers University, New Brunswick, NJ 08903.**

Readable—indeed, often well-written—scholarly pieces on topics such as "The Megamerger Wave of the 1980s: What Happened?" and "Changing Sales and Markets of American University Presses, 1960–1990."

Ring, Frances. *A Western Harvest: The Gatherings of an Editor.* **John Daniel and Co., P.O. Box 21922, Santa Barbara, CA 93121. 1991.**

As editor of *Westways*, Ring worked with Wallace Stegner, M.F.K. Fisher and a galaxy of other writers. This volume offers samples of their work along with backstage back-and-forth about editing and being edited.

***Rotten Reviews* and *Rotten Reviews II.* Edited by Bill Henderson. Pushcart Press/Norton, Box 380, Wainscott, NY 11975. 1986.**

Are reviewers dumping on you? Are you worried that they might? Look here to see the terrible things they said about William Faulkner, John Milton, Saul Bellow, Jane Austen and a host of others who proved them wrong.

Sensible Solutions' Judith Appelbaum and Florence Janovic. *The Writer's Workbook: A Full and Friendly Guide to Boosting Your Book's Sales.* Pushcart Press, P.O. Box 380, Wainscott, NY 11975. 1991.

A companion volume to the book you now have·in your hands, this is a collection of tips and worksheets for people who are working on trade books.

Stone, Bob. *Successful Direct Marketing Methods.* NTC Business Books, 4255 West Touhy Avenue, Lincolnwood, IL 60646-1975. Updated periodically.

By now a classic, Bob Stone's thorough and practical guide contemplates more sophisticated campaigns than you're likely to mount, but the principles and many of the tactics should prove useful.

Stone, Bob, and John Wyman. *Successful Telemarketing: Opportunities and Techniques for Increasing Sales and Profits.* NTC Business Books, 4255 West Touhy Avenue, Lincolnwood, IL 60646-1975. 1986.

Like the authors (high-level executives at Young & Rubicam and AT&T), the examples come from the big leagues. The advice, however, is applicable to small-scale operations as well.

Weiner, Richard. *Professional's Guide to Publicity.* Public Relations Publishing Company, 1633 Broadway, New York, NY 10019. Third edition, 1982.

An instruction manual from a pro, with plenty of tips and examples.

West, James L.W. *American Authors and the Literary Marketplace Since 1900.* University of Pennsylvania Press, Blockley Hall, 418 Service Drive, Philadelphia, PA 19104-6097; 800-445-9880, 1988.

Professor West's study offers fascinating perspectives on the publishing process then and now.

Williams, Jane A. *Selling to the Other Educational Markets.* Bluestocking Press, P.O. Box 1014, Placerville, CA 95667-1014. 1991.

How to approach people involved with alternative education—home study, correspondence schools and so on.

Tools

American Book Trade Directory. R. R. Bowker, 121 Chanlon Road, New Providence, NJ 07974. Updated periodically.

An alphabetical listing, by state (or Canadian province) and city, of approximately 25,000 book outlets in North America, plus listings of wholesalers, distributors and jobbers who provide conduits to readers. This is invaluable if you use it to identify stores where your work figures to sell well. Try your library for a copy; use the bookselling category index, and pay particular attention to large wholesalers and small bookstore chains.

American Bookseller. American Booksellers Association, 560 White Plains Road, Tarrytown, NY 10591; 800-637-0037. Published monthly.

The magazine of the American Booksellers Association can let you see how booksellers think and what they're thinking about.

American Library Directory. R. R. Bowker, 121 Chanlon Road, New Providence, NJ 07974. Updated periodically.

More than 38,000 public, academic, government and special libraries are listed here by state and Canadian province and by city.

American Wholesalers & Distributors Directory. Edited by Karin E. Koek. Gale Research Inc., P.O. Box 33477, Detroit, MI 48232-5477. 1991.

This brand-new resource provides a way to identify companies that carry products compatible with your book and reach people who should want it.

Author & Audience: A Readings and Workshops Guide. Poets & Writers, Inc., 72 Spring Street, New York, NY 10012. Updated periodically.

Groups in every state of the union sponsor programs that help poets and fiction writers connect with readers. Some 400 are listed in this handy guide, which also explains how to generate invitations to speak and round up people to listen.

Bacon's Publicity Checker. Bacon's, 332 South Michigan Avenue, Chicago, IL 60604. Updated annually.

Covering magazines in one volume and newspapers in another, the *Publicity Checker* is a good tool for preparing lists of reviewers and press release recipients.

Bacon's Radio/TV Directory. Bacon's, 332 South Michigan Avenue, Chicago, IL 60604. Updated annually.

Listings cover more than 10,000 stations and they're usefully annotated. *See* "The Self-Publishing Option Resources" for other Bacon's products and services.

Bodian, Nat G. *Bodian's Publishing Desk Reference.* Oryx Press, 4041 North Central at Indian School Road, Phoenix, AZ 85012-3397. 1988.

An old hand at professional and reference book publishing, Nat Bodian is the author of several marketing guides besides this "Comprehensive Dictionary of Practices and Techniques for Book and Journal Marketing and Bookselling." Especially useful for understanding people who talk to you in trade jargon.

Brands and Their Companies. Gale Research Inc., P.O. Box 33477, Detroit, MI 48232-5477. Updated periodically.

Have you identified a product or two or three or four or more that you might tie in with to boost your sales? Check here to see who makes it and distributes it.

Chain Store Guide, 425 Park Avenue, New York, NY 10022.

This company's publications may help you pinpoint wholesalers and retailers who reach your readers.

CMG Mailing List Catalog. CMG Information Services, 187 Ballardville Street, Suite B110, Winchester, MA 01887; 800-677-7959.

The College Marketing Group catalog, which is free, will lead you to lists of professors who teach specific courses, lists of library decision-makers, and lists of individuals who buy books in a variety of specified subject areas.

Contemporary Authors. Gale Research Inc., P.O. Box 33477, Detroit, MI 48232-5477. Updated periodically.

A good place to get yourself listed and to find addresses of writers you'd like to get blurbs from.

Crawford, Tad. *Business and Legal Forms for Authors & Self-Publishers*. Allworth Press, 10 East 23 Street, Suite 400, New York, NY 10010. 1990.

The title says it and Allworth has several other books of interest to writers so you might want to send for its catalog.

A Directory of American Poets and Fiction Writers. Poets & Writers, Inc., 72 Spring Street, New York, NY 10012. Updated periodically.

If you'd like to contact particular novelists and/or poets for pre-publication comments, here's affordable information on addresses and phone numbers. *See also The Writers Directory*, below, and check biographical dictionaries in the library for leads to other sorts of writers.

The Directory of Mail Order Catalogs. Richard Gottlieb, Editor. Grey House Publishing, Pocket Knife Square, Lakeville, CT 06039. Updated periodically.

Thousands of companies that sell products of every sort via printed materials are listed here. Get hold of the directory at your library to see which of them might do well with your book.

Directory of Personal Image Consultants. Edited by Jacqueline Thompson. Image Industry Publications, 10 Bay Street Landing, Suite 7F, Staten Island, NY 10301. Updated periodically.

The hundreds of consultants profiled are categorized under the headings "Speech Communication," "Wardrobe Analysis," "Personal Promotion" and "Motivation, Etiquette & Career Development." Consult the geographic index if you're looking for help of this sort in your area.

Directory of Special Libraries and Information Centers. Edited by Janice A. DeMaggio. Gale Research Inc., P.O. Box 33477, Detroit, MI 48232-5477. Updated periodically.

Using the subject index, you can construct your own mailing list of libraries that should be especially receptive to your book.

* *Encyclopedia of Associations*. Edited by Deborah M. Burek. Gale Research Inc., P.O. Box 33477, Detroit, MI 48232-5477. Updated periodically.

A first-class promotion tool whether you're being published or doing the publishing yourself, this is a conduit to 22,000 groups committed to all sorts of causes and activities. Get hold of it at your library and use the key word index to zero in on the people who will welcome news of your book and help you spread the word about it.

Gale Directory of Publications and Broadcast Media. **Gale Research Inc., P.O. Box 33477, Detroit, MI 48232-5477. Updated periodically.**

Thousands of newspapers, magazines and radio and TV stations are listed here, and indexed so it's easy to pinpoint special-interest market segments. Your library should have a copy.

Grants and Awards Available to American Writers.

See "Money Resources," and if you spot a way to become a winner, try it out. Both the credentials and the funds should come in handy at any stage of a writing project or a writing career.

Harris, Godfrey. *The Ultimate Black Book.* **The Americas Group, 9200 Sunset Blvd., Suite 404L, Los Angeles, CA 90069. 1988.**

A handy research tool, this little pamphlet lists 400 information sources under 34 subject headings, and indexes them by key words.

Kremer, John. *Book Marketing Made Easier: A Do-It-Yourself Marketing Kit for Book Publishers.* **Open Horizons, 51 N. Fifth Street, Fairfield, IA 52556. Updated periodically.**

Worksheets, sample letters and promotional pieces, checklists and many other handy forms accompany the savvy advice here. See above and below for some of Kremer's other books, and send for his catalog. His whole line is useful.

* Kremer, John, and Marie Kiefer. *Book Publishing Resource Guide.* **Ad-Lib Publications, 51½ West Adams, Fairfield, IA 52556. Updated periodically.**

This indispensable "directory of key contacts for marketing and promoting books" has more than 7,500 listings you can use in supplementing your publisher's marketing moves. An affordable book, it's considerably less expensive than *Literary Market Place* and, in this context, more useful.

Literary Bookstores: A Cross-Country Guide. **Poets & Writers, 72 Spring Street, New York, NY 10012. Updated periodically.**

An efficient way to locate 275 American bookstores that are hospitable to contemporary fiction and poetry.

Literary Market Place. R. R. Bowker, 121 Chanlon Road, New Providence, NJ 07974. Published annually.

Like *Book Publishing Resource Guide* (above), *LMP* can help you add to and reinforce whatever efforts your publisher plans to make on your behalf. *See* especially "Book Review, Selection & Reference," "Radio & Television" and "Public Relations Services."

Palder, Edward L. *The Catalog of Catalogs II: The Complete Mail Order Directory.* Woodbine House, 5615 Fishers Lane, Rockville, MD 20852; 800-843-7323. Updated periodically.

An affordable introduction to thousands of special-interest mail-order operations. Look under the subject(s) your work treats to find catalogs that might sell it to potential readers.

Poynter, Dan. *Business Letters for Publishers.* Para Publishing, P.O. Box 4232, Santa Barbara, CA 93140-4232. Updated periodically.

Letters directed to reviewers, catalog companies, ad media and the like will serve authors as well as publishers, and they're available on diskette for IBM PCs and compatibles. *See* "The Self-Publishing Option Resources" for other helpful Poynter products and write for information on the full range of first-rate goods and services he offers.

Radio-TV Interview Report. Bradley Communications Corp., 135 E. Plumstead, Lansdowne, PA 19050; 800-989-1400. Published monthly.

The Report, a collection of ads, goes to thousands of people who might book you on radio, as well as to hundreds of TV talk-show producers and selected newspaper feature editors. Rates are reasonable; results are mixed.

Research Centers Directory. Gale Research Inc., P.O. Box 33477, Detroit, MI 48232-5477. Updated periodically.

With the subject index, you can identify facilities that may want to order your book and/or help you spread the word about it. More than 12,000 research units are covered.

Siegel, Scott and Barbara. *The Celebrity Phone Book.* NAL/Plume, 375 Hudson Street, New York, NY 10014. 1990.

Names, addresses and phone numbers of famous people, plus advice on how to make contact that you can use to advantage once you've identified individuals who might help you promote your work.

Standard Periodical Directory. Edited by Matthew Manning. Gale Research Inc., P.O. Box 33477, Detroit, MI 48232-5477. Updated periodically.

Target special-interest publications listed here for reviews and other print publicity.

Star Guide. Axiom Information Resources, P.O. Box 8015, Ann Arbor, MI 48107. 1990.

Addresses for movie stars, sports celebrities, politicians, astronauts and more.

Tarila, Sophia. *New Marketing Opportunities*. First Editions, P.O. Box 2578, Sedona, AZ 86336; 800-777-4751. 1990.

This two-volume set covers the market often labeled "New Age." Lengthy listings include retailers, catalogs, associations, radio and TV shows, events, co-op mailings and quite a lot more.

Ulrich's International Periodicals Directory. R. R. Bowker, 121 Chanlon Road, New Providence, NJ 07974. Updated periodically.

Enough periodicals are listed here to make your head spin. Available in libraries.

Weiner, Richard. *Syndicated Columnists*. BPI Publications, 1515 Broadway, New York, NY 10036; 800-336-3533. Published annually.

This book can lead you to columnists who figure to like your work. If you get a mention in a column, prepare for soaring sales.

The Writers Directory. St. James Press, 233 E. Ontario Street, Chicago, IL 60611. Updated periodically.

Useful for getting in touch with people who might provide blurbs. *See also A Directory of American Poets and Fiction Writers* (above).

The Yearbook of Experts, Authorities & Spokepersons. Broadcast Interview Source, 2233 Wisconsin Avenue, NW, Washington, DC 20007. Updated periodically.

The idea is that producers look here to find experts they can invite to appear on their shows. Send for information on how to get listed.

People, Places and Programs

American Society of Journalists and Authors, 1501 Broadway, Suite 302, New York, NY 10036; 212-997-0947; fax: 212-768-7414.
Many ASJA members write for magazines. The group has meetings and a newsletter as well as the Dial-a-Writer Referral Service (*see* "Money Resources").

❋ The Authors Guild, Inc., 330 West 42 Street, New York, NY 10036; 212-563-5904; fax: 212-564-8363.
It's well worth joining this group of 6,500 professional writers and getting in as early in your career as you can, so request application forms. The Guild and its top-notch staff give writers power to deal with publishers by providing surveys of financial terms, seminars on current problems and opportunities for writers, a newsletter that disseminates solid, useful information, access to insurance, and sample forms, including model contracts.

Authors Unlimited, 31 East 32 Street, Suite 300, New York, NY 10016.
Founded by Arlynn Greenbaum, an experienced book publicist, this is a speakers' bureau for authors who can give useful and/or entertaining talks to a variety of audiences. Write to find out about the selection process and the registration fee.

BISAC, 160 Fifth Avenue, New York, NY 10010; 212-929-1393; fax: 212-929-7542.
The Book Industry Systems Advisory Committee, which performs many valuable services for book people, is now developing a "Standard Royalty Statement."

Communication Creativity. P.O. Box 909, 425 Cedar Street, Buena Vista, CO 81211-0909.
Marilyn and Tom Ross create books, tapes and services to help publishers and authors market books. Send for specifics.

International Women's Writing Guild.
See "Getting the Words Right Resources."

"Literary & Writers' Associations," *Literary Market Place*.
Listings here should lead you to groups you might join. *See also*

"Getting the Words Right Resources," "A Foot in the Door Resources" and "The Self-Publishing Option Resources."

The National Writers Club, 1450 South Havana, Suite 620, Aurora, CO 80012.

If you'd like to link up with other writers in your area, why not see if there's a chapter of this group nearby?

National Writers Union, 13 Astor Place, New York, NY 10003; 212-254-0279.

Unlike other writers' groups, this one is "a labor union" with an interest in collective bargaining, grievance resolution and boycotts.

NTC Business Books, 4255 West Touhy Avenue, Lincolnwood, IL 60646-1975; 708-679-5500; fax: 708-679-2494.

In addition to the Bob Stone books mentioned above, NTC publishes manuals on topics such as public relations writing and creative advertising. The catalog will give you details.

PEN American Center, 568 Broadway, New York, NY 10012; 212-334-1660; fax: 212-334-2181.

Known for its social conscience and its excellent grants directory (*see* "Money Resources"), PEN is an international writers' organization, with centers in various sites at home and abroad (*see* PEN West, below). Panel discussions, readings and other get-togethers keep members in touch and informed.

PEN Center USA West, 672 S. Lafayette Park Place, Suite 25, Los Angeles, CA 90057; 213-365-8500; fax: 213-365-9616.

This lively, rapidly growing group runs programs, issues an informative newsletter and generally makes life pleasanter and more productive for the writers it serves.

Poets & Writers.

See "Getting the Words Right Resources."

Poets House, 72 Spring Street, Second Floor, New York, NY 10012; 212-431-7920.

Poets and poetry lovers gather here for readings, workshops and celebrations. The group has an admirable library too.

Public Relations Society of America Information Center, 33 Irving Place, New York, NY 10003; 212-995-2230.

A large collection of materials for professional public relations people; open to the public for a modest fee. Call ahead to make an appointment.

Sensible Solutions, Inc., 275 Madison Avenue, Suite 1518, New York, NY 10016; 212-687-1761; fax: 212-986-3218.

Founded because readers of *How to Get Happily Published* asked for advice tailored to their particular books, Sensible Solutions is a consulting firm run by Judith Appelbaum and Florence Janovic. They confer with clients and then prepare target marketing plans designed to boost books' sales without big budgets.

Society of Children's Book Writers, P.O. Box 66296, Mar Vista Station, Los Angeles, CA 90066.

A sizable group offering an array of services. Write for details.

Tools of the Trade.

The easy way to get the books recommended here. *See* "Getting the Words Right Resources."

Women's National Book Association, 160 Fifth Avenue, New York, NY 10010; 212-675-7804.

Also open to men, WNBA has members who are writers, people in publishing, educators, librarians, artists, critics and booksellers. Send for information on the group's get-togethers and publications.

The Self-Publishing Option
Resources

O NE OF THE best ways for self-publishers to get help is by talking with other publishers, particularly smaller ones. Look below and in the local Yellow Pages for leads to those in your area. Other avenues to advice and assistance are also described below. For additional guidance, check back through the previous Resources section. See especially "A Foot in the Door Resources" (since the directories that help writers find publishers also help publishers find people who'll publicize their work and/or buy rights to it) and "The Sale and Its Sequels Resources" (since the ingredients for success through established publishing companies are very similar to the ingredients for success as a self-publisher).

Advice, Analysis and Reportage

* **Barker, Malcolm E.** *Book design & production for the small publisher.* **Londonborn Publications, 370 Fourth Street, P.O. Box 77246, San Francisco, CA 94107-7246. 1990.**

A book that gives pleasure along with knowledge. The design is exemplary and the tone unusually attractive. You get the feeling Barker doesn't just know his stuff; he's really rooting for you to grasp it too.

Beach, Mark, Steve Shepro and Ken Russon. *Getting It Printed: How to Work with Printers and Graphic Arts Services to Assure Quality,*

Stay on Schedule, and Control Costs. Coast to Coast Books, 2934 Northeast 16th Avenue, Portland, OR 97212, 1986.

A clear, detailed primer that's applicable to books although it doesn't often focus on them. Use it to see what your options are and to get help in exercising the ones that make sense for your project.

Bloch, Douglas (with Robert Brock). *Phone Power: How to Successfully Telemarket Your Product or Service.*
See "The Sale and Its Sequels Resources."

Blue, Martha. *By the Book: Legal ABCs for the Printed Word.* Northland Publishing Co., P.O. Box N, Flagstaff, AZ 86002. 1990.

Readable advice from an expert. Blue's goals here are to teach publishers enough about relevant matters of law so that they can minimize legal problems, expedite the handling of those that do arise, and spend less on legal fees. *See also* the legal guides listed in "Getting the Words Right Resources."

Book, Albert C. and C. Dennis Schick. *Fundamentals of Copy & Layout.* NTC Business Books, 4255 West Touhy Avenue, Lincolnwood, IL 60646-1975. 800-323-4900. Second edition, 1991.

Written for people who create ads (by no means a book's best selling tool); useful for producing flyers and mailing pieces as well (which figure to work better) and full of instructive examples.

Burgett, Gordon. *Self-Publishing to Tightly-Targeted Markets.* Communication Unlimited, P.O. Box 6405, Santa Maria, CA 93456. 1989.

Target marketing is a self-publisher's best bet, and Burgett's system will be useful even for loosely targeted titles.

Crispell, Diane. *The Insider's Guide to Demographic Know-How: How to Find, Analyze, and Use Information About Your Customers.* American Demographics Press, 108 N. Cayuga Street, Ithaca, NY 14850. 1990.

Use the introductory essays when you're figuring out what sort of market research to do, and consult the Sources sections when it's time to go after your data.

Dessauer, John P. *Book Publishing: A Basic Introduction.* Continuum Publishing Company, 370 Lexington Avenue, New York, NY 10017. 1989.

By the author of the classic *Book Publishing: What It Is, What It Does.* *See* "The Sale and Its Sequels Resources" for a fuller description.

Dill, Barbara. *The Journalist's Handbook on Libel and Privacy.* **The Free Press, 866 Third Avenue, New York, NY 10022. 1986.**

Both lively and informative, Dill's handbook grew out of seminars given for reporters and editors. *See* the Q-and-A section at the back for a quick fix on basic guidelines.

Direct Mail and Mail Order Handbook. **Edited by Richard S. Hodgson. Dartnell Corporation, 4660 Ravenswood Avenue, Chicago, IL 60640. Third edition, 1980.**

A giant helping of information on doing business through the mail.

Doty, Betty. *Publish Your Own Handbound Books.* **The Bookery, 6899 Riata Drive, Redding, CA 96002. 1980.**

Both an instruction manual and a kit for producing one small book (for starters), this engaging and encouraging self-published work gives you the chance to control one more phase of the publishing process. Doty's new manual, *Hey Look . . . I Made a Book,* is in the works at this writing and expected to show up in due course at crafts stores as well as bookstores.

Editor & Publisher International Yearbook.
    See "A Foot in the Door Resources."

Fletcher, Tana, and Julia Rockler. *Getting Publicity: A Do-It-Yourself Guide for Small Business and Non-Profit Groups.* **Self-Counsel Press, 1704 N. State Street, Bellingham, WA 98225. 1990.**
    See "The Sale and Its Sequels Resources."

Folio: The Magazine for Magazine Management. **Folio Publishing Corporation, Six River Bend, P.O. Box 4949, Stamford, CT 06907-0949. Published monthly.**

A magazine for people who publish and edit periodicals, with some articles and news items that will interest book publishers too.

Follett, Robert. *Financial Feasibility in Book Publishing.* **Alpine Guild, P.O. Box 183, Oak Park, IL 60303. 1988.**

An accomplished publisher, Follett gives practical, easy to follow advice not only in this primer but also in a 19-lesson home-study course, *The Financial Side of Book Publishing* (Alpine Guild, as above).

Fulton, Len, and Ellen Ferber. *American Odyssey: A Bookselling Travelogue.* **Dustbooks, P.O. Box 100, Paradise, CA 95969; 800-477-6110. 1975.**

Fulton visited bookstores across the country in order to see what selling his own work would be like. His account of the experience is both instructive and entertaining.

Garst, Robert E., and Theodore M. Bernstein. *Headlines and Deadlines: A Manual for Copy Editors.* **Columbia University Press, 562 West 113th Street, New York, NY 10025. Updated periodically.**

The copy editors of the title are newspaper copy editors—who do far more general editing than their namesakes in book and magazine publishing—and the book discusses such matters as writing leads, developing stories and cutting copy. Use the lengthy "Headline Vocabulary" to decrease dependence on overused words.

Glenn, Peggy. *Publicity for Books and Authors.*
See "The Sale and Its Sequels Resources."

Hodgson, Richard S. *The Greatest Direct Mail Sales Letters of All Time.* **The Dartnell Corporation, 4660 Ravenswood Avenue, Chicago, IL 60640. 1986.**

Hodgson, a direct marketing ace, tells "How They Were Created. Why They Succeeded. How You Can Create Great Sales Letters, too!"

"How to Submit Your Books to Book-of-the-Month Club." **Book-of-the-Month Club, Inc., 1271 Avenue of the Americas, New York, NY 10020; 212-522-4200.**

If you're interested in approaching one or more of the eight BOMC clubs (and you certainly should be), call or write to get this sheet of instructions.

Hubbard, J.T.W. *Magazine Editing for Professionals.* **Syracuse University Press, 1600 Jamesville Avenue, Syracuse, NY 13244-5160. Second edition, 1989.**

Detailed, well illustrated advice deals with production and management as well as editorial matters.

✱ **Huenefeld, John.** *The Huenefeld Guide to Book Publishing.* **Mills & Sanderson, Publishers, 442 Marrett Road, Suite 6, Lexington, MA 02173. Updated periodically.**

John Huenefeld has been helping small publishers manage their operations for a good long time through consulting services and seminars (see below), through his newsletter (see the next listing) and through this sizable volume, which discusses everything from starting a book-publishing venture to selling one.

The Huenefeld Report, **The Huenefeld Company, Inc., 41 North Road, Suite 201. Bedford, MA 01730. Published fortnightly.**

Huenefeld's newsletter is virtually unique as a source of information and ideas on running a "modest-sized book publishing" company. Write for information and a sample copy.

Judd, Karen. *Copyediting: A Practical Guide.* **Crisp Publications, Inc., 95 First Street, Los Altos, CA 94022. Second edition, 1990.**

A delightful primer. *See* "Money Resources."

✱ **Kamoroff, Bernard.** *Small-Time Operator: How to Start Your Own Small Business, Keep Your Books, Pay Your Taxes, & Stay Out of Trouble.* **Bell Springs Publishing, P.O. Box 640, Laytonville, CA 95454. Updated periodically.**

A self-publishing success story, Kamoroff's guide provides excellent guidance on managing financial affairs.

Kavka, Dorothy. *Selling Your Book: The Writer's Guide to Publishing and Marketing.* **Evanston Publishing, Inc., 1216 Hinman Avenue, Evanston, IL 60202. 1991.**

Good advice generously laced with specifics. See below for services available from Kavka's Evanston Publishing company.

Kramer, Felix and Maggie Lovaas. *Desktop Publishing Success: How to Start and Run a Desktop Publishing Business.* **Business One Irwin/ DTP Success, P.O. Box 844, Cathedral Station, New York, NY 10025; 800-541-2318. 1991.**

If you're using desktop publishing equipment, you'll benefit by reading this well-organized, encouraging, practical guide.

✱ **Kremer, John.** *1001 Ways to Market Your Books—For Publishers and Authors.* **Open Horizons, 51 N. Fifth Street, Fairfield, IA 52556. Updated periodically.**

One good idea after another, dealing with all aspects of marketing, including editorial and production matters. Kremer's bimonthly news-letter, *Book Marketing Update,* complements the advice here and in his other books, listed elsewhere in this section.

Levinson, Jay Conrad. *Guerrilla Marketing Weapons: 100 Affordable Marketing Methods for Maximizing Profits from Your Small Business.* **Penguin/Plume, 375 Hudson Street, New York, NY 10014, 1990.**

Great for people who have lots of energy and relatively little money to invest in marketing. Levinson is also the author of *Guerrilla Marketing* and *Guerrilla Marketing Attack.*

McVay, Barry L. *Getting Started in Federal Contracting: A Guide Through the Federal Procurement Maze.* **Panoptic Enterprises, P.O. Box 1099, Woodbridge, VA 22193-0099. Second edition, 1987.**

Brisk straight talk from a former Department of Defense contracting officer about getting the government as a customer. McVay provides consulting services too.

Miller, Casey, and Kate Swift. *The Handbook of Nonsexist Writing.* **HarperCollins, 10 East 53 Street, New York, NY 10022. Second edition, 1988.**

Whoever does your editing, copy-editing and copy writing should use this book. Miller and Swift make it easy to avoid offensive sexist terms without calling attention to the effort.

The New York Times Manual of Style and Usage. **Edited by Lewis Jordan. Random House, 201 East 50 Street, New York, NY 10022. Updated periodically.**

A standard reference work. Entries are arranged alphabetically rather than topically.

✱ **Parker, Roger C.** *Looking Good in Print: A Guide to Basic Design for Desktop Publishing.* **Ventana Press, Inc., P.O. Box 2468, Chapel Hill, NC 27515. 1990.**

Once you've got your desktop publishing software up and running, consult Parker's excellent illustrated guide for ways to use it to best advantage.

Personal Publishing. **P.O. Box 3019, Wheaton, IL 60189. Published monthly.**

A magazine by, for and about desk-top publishers.

Perle, E. Gabriel, and John Taylor Williams. *The Publishing Law Handbook.* **Prentice Hall Law & Business, 270 Sylvan Avenue, Englewood Cliffs, NJ 07632. Updated periodically.**

Your lawyer should, and probably will, be familiar with this hefty, handily organized volume, and its discussions will be understandable to you. It's $80 so you may want to try nearby libraries for a copy when you need information on specific legal issues.

Playle, Ron. *Selling to Catalog Houses.* **Playle Publications, Inc., P.O. Box 775, Des Moines, IA 50303. Updated periodically.**
  See "The Sale and Its Sequels Resources."

✽ **Poynter, Dan.** *Book Fairs: An Exhibiting Guide for Publishers.* **Para Publishing, P.O. Box 4232, Santa Barbara, CA 93140-4232. Updated periodically.**
  A knowledgeable guide that answers the essential questions about promoting and selling books through exhibits. See below for other Poynter products and services.

✽ **Poynter, Dan.** *The Self-Publishing Manual: How to Write, Print & Sell Your Own Book.* **Para Publishing, P.O. Box 4232, Santa Barbara, CA 93140-4232. Updated periodically.**
  This is the best self-publishing manual on the market. Poynter offers more information per paragraph than many handbooks put on a page, and it's all clear and easy to follow. Highly recommended.

Publish, **P.O. Box 51966, Boulder, CO 80321. Published monthly.**
  A desktop publishers' periodical with an annual buyers' guide.

Publishing Research Quarterly. **Transaction Publishing Consortium, Rutgers University, New Brunswick, NJ 08903. Published quarterly.**
  Scholars and others who've done some digging for hard data about the book world report their findings here.

✽ *The Publish-It-Yourself Handbook: Literary Tradition and How-To.* **Edited by Bill Henderson. Pushcart Press, P.O. Box 380, Wainscott, NY 11975. Revised edition, 1980.**
  By now a classic, this collection of spirited essays by self-publishers and their supporters should serve to embolden authors considering the self-publishing option and to entertain and inform readers of all sorts.

Ross, Marilyn and Tom. *How to Make Big Profits Publishing City & Regional Books: A Guide for Entrepreneurs, Writers and Publishers.* **Communication Creativity, P.O. Box 909, 425 Cedar Street, Buena Vista, CO 81211-0909; 800-331-8355. 1987.**
  Ringing changes on their *Complete Guide to Self-Publishing* (see

below), Marilyn and Tom Ross provide an array of examples here that's wondrous to behold. Obviously, lots of people now realize that it's easier to publish for limited geographical markets than for the widely dispersed (and probably mythical) general reader.

Ross, Tom and Marilyn. *The Complete Guide to Self-Publishing.* **Writer's Digest Books, 1507 Dana Avenue, Cincinnati, OH 45207. Second edition, 1989.**
Subtitled "Everything You Need to Know to Write, Publish, Promote, and Sell Your Own Book," this is a good source of sound, detailed advice.

Scholarly Publishing: A Journal for Authors and Publishers. **University of Toronto Press, Toronto, Canada M5S 1A6. Published quarterly.**
Consistently interesting and well edited, this journal has new ideas, new information and new perspectives to offer publishers whether they're scholarly or not.

Sitarz, Daniel. *The Desktop Publisher's Legal Handbook.* **Nova Publishing Co., 1103 West College Street, Carbondale, IL 62901. 1989.**
A thorough self-help guide by a lawyer who's a publisher too.

✱ *Small Press: The Magazine of Independent Publishing.* **Small Press, Inc., Colonial Hill/RFD 1, #165, Mt. Kisco, NY 10549-9871. Published quarterly.**
With Jennifer Moyer and Wendy Crisp as its new publisher and editor, respectively, *Small Press* offers news, reviews, opinion, instruction, information and samples of the best work today's smaller publishers are putting out. Let them know what you're doing, and subscribe to keep up with events, trends and kindred spirits.

Stone, Bob. *Successful Direct Marketing Methods,* **and Bob Stone and John Wyman,** *Successful Telemarketing.*
See "The Sale and Its Sequels Resources."

Strong, William S. *The Copyright Book: A Practical Guide.* **MIT Press, 55 Hayward Street, Cambridge, MA 02142. Third edition, 1990.**
A thorough, orderly introduction to copyright by a lawyer whose specialty it is.

White, Jan V. *Editing by design: A guide to effective word-and-picture communication for editors and designers.* R.R. Bowker, 121 Chanlon Road, New Providence, NJ 07974. Second edition, 1982.

Lavishly illustrated in black-and-white, this well-established handbook is geared to magazines.

Williams, Jane A. *Selling to the Other Educational Markets.* Bluestocking Press, P.O. Box 1014, Placerville, CA 95667-1014. 1991.

Look here if you want to reach correspondence schools and people involved with other sorts of home study.

Wills, F. H. *Fundamentals of Layout, for Newspaper and Magazine Advertising, for Page Design of Publications and Brochures.* Dover Publications, Inc., 180 Varick Street, New York, NY 10014. 1965.

The focus is on ads, but the principles and techniques revealed are applicable to the design of books and periodicals. A thorough and readable primer with a wealth of captioned illustrations that teach important lessons pleasurably.

Tools

American Bookseller.
See "The Sale and Its Sequels Resources."

American Book Trade Directory. R. R. Bowker, 121 Chanlon Road, New Providence, NJ 07974. Updated periodically.

The listings here will let you target bookstores—and large and small bookstore chains—where your work figures to sell well. Available in libraries.

American Library Directory. R. R. Bowker, 121 Chanlon Road, New Providence, NJ 07974. Updated periodically.

As above, a fine tool for targeting.

"Book Review, Selection & Reference," *Literary Market Place.* R. R. Bowker, 121 Chalon Road, New Providence, NJ 07974.

A useful checklist when the time comes to start sending out review copies.

Bowker Catalog. R. R. Bowker, 121 Chanlon Road, New Providence, NJ 07974.

Like its counterpart from Gale (see below), this free catalog should stimulate your thinking about promotional possibilities.

Brands and Their Companies. Gale Research Inc., P.O. Box 33477, Detroit, MI 48232-5477. Updated periodically.

Good leads for special sales. *See* "The Sale and Its Sequels Resources."

Cassell & The Publishers Association. *Directory of Publishing.* Cassell Publishers Ltd., Villiers House, 41-47 Strand, London, WC2N 5JE, England. Updated periodically.

Information about publishers, agents and others in the U.K. and elsewhere around the world who might help you get your work known overseas.

The Chicago Manual of Style, for Authors, Editors, and Copywriters. The University of Chicago Press, 5801 South Ellis Avenue, Chicago, IL 60637. Updated periodically.

The aristocrat of style manuals, this one is favored by many academics and professional copy editors.

Crawford, Tad. *Business & Legal Forms for Authors & Self-Publishers.* Allworth Press, 10 East 23 Street, New York, NY 10010; 800-283-3572.

Why reinvent the wheel when this affordable book is available, and toll-free too.

Directory of Book Printers. Edited by John Kremer and Marie Kiefer. Ad-Lib Publications, 51½ West Adams, Fairfield, IA 52556. Updated periodically.

An extremely useful, intelligently indexed directory that covers roughly 800 printers and tells you how to approach them. Ads are interspersed among the listings.

Directory of Mail Order Catalogs.
See "The Sale and Its Sequels Resources."

Directory of Publications Resources: A Guide to Selected Books, Periodicals, Software, Courses, Organizations, Contests, Grammar Hotlines, and Tools. **Editorial Experts, Inc., 66 Canal Center Plaza, Suite 200, Alexandria, VA 22314-1538. Updated periodically.**

Designed for people who write, edit and publish, this is a handy, compact roundup.

Dustbooks, P.O. Box 100, Paradise, CA 95967; 800-477-6110.

Get your publications listed in the Dustbooks Small Press Information Library (which includes *The International Directory of Little Magazines and Small Presses*), and use these volumes to identify small publishers in your area who might be willing to give you advice and moral support.

"Editorial Services," *Literary Market Place.* **R. R. Bowker, 121 Chanlon Road, New Providence, NJ 07974.**

A list you can use to find editorial aid nearby. Be sure to get samples, check references and compare prices before you make a deal.

* *Encyclopedia of Associations.* **Gale Research, Inc., P.O. Box 33477, Detroit, MI 48232-5477. Updated periodically.**

A stellar source of information about people who will want your work. *See* "The Sale and Its Sequels Resources."

Fenton, Erfert, and Christine Morrissett. *Canned Art: Clip Art for the Macintosh.* **Peachpit Press, Inc., 1085 Keith Avenue, Berkeley, CA 94708. 1990.**

This giant catalog, arranged by vendor, displays the wares of clip art companies—i.e., places you can get artwork that's in the public domain and therefore usable without permission or fee. Even if your book is being produced on something other than a Mac, you might find leads here to useful illustrative material.

Gale Research Catalog. **Gale Research, Inc., P.O. Box 33477, Detroit, MI 48232-5477.**

First-rate stimulation when you need ideas about getting in touch with readers. Write to request a copy.

International Literary Market Place. **R. R. Bowker, 121 Chanlon Road, New Providence, NJ 07974. Updated periodically.**

Listings include publishers, booksellers, libraries, book clubs, literary agents and organizations in 160 countries outside the United States. Go through the book at your library if your work might sell overseas.

Kremer, John. *Book Marketing Made Easier: A Do-It-Yourself Marketing Kit for Book Publishers*. Open Horizons, 51 N. Fifth Street, Fairfield, IA 52556. Updated periodically.

A compendium of basic forms for publishers to use in acquiring books and shepherding them to readers.

* Kremer, John, and Marie Kiefer. *Book Publishing Resource Guide*. Ad-Lib Publications, 51½ West Adams, Fairfield, IA 52556. Updated periodically.

This directory is an even more valuable resource for book publishers than *Literary Market Place*. Created by people who know how publishing really works, it provides information on wholesalers, retailers, catalogers, sales reps, publicity and marketing services, reviewers, radio and television shows and on and on.

Literary Bookstores.
See "The Sale and Its Sequels Resources."

* *Literary Market Place*. R. R. Bowker, 121 Chanlon Road, New Providence, NJ 07974. Updated annually.

Like *Book Publishing Resource Guide* (above), *LMP* is replete with useful information. Since it's more expensive but also more likely to be available in libraries, you'd be smart to use it there if you can buy only one.

Logos. Whurr Publications Ltd., 19B Compton Terrace, London, N1 2UN, United Kingdom. Published quarterly.

A new "Professional Journal for the Book World," *Logos* publishes opinion pieces by book industry insiders from many nations.

Mailing lists.
See Book Publishing Resource Guide and *Literary Market Place*, above, and Standard Rate and Data Service, below.

Palder, Edward L. *The Catalog of Catalogs: The Complete Mail Order Directory*. Woodbine House, 5615 Fishers Lane, Rockville, MD 20852; 800-843-732320895. Updated periodically.

An affordable guide you can use to identify and approach mail-order operations suitable for your subject.

The Publicity Process. **Edited by Christine Friesleben Goff. Iowa State University Press, 2121 S. State Avenue, Ames, IA 50010. Third edition, 1989.**

Thoughtful essays by Iowa State faculty members on both the theoretical and the practical aspects of publicity.

Publishers Weekly, **249 West 17th Street, New York, NY 10011.**

If you have arranged to distribute your book to stores around the country, send a review copy to *PW* at least three months before its official pub date. Check the masthead at the beginning of the "Forecasts" section to find the proper editor, and be sure to include information about your distribution setup along with other background data in your covering letter. *PW* is also a window on publishing events and trends; a subscription will keep you up to date, and if you can sell one of the magazine's departmental editors on a story idea you'll boost your book's chances in bookstores.

Publishing Agreements: A Book of Precedents. **Edited by Charles Clark. New Amsterdam Books, 171 Madison Avenue, New York, NY 10016. Third edition, 1988.**

Clark is an English lawyer turned editor and publisher. His compendium of contracts includes a book club rights agreement, an electronic publishing agreement, a translator's agreement and much more.

Radio-TV Interview Report. **Bradley Communications Corp., 135 East Plumstead, Lansdowne, PA 19050; 800-989-1400. Published monthly.**

See "The Sale and Its Sequels Resources."

Smith, Peggy. *Mark My Words: Instruction and Practice in Proofreading* and *Simplified Proofreading: How to Catch Errors Using Fewer Marks.* **Editorial Experts, Inc., 66 Canal Center Plaza, Suite 200, Alexandria, VA 22314-1538. 1987 and 1991, respectively.**

Any typo, any misspelling, any grammatical glitch sends a signal to your readers that maybe you're not to be trusted. With this practical manual, you can avoid conveying that impression by learning to catch mistakes and to communicate clearly with the people who are supposed to correct them.

* *Stock Photo Deskbook: Your Instant Key to Over 150 Million Images.* The Photographic Arts Center, 163 Amsterdam Avenue, #201, New York, NY 10023. Updated periodically.

Would pictures of Africa, carousels, honeymoons or nursing homes enhance your text? Would pictures of anything else? Chances are, you can find them by using the Subject Matter Index in this guide to "existing images." Entries include fax numbers as well as phone numbers, and some of the artwork you're interested in may be quite inexpensive, or even free.

Talab, R. S. *Commonsense Copyright: A Guide to the New Technologies.* McFarland & Company, Inc., Publishers, Box 611, Jefferson, NC 28640. 1986.

Especially useful if what you're publishing is a collection of previously published work and/or if non-print media figure in your publishing plans.

Tarila, Sophia. *New Marketing Opportunities.* First Editions, P.O. Box 2578, Sedona, AZ 86336; 800-777-4751. 1990.

A two-volume directory covering "New Age" retailers, organizations, media, events and more.

Trade Shows Worldwide. Gale Research, Inc., P.O. Box 33477, Detroit, MI 48232-5477. Updated periodically.

Trade shows are useful not only for actually selling books (if exhibitors' costs are not prohibitively high) but also for learning your way around an industry with a view toward eventually using the promotion, publicity and sales possibilities it offers.

Weiner, Richard. *Syndicated Columnists.* BPI Publications, 1515 Broadway, New York, NY 10036. Published annually.

Entries, arranged under subject headings, include column titles and columnists' addresses and phone numbers.

The H. W. Wilson Company Catalog. H. W. Wilson Company, 950 University Avenue, Bronx, NY 10452-9978.

Reference books by the dozens, some of which may be grist for your mill.

Working Press of the Nation. National Research Bureau, Directory Division, 225 W. Wacker Drive, Suite 2275, Chicago IL 60606-1229. Updated annually.

The subject indexes and the amount of information included in each listing make this five-volume set valuable. Explore it at your library for leads to receptive people in radio and TV as well as in periodical publishing.

People, Places and Programs

About Books, Inc., P.O. Box 1500, 425 Cedar Street, Buena Vista, CO 81211-1500; 719-395-2459; fax: 719-395-8374.

Tom and Marilyn Ross offer consulting services, books, tapes, seminars and a "Maverick Mail Order Bookstore" catalog you can use to order their books and plenty of others toll-free.

Acanthus Associates, 19 Rector Street, Suite 1102, New York, NY 10006; 212-425-1880; fax: 212-425-1788.

Desktop publishing production services. Maggie Lovaas, who heads this company, is co-author of *Desktop Publishing Success*; see above, and *see also* Kramer Communications.

Adams Press, 500 N. Michigan Avenue, Suite 1920, Chicago, IL 60611; 708-676-4326.

A well-established printer of short-run books for self-publishers and others, the Adams Press also offers help with Library of Congress catalog card numbers, ISBNs, bar codes and other such items. Send for the "Book Printing" brochure and the price list.

Allworth Press, 10 East 23 Street, New York, NY 10010.

Tad Crawford started Allworth to provide "practical information to creative professionals." Check his catalog to see which books meet your needs.

The Authors Guild, Inc., 330 West 42 Street, New York, NY 10036.

When and if you decide to publish other people's work as well as your own, ask for a copy of the Guild's model trade book contract and consider basing your contract on it. After all, who has better reason to be fair to authors than a self-publisher?

Bacon's Information, Inc., 332 South Michigan Avenue, Chicago, IL 60604; 800-621-0561.

Bacon's has mailing services and a clipping service plus its well-known media directories (*see* "The Sale and Its Sequels Resources").

Bar Codes.

Some booksellers still can't scan bar codes but these machine-readable IDs do streamline sales for booksellers who can, and they bolster your image as a serious, professional publisher in every retailer's eyes. *See* BISAC, GGX Associates and Precision Photography, below.

Malcolm E. Barker Consulting Services, P.O. Box 77246, San Francisco, CA 94107-0246.

Barker, author of the much (and deservedly) praised *Book design & production for the small publisher*, offers guidance in person as well as in print.

Henry Berry, Publishing Consultant, P.O. Box 176, Southport, CT 06490; 203-268-4878.

Berry writes a column for *The COSMEP Newsletter*, puts out *The Small Press Book Review* and shares his expertise via phone and written reports.

BISAC (Book Industry Systems Advisory Committee), 160 Fifth Avenue, New York, NY 10010.

BISAC has been helping to streamline ordering and fulfillment procedures for some time now, and they've recently begun to develop a model royalty statement. Write for information about the group and its activities and ask for the pamphlet called "Machine-Readable Coding Guidelines for the U.S. Book Industry" if you want to be fully informed about bar codes.

Book Industry Study Group, Inc., 160 Fifth Avenue, New York, NY 10010; 212-929-1393.

Publishers, booksellers, manufacturers, librarians and others who work with books come together through BISG to gather and disseminate data about the book business.

BookMasters, Inc., 638 Jefferson Street, P.O. Box 159, Ashland, OH 44805; 800-537-6727.

BookMaster's services include typesetting, printing and binding, warehousing and fulfillment.

Cataloging in Publication Division, Library of Congress, Washington, DC 20540.

Send for the "PCN Publishers Manual" and for the form called "Request for Preassignment of Library of Congress Catalog Card Number" well in advance of publication.

Copyright Office, Library of Congress, Washington, DC 20559; hotline for ordering application forms 202-287-9100.

You'll want the "Copyright Basics" pamphlet (Circular 1) and Form TX—the application for copyright registration for a nondramatic literary work—as early as possible. (If you need applications for other kinds of creative work, the Copyright Office will supply them too.)

* **COSMEP, The International Association of Independent Publishers. P.O. Box 420703, San Francisco, CA 94142-0703.**

The *COSMEP Newsletter* is itself worth the price of admission, and the organization functions as a highly effective channel of communication. Its members, who come from all 50 states and 11 foreign countries, work with both books and magazines.

Council of Literary Magazines and Presses, 154 Christopher Street, Suite 3C, New York, NY 10014-2839.

Formerly CCLM (the Coordinating Council of Literary Magazines), CLMP is dedicated to preserving, supporting and promoting literary periodicals and presses.

Crane Duplicating Service, Inc., 1611 Main Street, West Barnstable, MA 02668.

Those "bound galleys" that reviewers like can come from printers who produce early copies with unadorned covers, or you can get them here. The company is so well-known for bound galleys that "Cranes" has become a synonym for them.

Delta Lithograph Co., 28210 N. Avenue Stanford, Valencia, CA 91355-1111; 800-32DELTA.

Delta offers a variety of printing and publishing services. Send for information and for the "21 Ways to Save Money on Your Next Publication" Idea Report.

Direct International Inc., 150 East 74 Street, New York, NY 10021; 212-861-4188; fax: 212-988-1632.

Write to become acquainted with this company's publications and services for "the international direct marketing executive" if that's a label that sometimes fits you.

Distributors.

See Book Publishing Resource Guide and *Literary Market Place*, above, for listings of distributors, and consult the *Subject Guide to Books in Print* to find publishers who might function as distributors for you because they issue books like yours.

DOT Graphic Supply Co., 1612 California Street, P.O. Box 369, Omaha, NE 68101.

DOT's catalog offers office supplies and ink-color charts that any self-publisher is likely to find useful, along with the materials necessary for the paste-up style of production that some may still favor.

Editorial Freelancers Association, P.O. Box 2050, Madison Square Station, New York, NY 10159; 212-677-3357.

If you call the Editorial Freelancers Job Phone (given above) to describe the services you need, you'll hear from experienced people who want the work. As you would with any job applicant, ask for samples and check references.

Evanston Publishing, Inc., 1216 Hinman Avenue, Evanston, IL 60202; 708-492-1911.

Evanston handles publishing tasks from editing through printing and binding.

GGX Associates, Inc., 11 Middle Neck Road, Great Neck, NY 11021; 516-487-6370; fax: 516-487-6449.

Teri Bice's company produces bar codes for publishers large and small.

GRT Book Printing, 3960 East 14th Street, Oakland, CA 94601; 415-534-5032.

GRT specializes in producing small editions—200 to 2,000 copies—at reasonable prices. Send for "A Closer Look at GRT Book Printing"; it presents a great deal of sensible advice as it spells out the company's capabilities.

Hunter House, Inc., P.O. Box 847, Claremont, CA 91711.

Production services for books, manuals and newsletters are available from this trade-book publisher.

Indexers.

If your book is nonfiction and you'd like to maximize library sales, make sure it has a good index. Leads are available through the Editorial Freelancers Association (see above), through *Literary Market Place* and through the American Society of Indexers, 1700 18th Street, NW, Washington, DC 20009.

Inprint Graphic Design, P.O. Box 1600, East Hampton, NY 11937; 516-329-7600.

Judith Grossman designs and produces newsletters, books, stationery, brochures, whatever print products you need.

ISBN [International Standard Book Number], R. R. Bowker, 121 Chanlon Road, New Providence, NJ 07974; 908-665-6770; fax: 908-464-3553.

By assigning a unique number to each published book, the ISBN system simplifies ordering, shipping and billing. To get your number as soon as possible, send the agency the data on your title page along with the name and address of your press and a SASE; they'll send you the proper forms.

ISSN [International Standard Serial Number], Library of Congress National Serials Data Program, Washington, DC 20540; 202-287-6452.

The periodical world's equivalent of the ISBN.

Kramer Communications, P.O. Box 844 Cathedral Station, New York, NY 10025; 212-866-4864.

Felix Kramer, coauthor of *Desktop Publishing Success*, provides "start-to-finish" desktop publishing services, including training for those who want to do as much as possible themselves.

John Kremer, Book Marketing Consultant, 51 N. Fifth Street, P.O. Box 1102, Fairfield, IA 52556-1102; 515-472-6130.

Advice of the sort you'll find in Kremer's books (above) is available from Kremer in person by the hour, day or project.

Laing Communications/Laing Research Services, 16250 NE 80th Street, Redmond, WA 98052; 206-869-6313; fax: 206-869-6318.

Norman Bolotin and his associates offer consulting services to book, periodical and software publishers at all stages of the publishing process. The company also produces a variety of studies on "The Business of Publishing," including "Sales and Distribution Practices of Independent Presses."

Jeffrey Lant Associates, 50 Follen Street, Suite 507, Cambridge, MA 02138.

Lant, author of *The Unabashed Self-Promoter's Guide* and other books, follows his own advice with abandon. His "Sure-Fire Business Success" catalog is free on request.

National Association of Desktop Publishers, P.O. Box 508 Kenmore Station, Boston, MA 02215-9998; 617-437-6472.

Membership brings you a journal, a newsletter, a directory of courses, and assorted other benefits.

National Association of Independent Publishers, P.O. Box 850, Moore Haven, FL 33471; 813-946-0293.

The group, which issues a newsletter, aims to be a supportive source of information.

Panoptic Enterprises, 3911 Findley Road, P.O. Box 1099, Woodbridge, VA 22193-0099; 703-670-2812.

Advice on contracting with the federal government from a company run by Vivina and Barry McVay (*see* McVay's *Getting Started in Federal Contracting*, above).

* **Para Publishing, P.O. Box 4232, Santa Barbara, CA 93140-4232; 805-968-7277; fax: 805-968-1379.**

Dan Poynter's Para Publishing supplies an ever-expanding collection of clever, practical products and services for book publishers, including weekend workshops in a hilltop home overlooking the Pacific Ocean. *See* "Resources" passim and write right now for Para's free self-publishing information kit.

Peachpit Press, 2414 Sixth Street, Berkeley, CA 94710; 800-283-9444.

Ted Nace's publishing company specializes in books that help people use computers to advantage. Send for the catalog.

Poets & Writers.

See "Getting the Words Right Resources."

Poets House.

See "The Sale and Its Sequels Resources."

Precision Photography, Inc., 1150 North Tustin Avenue, Anaheim, CA 92807; 800-UPC-9988.

One source for bar codes for your book covers; *see* "Bar Codes," above.

* **Publishers Marketing Association, 2401 Pacific Coast Highway, Suite 109, Hermosa Beach, CA 90254; 213-372-2732; fax: 213-374-3342.**

PMA works hard—and effectively—to help smaller publishers market their books. Write or call Jan Nathan for detailed information on publications, programs, and other benefits of membership.

Quality Books, Inc., 918 Sherwood Drive, Lake Bluff, IL 60044-2204; 708-295-2010; fax: 708-295-1556.

Quality Books distributes adult nonfiction from small publishers to libraries. They're selective; call or write to get more information about the various services they offer, and to find out how to submit a copy of your book for consideration.

Ripinsky & Company, Production Services, Obtuse Road, Newtown, CT 06570; 203-426-1650, 212-529-3600.

Harriet Ripinsky (whose experience includes a tour of duty as director of production at Simon & Schuster) now provides production services to small and self-publishers through her own company.

Sensible Solutions, Inc., 275 Madison Avenue, Suite 1518, New York, NY 10016; 212-687-1761; fax: 212-986-3218.

The consulting firm that grew out of *How to Get Happily Published*, Sensible Solutions handles marketing for self-publishers, among others. *See* "The Sale and Its Sequels Resources."

Small Press Center, 20 West 44 Street, New York, NY 10036; 212-764-7021.

A mid-Manhattan site that small publishers and self-publishers can use to exhibit their books inexpensively. Titles must have "literary, artistic or social value."

Standard Rate and Data Service, 3004 Glenview Road, Wilmette, IL 60091; 800-323-4588.

SRDS publications are designed to give people the facts they need to place ads intelligently on radio and TV and in newspapers, magazines, shopping guides, bus shelters, card decks and more. Check at your library or call SRDS to find out which of their general-interest and/or special-interest guides meet your specific needs.

Stars and Stripes, 252 Seventh Avenue, Room 401, New York, NY 10001; 212-620-3333.

These people buy books and magazines for sale to members of our armed forces. If you'd like yours considered (and why wouldn't you?), send them a copy along with a discount schedule for quantities up to at least 1000.

The Town House Press, Inc., 552 Fearington Post, Pittsboro, NC 27312; 800-525-5470.

Alvin Schultzberg, who runs The Town House Press, will handle all aspects of production for small editions and, if you like, he'll steer you toward help with publicity and sales.

Ventana Press, P.O. Box 2468, Chapel Hill, NC 27515; 919-942-0220; fax: 919-942-1140.

Ventana is a publisher "committed to producing readable, timely computer titles." Take a look at the catalog to see which of their books can help you.

Volunteer Lawyers for the Arts.

See "Money Resources."

Wholesalers.

See Book Publishing Resource Guide and *Literary Market Place*, and pay special attention to the national giants, Baker & Taylor and Ingram.

Women's National Book Association.

See "The Sale and Its Sequels Resources" and call to find out if there's a nearby WNBA chapter you might join.

Money Resources

TO EARN MORE money from writing, first figure out how to recycle material for multiple markets; then use the resources in previous sections to attract as many different buyers as you can. To win money, save money and stretch the dollars you have, see the resources listed below.

Advice, Analysis and Reportage

Adams, Jane. *How to Sell What You Write.* **Putnam/Perigee, 200 Madison Avenue, New York, NY 10016. 1984.**
Sprightly, incisive tips on recycling.

Alvarez, Mark. *The Home Office Book: How to Set Up and Use An Efficient Personal Workspace in the Computer Age.* **Goodwood Press, 33 Washington Avenue, P.O. Box 942, Woodbury, CT. 06798. 1990.**
Alvarez has thought of just about everything. His likable, knowledgable guide is geared to creating a work environment that's not only technologically appropriate for your tasks and your budget, but also personally pleasing. And he gives you a buyer's guide along with his good advice.

Barbara Brabec's National Home Business Report, **P.O. Box 2137, Naperville, IL 60567. Published quarterly.**
Information and tips from an entrepreneur who believes in encouraging and empowering others.

Burgett, Gordon, and Mike Frank. *Speaking for Money.* Communication Unlimited, P.O. Box 6405, Santa Maria, CA 93456. 1985.

Burgett covers seminars and Frank covers speeches in this detailed, common-sensical manual.

Crawford, Tad. *The Writer's Legal Guide.* Allworth Press, 10 East 23 Street, Suite 400, New York, NY 10010. 1978.

Crawford, a lawyer-writer, offers some good guidance on money matters and presents a sample ledger you can use to get into the habit of recording your expenses so you're prepared at tax time.

Davidson, Jeffrey P. *Marketing for the Home-Based Business.* Bob Adams, Inc., 260 Center Street, Holbrook, MA 02343. 1990.

Solid, specific pointers with lots of real-life examples and handy lists, including one called "When to Call" that tells you the times when certain people—accountants, bankers, pharmacists, priests, etc.—are most accessible.

Edwards, Paul and Sarah. *Working from Home: Everything You Need to Know about Living and Working Under the Same Roof.* Jeremy P. Tarcher, Inc., 5858 Wilshire Boulevard, Suite 200, Los Angeles, CA 90036. Revised edition, 1990.

A useful common-sense guide on setting up and managing any kind of home-based business.

Hanson, Nancy Edmonds. *How You Can Make $25,000 a Year Writing (No Matter Where You Live).* Writer's Digest Books, 1507 Dana Avenue, Cincinnati, OH 45207. Revised edition, 1987.

This peppy, can-do manual focuses on the kinds of writing you do primarily for money. Hanson makes the very good point that writers outside New York have at least as much chance of making it as writers in the city.

Judd, Karen. *Copyediting: A Practical Guide.* Crisp Publications, Inc., 95 First Street, Los Altos, CA 94022. Second edition, 1990.

Speaking from experience at Random House and elsewhere, Karen Judd shows how to get manuscripts ready for publication. A delightful, effective primer for anyone who'd like to make money polishing other people's prose.

* Kamoroff, Bernard. *Small-Time Operator: How to Start Your Own Small Business, Keep Your Books, Pay Your Taxes, & Stay Out of Trouble!* Bell Springs Publishing, P.O. Box 640, Laytonville, CA 95454. Updated periodically.

Kamoroff has years of experience as a financial adviser and tax accountant for small businesses and years of experience running small businesses of his own. This very popular guide covers everything from getting started (figuring out how much money you need and then getting your hands on it) to bookkeeping to the legal and financial technicalities of partnerships, payrolls and, yes, taxes. Bell Springs has other books about small businesses too; ask for the brochure.

Kramer, Felix, and Maggie Lovaas. *Desktop Publishing Success: How to Start and Run a Desktop Publishing Business.* Business One Irwin/ DTP Success, P.O. Box 844, Cathedral Station, New York, NY 10025; 800-541-2318. 1991.

Remarkably thorough, readable and friendly, this is a book you'll want to buy if you're thinking of cashing in on desktop expertise. Both authors are experienced enough to really know what they're talking about and generous enough to tell you what you need to know to compete with them.

Levinson, Jay Conrad. *Guerrilla Marketing Weapons.*
See "The Self-Publishing Option Resources."

Poet's Market: Where & How to Publish Your Poetry.
See "A Foot in the Door Resources."

Publication Grants for Writers & Publishers. Oryx Press, 4041 North Central at Indian School Road, Phoenix, AZ 85012-3397. 1991.

A handbook rather than a directory, this explains how to write and submit proposals to the federal government, to selected foundations and to several less conventional funding sources.

Rubin, Mary, and the Business and Professional Women's Foundation. *How to Get Money for Research.* The Feminist Press, 311 East 94th Street, New York, NY 10128. 1983.

The advice in Rubin's short primer is directed to women and people doing research about women but it can be applied to a variety of projects.

Seltzer, Michael. *Securing Your Organization's Future: A Complete Guide to Fundraising Strategies.* **The Foundation Center, 79 Fifth Avenue, New York, NY 10003. 1987.**

Because it's so comprehensive, so imaginative and so well written, Michael Seltzer's handbook can help individuals (including writers) as well as groups (for which it's designed) to amass the funds they need.

Shaw, Eva. *Ghostwriting: How to Get Into the Business.* **Paragon House, 90 Fifth Avenue, New York, NY 10011. 1991.**

Drawing on her own fund of experience, Shaw explains the whole process of ghostwriting—not just how to get into the business, as the subtitle says, but how to structure and price your services as a literary ghost and how to work with the source of your material.

Smith, Peggy. *Mark My Words: Instruction and Practice in Proofreading.* **Editorial Experts, Inc., 66 Canal Center Plaza, Suite 200, Alexandria, VA 22314-1538. 1987.**

Those of you who like catching typos and other errors can upgrade proofreading skills through the exercises in here, and sell them when they're good and strong. Smith is also the author of *Simplified Proofreading: How to Catch Errors Using Fewer Marks*, from Editorial Experts.

Stoughton, Mary. *Substance & Style: Instruction & Practice in Copyediting.* **Editorial Experts, Inc., 66 Canal Center Plaza, Suite 200, Alexandria, VA 22314-1538. 1989.**

Primarily a book of exercises, *Substance & Style* also includes interesting short essays on topics such as "Is It Wrong to Tamper with a Quotation?" and "Fair Use and Copyright."

Tools

Author & Audience: A Readings and Workshops Guide. **Poets & Writers, 72 Spring Street, New York, NY 10012. Updated periodically.**

The listings here will help you pinpoint places to give your own readings and/or workshops, and the advice in the book will be helpful too.

Awards, Honors, and Prizes. **Edited by Gita Siegman. Gale Research Inc., P.O. Box 33477, Detroit, MI 48232-5477. Updated periodically.**

This is a two-volume general reference work about all kinds of awards in the United States and abroad. Its subject index will lead you to those for which you're eligible. Entries are sensibly annotated.

Communication Unlimited Catalog, **P.O. Box 6405, Santa Maria, CA 93456.**

Featuring the works of Gordon Burgett, Communication Unlimited sells tapes and reports as well as books on topics that include writing greeting cards, setting up seminars and marketing mailing lists.

Follett, Robert J. R. *The Financial Side of Book Publishing: A Home/ Office Study Course on Financial and Business Analysis for the Non-Accountant in Book Publishing.* **Alpine Guild, P.O. Box 183, Oak Park, IL 60303. Revised edition, 1988.**

An experienced publisher who learned financial terms, techniques and skills the hard way, Follett now makes it easy for beginners to get the hang of them.

The Foundation Center Catalog. **The Foundation Center, 79 Fifth Avenue, Dept. CE, New York, NY 10003-3050.**

If the world of grants is new to you, start by ordering *The Foundation Center's User-Friendly Guide,* a helpful booklet, and/or by going to one of the Center's collections, browsing around and asking questions (*see* "People, Places and Programs," below). Then zero in on appropriate entries in *The Foundation Directory, The Foundation Grants Index, Foundation Grants to Individuals* and any of the specialized Foundation Center publications that fit your needs.

* *Grants and Awards Available to American Writers.* **P.E.N. American Center, 568 Broadway, New York, NY 10012. Updated periodically.**

An indispensable—and inexpensive—reference for writers in search of funds. Well worth perusing whether you write fiction, nonfiction, poetry, children's books, plays or all of the above.

Lant, Jeffrey. *Sure-Fire Business Success Catalog,* **Jeffrey Lant Associates, 50 Follen Street, Suite 507, Cambridge, MA 02138.**

The author of *The Unabashed Self-Promoter's Guide* unabashedly uses his books as tools for promoting himself. Fortunately, he also supplies canny tips and he's able to poke fun at his own audacity. If the brashness doesn't turn you off, his publications may embolden you to spot and pull all the strings you can for your book, magazine or whatever. The catalog is free.

Lesko, Matthew. *Getting Yours: The Complete Guide to Government Money.* **Viking Penguin, 40 West 23rd Street, New York, NY 10010. Third edition, 1987.**

Good leads to state and federal funds. Be sure to check the lengthy index for the subject(s) your work covers.

Literary Market Place. **R. R. Bowker, 121 Chanlon Road, New Providence, NJ 07974. Updated annually.**

LMP comes in handy in two ways where money is concerned: it has lists that you can consult to find funding (*see* "Literary Awards, Contests & Grants" and "Employment Agencies"), and it has lists that you can get on to earn fees, given relevant skills (*see* "Typing & Word Processing Services," "Electronic Publishing Consultants" and "Editorial Services," including its subdivisions for copy editing, ghost writing, line editing, proofreading, research, rewriting and special assignment writing).

Million Dollar Directory. **Dun's Marketing Services, A Division of Dun & Bradstreet, Three Century Drive, Parsippany, NJ 07054. Updated periodically.**

Businesses often need writers—to prepare annual reports, speeches, feature stories, newsletters and manuals. Try using the geographic and industry classification indexes in this multivolume work to zero in on companies that might hire you. Entries cover more than 160,000 U.S. businesses with net worths over $500,000.

Research Centers Directory. **Edited by Karen Hill. Gale Research Inc., P.O. Box 33477, Detroit, MI 48232-5477. Updated periodically.**

By affiliating with institutions, individuals can become eligible for some grants offered to non-profit groups. To find the centers most likely to take you under their wing, look up your project's subject in the directory's index and then study the description of each group listed under that heading.

Thomas Register of American Manufacturers. **Thomas Publishing Company, One Penn Plaza, New York, NY 10001-0107. Updated periodically.**

A great source of leads to companies that might buy your work in bulk. The *Thomas Register*, a twenty-six-volume set, is available in libraries.

"Writer's Profit Catalog,".™ 174 Holland Avenue, New Milford, NJ 07646.

Bob Bly, author of *Secrets of a Freelance Writer: How to Make $85,000 a Year*, *Technical Writing: Structure, Standards, and Style* and several other titles designed to boost writers' revenues, offers them all via this catalog. He's created an audiotape program too—"The High-Profit Writer."

People, Places and Programs

American Book Producers Association, 41 Union Square West, Suite 1327, New York, NY 10003; 212-645-2368.

If you have enough expertise and writing credits to work for a book packager, or if you think you'd like to become one, get in touch with this group. Its members think up and produce all sorts of titles.

Associated Writing Programs, Old Dominion University, Norfolk, VA 23529-0079.

For a small membership fee, the creative writer can take advantage of a number of income-generating programs sponsored by AWP, including a placement service.

Authors Unlimited, 31 East 32 Street, Suite 300, New York, NY 10016.

A speakers' bureau that's not just—or even primarily—for celebrity authors. Arlynn Greenbaum, who runs it, is selective, of course, but if you're a good speaker, get in touch.

CLMP, 154 Christopher Street, Suite 3C, New York, NY 10014-2389; 212-741-9110; fax: 212-741-9112.

Contact the Council of Literary Magazines and Presses if fine writing is what you aim to publish. Originally the Coordinating Council of Literary Magazines, CLMP offers financial and moral support.

Dial-a-Writer Referral Service, American Society of Journalists and Authors, 1501 Broadway, Suite 302, New York, NY 10036; 212-997-0947; fax: 212-768-7414.

Some people ask the Dial-a-Writer referral service to find them collaborators and ghosts. A writer who pays the price of admission to the

ASJA can see who candidates are, what they want and whether any of their projects is attractive, financially and otherwise.

Editorial Experts, Inc., 66 Canal Center Plaza, Suite 200, Alexandria, VA 22314-1538; 703-683-0683; fax: 703-683-4915.

A publications consulting company that provides writers, editors, proofreaders and and word and data processors for its clients, Editorial Experts also has an informative newsletter, "The Editorial Eye."

Editorial Freelancers Association, P.O. Box 2050, Madison Square Station, New York, NY 10159; 212-677-3357.

Members have access to information about job opportunities through a telephone bulletin board. The EFA also offers a newsletter, a directory and insurance at group rates, plus educational and supportive meetings.

The Foundation Center, 79 Fifth Avenue, New York, NY 10003-3050; 212-620-4230; 1001 Connecticut Avenue, NW, Suite 938, Washington, DC 20036, 202-331-1400; 312 Sutter Street, San Francisco, CA 94108, 415-397-0902; 1356 Hanna Building, 1422 Euclid Avenue, Cleveland, OH 44115, 216-861-1934.

With national offices in New York and Washington, field offices in San Francisco and Cleveland and cooperating collections in libraries throughout the United States and abroad, the Foundation Center is a splendid source of information about thousands of foundations that offer grants to individuals and groups. *See* "Tools," above, for information on the Center's publications.

International Association of Business Communicators, One Hallidie Plaza, Suite 600, San Francisco, CA 94102; 800-776-4222; fax: 415-362-8762.

Are you working part-time for big business to pay the bills, or thinking of doing that? If so, consider joining IABC. It offers seminars, a job hotline, a speakers bureau and excellent opportunties to network through local chapters.

Poets & Writers, Inc., 72 Spring Street, New York, NY 10012.

Through their publications and referral services, Poets & Writers can boost the income as well as the spirits of people who write fiction and poetry.

State councils for the arts.

The best way to find out whether your state has an arts council is by writing your governor's office. If it does, ask for full information about the council's programs.

U.S. government.

Federal agencies engaged in all sorts of activities have libraries and issue press releases about where funds are going and what they've been earmarked for. There's grist for sales and promotion plans when and if money is allocated to a particular region for study of the particular subject you've written about, so ask to be put on the mailing lists of agencies whose bailiwicks are relevant to your writing/publishing efforts. And find out if they have special-interest libraries that might buy your book.

Volunteer Lawyers for the Arts, 1285 Avenue of the Americas, Third Floor, New York, NY 10019 and other locations (see below).

Founded in New York to provide legal services for artists who can't afford lawyers' fees, Volunteer Lawyers for the Arts has affiliates across the country—in California (San Francisco, Los Angeles and La Jolla), Colorado (Denver), Connecticut (Hartford), the District of Columbia, Florida (Clearwater, Fort Lauderdale, Miami and Tallahassee), Georgia (Atlanta), Illinois (Chicago), Iowa (Cedar Rapids and Dubuque), Kentucky (Lexington and Louisville), Louisiana (New Orleans), Maine (Augusta), Maryland (Baltimore), Massachusetts (Amherst and Boston), Minnesota (Minneapolis), Missouri (St. Louis), Montana (Missoula), New Jersey (Trenton), New York (Albany, Buffalo, Huntington and Poughkeepsie, as well as New York City), North Carolina (Raleigh), Ohio (Cleveland and Toledo), Oklahoma (Oklahoma City), Pennsylvania (Philadelphia), Rhode Island (Narragansett), South Carolina (Greenville), Tennessee (Nashville), Texas (Austin and Houston), Utah (Salt Lake City) and Washington (Seattle). And there's an office in Toronto too. Write or call the affiliate nearest you to find out about services and costs, or send $10 to the NYC office for the group's directory.

Women in Communications, 2101 Wilson Boulevard, Suite 417, Arlington, VA 22201; 703-528-4200; fax: 703-528-4205.

Job hotlines and programs that hone professional skills are just two of the benefits Women in Communications offers members. Contact national headquarters for information on nearby chapters.

Writers' groups.

Like IABC and Women in Communications, the Authors Guild, PEN and several other writers' groups help writers save money, by offering medical insurance at group rates, for example. *See* entries in "The Sale and Its Sequels Resources" and be sure to find out how groups you belong to can make your dollars stretch.

Index